Social Assessment Manual

Other Titles in this Series

The Changing Economics of World Energy, edited by Bernhard J. Abrahamsson

Natural Resources and a Democratic Society: Public Participation in Decision-Making, edited by Albert Utton, W. R. Derrick Sewell, and Timothy O'Riordan

The Nuclear Impact: A Case Study of the Plowshare Program to Produce Natural Gas by Underground Nuclear Stimulation in the Rocky Mountains, Frank Kreith and Catherine B. Wrenn

Earthcare: Global Protection of Natural Areas, edited by Edmund A. Schofield

Indonesia's Oil, Sevinc Carlson

Westview Special Studies in
Natural Resources and Energy Management

Social Assessment Manual: A Guide to the Preparation of the Social Well-Being Account for Planning Water Resource Projects

Stephen J. Fitzsimmons, Lorrie I. Stuart, and Peter C. Wolff

A Social Well-Being Account is the product of an assessment of the comparative beneficial and adverse social effects likely to occur as a result of implementing—or not implementing—a particular development plan. This volume establishes procedures for conducting research and analyzing data in order to make this assessment for water development plans, and it provides planners with instructions for completing a formal Social Well-Being Account in accordance with guidelines established in 1973 by the Water Resources Council.

In developing this manual, researchers conducted an intensive review and analysis of the literature in sociology, social psychology, and water resources development, and then systematically identified where important social and water considerations existed. The result is a basis for meaningful social assessment, developed out of theory, research, and program experience and consistent with federal requirements in this realm.

Stephen J. Fitzsimmons, vice-president for social research development with Abt Associates Inc., has done extensive research in the areas of community theory and social research, delivery of human services, and water resources development. Lorrie Stuart has worked as an analyst on numerous Abt projects, among them a social impact assessment of the Tulatin Dam Project in Oregon. Peter C. Wolff is a project director with Abt Associates. His research includes a number of social impact analyses for the Bureau of Reclamation and the Department of Transportation.

Other Abt Associates Studies in Applied Social Research published by Westview Press:

The College Guide for Students with Disabilities, Elinor Gollay and Alwina Bennett

Man and Water: A Social Report, Stephen J. Fitzsimmons and Ovadia Salama

Rural America: A Social and Educational History of Ten Communities, edited by Stephen J. Fitzsimmons, Peter C. Wolff, and Abby J. Freedman

Guidance Manual to Providing Neighborhood Services, Stephen J. Fitzsimmons, Barbara C. Sampson, and M. Brigid O'Farrell

Social Assessment Manual

A Guide to the Preparation of the Social Well-Being Account for Planning Water Resource Projects

An Abt Associates Study
in Applied Social Research
by Stephen J. Fitzsimmons,
Lorrie I. Stuart,
and Peter C. Wolff

Routledge
Taylor & Francis Group
LONDON AND NEW YORK

First published 1977 by Westview Press, Inc.

Published 2019 by Routledge
52 Vanderbilt Avenue, New York, NY 10017
2 Park Square, Milton Park, Abingdon, Oxon OX14 4RN

Routledge is an imprint of the Taylor & Francis Group, an informa business

Library of Congress Cataloging in Publication Data

Fitzsimmons, Stephen J.
Social assessment manual.

(An Abt Associates study in applied social research)
Bibliography: p.
1. Water resources development—Social aspects—Research. I. Stuart, Lorrie I., joint author. II. Wolff, Peter C., joint author. III. Title.
HD1691.F56 309.2'12 76-58332

ISBN 13: 978-0-367-28745-0 (hbk)
ISBN 13: 978-0-367-30291-7 (pbk)

Contents

Figures and Tables

Figures

Tables

Preface

This book deals with the assessment of the comparative future beneficial and adverse *social* effects likely to occur as a result of implementing various water development plans, or as a result of not implementing a plan. It provides planners with an orientation to conducting a social assessment and with instructions for completing a formal Social Well-Being (SWB) Account, in accordance with guidelines established in 1973 by the Water Resources Council. This work has been completed for the U.S. Bureau of Reclamation, which earlier played a pioneering role in economic assessments through development and refinement of cost-benefit analysis. Just as cost-benefit analysis has been extended to a variety of uses beyond those related to water development, so it is hoped that the results of the present work in social assessment will have widespread applicability in a variety of public investments.

Present-day capabilities to effectively assess the social implications of public investments were greatly aided as a result of important, socially oriented legislation and programs conducted during the 1960s. Here, improvement of the quality of life of people, the social well-being of communities, and the equity among citizens were all prime societal goals. In a sense, such experience provided the minimum necessary conditions to move into the complex area of social assessment. However, this alone was not sufficient to achieve effective assessments. Research, theory, and actual program experience were necessary to conceptualize sound social assessment.

In preparation for the development of this book, an intensive review and analysis was required of the theory and research of the fields of sociology and social psychology; a similar review of the broad range of water resources planning and development literature was also completed. In turn, these two separate areas were brought together in order to systematically identify where important social and water considerations existed. Finally, a series of preliminary measures of these relationships were identified. The study examined man's needs for water resources development, and conversely, the impacts, both positive and negative, direct and indirect, of water development plans upon man (see Fitzsimmons and Salama, 1974). Building upon this research, the present book provides a basis for meaningful social assessment, developed out of theory, research, and program experience and consistent with various federal requirements in this realm. The result is a comprehensive, systematic, and representative basis for social assessment.

The *Social Assessment Manual* has been designed with the needs of the water resources planning officer in mind. While a general orientation is provided, much of the book is devoted to materials and procedures necessary to prepare a Social Well-Being Account in multiple objective planning. The major objectives guiding the authors were clarity, the representativeness of social concerns, and the feasibility of achieving a useful and accurate social assessment.

The authors wish to express their appreciation to Dr. Darrell Adams, who served as Project Officer, Mr. Ira Watson, and Mr. Edmund Barbour, all of the Division of Planning Coordination, Engineering and Research Center, Bureau of Reclamation, U.S. Department of the Interior, for their continued support and constructive suggestions in the development of this document. The assistance of Ms. Abby Freedman in editing these materials is gratefully acknowledged.

Part 1
Orientation to the Social Assessment

1
Introduction, Purpose of This Book, and Organizing Assumptions

This book has been designed to be used by water resources planners for purposes of assessing the probable social effects of implementing alternative water development plans. Its fundamental purpose is to enable a planning office to conduct the research and analyze the data in order to complete a Social Well-Being Account (SWB). All of the information necessary to conduct a social assessment, analyze data, present findings, and make recommendations is contained within this book. These procedures are consistent with the mandate of the Water Resources Council's *Principles and Standards for Planning Water and Related Land Resources* (1973)[1] as they apply to the completion of a Social Well-Being Account.

The materials provided in this book have been developed with the needs and resources of a federal water resource planning agency in mind. The following assumptions underlie the development of this book.

1. Hereafter cited as U.S. WRC, *Principles and Standards*, 1973.

This social assessment is to be administered in coordination with or as part of a larger assessment process which may include economic, environmental, and regional assessments.

Certain basic parameters (e.g., geographic area, time frame of analysis, and specific plans and alternatives) are present in all social assessments.

The assessment should be capable of application to a range of water development plans, varying in size and complexity.

The social assessment should be applicable to a variety of community settings: rural and urban, large and small.

The planning agency will have limited resources in terms of staff, time, and money to apply to this assessment.

The social assessment, by virtue of representing one of a number of concerns, will contribute to a final "overall" assessment, but will not in and of itself be the only determinant as to which of a variety of alternatives is deemed "best."

While the social assessment will be able to deal with the projected social benefits and costs of alternative plans for the area in question, larger social issues may exist beyond the immediate impact area which cannot be adequately addressed by this assessment.

These assumptions amount to the following. A social assessment is conducted along with economic, environmental, and regional assessments, which together form the basis upon which alternative water resource plans are assessed. A typical planning office should be able to conduct this assessment within reasonable resource constraints in a variety of plan situations and to draw appropriate conclusions. Final recommendation of a plan may be influenced by social effects which occur outside the area immediately affected by the proposed plans.

It is useful at the outset to define certain terms which are used in connection with the Social Well-Being Account.

Social Assessment Manual: This defines the purpose of social assessment and gives procedures for completing the Social Well-Being Account.

Social Assessment: The process of gathering data and developing the Social Well-Being Account.

Social Well-Being Account: A formal document on the beneficial and adverse social effects of alternative water development plans.

Social Impacts: Those changes in social structures or behaviors which are forecasted to occur as a direct or indirect result of implementing a plan; e.g., a forecasted change in income distribution.

Adverse and Beneficial Social Effects: The social evaluation of any given impact in terms of its relative "goodness" or "badness" for the planning area; e.g., the social value of a forecasted redistribution of income to a community and its residents. More than one effect can be assigned to any impact if it means different things for different people in the planning area. This will be further described in Chapter 2.

In order to facilitate the preparation of a Social Well-Being Account, this book has been divided into three parts. Part 1 contains a discussion of the context of multi-objective planning (Chapter 2), the function of the Social Well-Being Account (Chapter 3), the theoretical and methodological bases for preparing the Account (Chapter 4), and the structure of the Account (Chapter 5). It is important to read Part 1 before Part 2 in order to understand the terminology and procedures described in Part 2. In Part 2, Chapter 1, instructions are given for organizing the tasks of the social assessment. In Chapters 2–6, the five consecutive steps in preparing the Social Well-Being Account are described in detail. In Part 3, tables to be used in completing the Social Well-Being Account are provided.

2
The Social Well-Being Account Within the Multiple Objectives Planning Context

The term *multi-objective planning* is a shorthand reference for the conceptual approach contained in the Interagency Report prepared for the U.S. Water Resources Council (WRC) in July 1970 for the purpose of unifying, codifying, and broadening methods and procedures. This document was widely distributed in the United States and represents the first and most comprehensive articulation of the concept of multi-objective planning. The concept evolved as a logical response to shifts in public values on the role of increasingly scarce water resources and their relationship to environmental, social, and economic concerns. Citizens became increasingly concerned that people and their communities should not be viewed solely in economic and material terms; i.e., that it was necessary for government and other major institutions of society to consider the quality of life of the individual, the social well-

Much of Chapter 2 draws heavily, in words and content, on "Multiobjective Water Resource Planning," a paper by Edmund Barbour, chief, Resource Analysis Branch in the Bureau of Reclamation, delivered in December 1974 at the Second World Congress on Water Resources in New Delhi, India.

being of communities, and equity among people. A general feeling emerged that there was a disproportionate emphasis on economic considerations which, instead of improving family and community life, left man more at the mercy of technology and government. As part of this change in values, there was also widespread concern about exploitation of the environment and man's natural resources. Whereas the development of the environment for economic purposes had dominated much of natural resources planning in the past, there began to be increasing concern to protect it. Again, human values were involved. This new value or ethic maintained that, in the long run, man must live in harmony with the environment rather than exploit it.

Important stimuli to change were provided in the late 1960s by a number of highly controversial preservation issues involving large water projects and by the enactment of major pieces of environmental protection legislation. Economic development goals, expressed as simple benefit-cost ratios in monetary terms, became less important, and greater attention was given to quality of life considerations. This restatement and broadening of criteria was the answer to the charge given to the WRC when it was created in 1965 to develop uniform policies and procedures that could be consistently applied by the many entities involved in national water planning.

The implication of these changes in values may be summarized as follows:

> Too often in the past man's role has been restricted by the planner to that of a "homo economicus," that is, a producer and consumer of goods and services with pre-specified objectives of utility and profit maximization. Today, governmental decision makers are aware of the fact that beyond these limited economic objectives, the policies and programs they establish, as well as the resources they allocate, significantly affect the quality of life, the social well-being, and the equity of different groups of people. . . .
>
> . . . legislators [need] to assess the social impacts of

> spending committed in the name of the public interest. The United States Water Resources Council's *Principles and Standards for Planning Water and Related Land Resources* illustrates and emphasizes the concern over these social impacts, as it calls for the systematic identification of non-economic effects along with traditional profitability measures when considering the development of future use of the country's natural resources (Fitzsimmons & Salama, 1973, p. v).

In order to do multi-objective planning, it is necessary to consider three different features of such planning: first, a set of national objectives—different plans will emphasize different national objectives; second, a set of accounts which display how and to what extent a given plan affects various areas of concern; third, planning has different stages, from the initial general investigations to the last, detailed plan implementation. Below, we will discuss all three features of multi-objective planning. The first section will deal with national objectives, the second with a system of accounts, and the last with the Bureau of Reclamations's planning procedures.

The Formulation of Plans Serving Different Objectives

The Original Four Objectives

Initially, the following four national objectives were specified as guideposts for formulating water resource plans: national economic development (NED), having to do with increases in goods, services, and production efficiency; environmental quality (EQ), involving protecting and enhancing natural, cultural, and ecological systems; regional development (RD), covering improvements in a broad spectrum of economic and social factors, identifiable with users in a localized, less than national setting; social well-being (SWB), concerned with standards of living, health and safety, and emergency preparedness. Although there are obvious overlaps in the definitions, significant distinctions were made by careful delineation of *sub-objectives* or *components* which form the focal points in the planning process.

To determine how effectively various plans served the four objectives, a parallel four-account evaluation system was provided. By analyzing the results of the accounting system and comparing trade-offs among alternative plans, a decision-maker could determine to what extent an objective was "optimized" or at least "emphasized" in each plan. The number of plans and the objectives to be emphasized depended largely on the problems, needs, and competitive uses involving water and its related land resources in a particular planning setting; there could be as many as four or five plans, or possibly only one. Although all plans would not emphasize the same objective and one or more might represent different levels of compromise, all plans have effects on the four objectives and in each case these effects are to be measured by using the four-account evaluation procedure.

New standards were proposed which attempted to formally articulate the various objectives, to encourage the development of alternative plans where competition in resource use occurred, and to provide an improved evaluation system that could better identify the trade-offs among plans. It was and still is hoped that this approach will promote public scrutiny and facilitate the democratic processes in making better decisions on managing precious water supplies.

Two Objectives

The finally approved *Principles and Standards* of September 1973 listed only two national objectives: national economic development (NED) and environmental quality (EQ). The four-account system, which had been developed to evaluate how the original four objectives were emphasized in the plans, remained essentially unchanged. Measurements of impacts are to be made for the two national objectives of NED and EQ plus the two accounts of RD and SWB. One component of the regional development objective which had been included in the proposed standards–use of unemployed or underemployed resources–was given slight recognition under the NED objective. Special beneficial effects for the NED objective were claimed when implementation of a plan used otherwise unemployed or underemployed resources in planning regions designated by the WRC.

The major components of the two objectives serving as focal points in the planning process were these:

- National economic development (NED) components:
  Those identified with direct users, including conventional purposes such as flood control, hydropower, irrigation, municipal and industrial water supplies, fish and wildlife, recreation, drainage, etc.
  External economies relating to increased production efficiency
- Environmental quality components (EQ):
  Areas of natural beauty and human enjoyment such as open space and greenbelts, stream systems, lakes, wilderness, estuaries, etc.
  Archeological, historical, and cultural resources
  Biological, geological, and ecological resources
  Water, air, land, visual, and noise quality

Alternative Plans

In an abstract situation, the planners only have to formulate two plans and choose between them: an NED plan and an EQ plan. In actual practice, however, the planners will have to choose between a larger number of alternative plans. Where there are resource use conflicts, a plan emphasizing national economic development and another plan emphasizing environmental quality will ordinarily be formulated. In addition, however, there can also be other plans; some will emphasize national economic development more than others, and concomitantly, some will emphasize environmental quality more than others. These other plans will, in other words, strike some sort of compromise between the two national objectives and may cover a considerable portion of the spectrum between ignoring one of the objectives almost totally and emphasizing it almost exclusively.

Another "plan"—or more correctly, alternative—that needs to be considered by the planners is "No Plan." That is, the planners need to consider what would happen if no plan at all were to be implemented. Since the effects of any plan in which the planners are interested would be *future* effects, the future effects of *no* plan must also be considered. Thus, the decision not to implement any plans does not mean that everything in the planning area would remain exactly the same as it is now. As time goes on, existing social (and other) trends would make themselves felt, and sometime in the future the planning area will be quite different from what it is now, even in the absence of any plan implementation. The planner will display a four-account system of effects for the NED and EQ oriented plans, as well as for any other alternative plans developed, including the No Plan.

Four-Account System

A brief summary of the four-account system may be helpful at this point. In order to evaluate the relative merits of alternative plans, the beneficial and adverse effects on economic development, environmental enhancement, regional development, and social well-being must be accounted for and displayed. Again, it should be remembered that all plans are multi-objective in their effects, regardless of which objective is being emphasized. Vital to the display and ultimate selection is that alternative plans, whether structural or nonstructural, be analyzed comparably and that the accounts for each plan be covered in the same relative degree of detail. The accounts are not additive, but rather attempt to present the best information available on the effects for each of the four accounts.

> This system of four accounts "calls attention to the important aspects of information which must be generated and displayed if the decision-making process is to be effective. The evaluation framework through the system of accounts provides for a systematic investigation of the full range and extent of effects of a plan and provides for a display of this information in a format which is clear and useful to all participants in the decision process" (U.S. WRC, *Principles and Standards,* 1973, p. 108).

National Economic Development (NED) Account

The NED account is measured in wholly monetary terms, reflecting direct or primary income gain to first users. Present procedures for measuring direct effects of conventional water purposes are useful here, such as increased farm income, prevention of damages, market values of direct outputs, values of likely alternatives, etc.

Regional Development (RD) Account

The RD account measures both monetary and nonmonetary effects. It encompasses the NED effects and attempts to identify the second-round effects as well, not only in dollars but also in descriptive terms; e.g., the number of jobs created. A unique aspect of the account is that it identifies beneficiaries to a greater degree than ever before; it also locates the effects between the region involved and the rest of the nation. Unless there are regional unemployed or underemployed resources identified in the account, the second-round effects are usually considered to be transferred from one region to another. This assumption of transfer is one of the most significant conceptual changes from past economic evaluations. There still remains a controversy over whether utilizing unemployed and underemployed resources represents a net national gain.

Environmental Quality (EQ) Account

The EQ account has received the greatest attention in developing evaluation procedures because of the past lack of generally accepted methodology. The EQ evaluation system that resulted from the Bureau of Reclamation efforts in preparing guidelines and field testing is a significant accomplishment (U.S. Dept. of Interior, Bureau of Reclamation, *Guidelines for Implementing Principles and Standards for Multi-Objective Planning of Water Resources,* 1972).[1] It employs descriptors and numerical factors to rate aspects of quantity, quality, and human influence. Quantity factors are expressed in terms of acres, miles, volumes, and number of units. Both

1. Hereafter referred to as the *Yellow Book.*

quality and human influence factors are assigned arbitrary numbers on a 0-10 scale. Zero represents the worst known and 10 the best known factor. The irreversibility of action programs on EQ and the relative uniqueness of the resources are also rated on a 0-10 scale. Detailed guidelines and worksheets are provided to planners to assist in evaluating each of the three factors for the 19 environmental components.

Social Well-Being (SWB) Account

The Social Well-Being Account is both quantitative and descriptive; it incorporates statistical data as necessary to show effects on the components, such as those on income distribution or on health and safety. The *Principles and Standards* notes that "most water and land resource plans have beneficial and adverse effects on social well-being." It continues:

> Beneficial effects on social well-being are contributions to the equitable distribution of real income and employment and to other social opportunities. . . . Adverse effects of a plan on social well-being have detrimental impacts on the equitable distribution of real income and employment or otherwise diminish or detract from the attainment of other social opportunities. Additionally, such adverse effects include not only those incurred in the designated planning area, but also include adverse consequences elsewhere in the Nation resulting from implementation of the plan (U.S. WRC, *Principles and Standards,* 1973, p. 81).

One of the purposes of the present book is to elaborate upon and augment the concepts developed in the *Principles and Standards* to enable a clearer articulation of the complex social impacts and effects of alternative plans to be analyzed and displayed in a way which is consistent with the *Yellow Book.* The book has been designed to guide planners in identifying and measuring social effects resulting from plans emphasizing different national objectives by preparing the Social Well-Being Account. The steps for completing the Social Well-Being

Account are described in detail in Part 2. In Figure 1 the guidelines for preparing the Social Well-Being Account, as described in this book, are presented.

Different Planning Levels

In the general planning process which the Bureau of Reclamation goes through, there are three major kinds of studies which need to be prepared. First, early in the planning process is an *Appraisal Study,* which is in the nature of a reconnaisance effort. The Appraisal Study is an investigation conducted at the regional level, upon authorization by the Commissioner, when local people have requested such a study. Beneficial and adverse social effects will be of concern in such an appraisal, but the study is of a preliminary kind; the social concerns will be expressed in general rather than in specific terms.

The second kind of study is a *Feasibility Study.* The Social Well-Being Account (and the other three accounts) are developed mainly for the purposes of the Feasibility Study. The investigation of feasibility is a fairly lengthy process, involving perhaps from one to three years. In the course of the study, the different plans mentioned on pp. 9-14 (NED, EQ, Alternative Plans, and No Plan) will be examined, and the four accounts will be set up to indicate what the effects of the different plans are for national economic development, for environmental quality, for regional development, and for social well-being.

The Feasibility Study, when it has been completed, results in a Feasibility Report. If the plan is ultimately found to be feasible, if it is approved by the Commissioner and by the Secretary of the Interior, and if Congress appropriates funds (this is a very much shortened description of the planning process), then another report is prepared, namely, a *Definite Plan Report.* Beneficial and adverse effects on social well-being will once more be considered, and the Social Well-Being Account (and the *Social Assessment Manual*) once more comes into use. Since the major considerations of social well-being would obviously have been made in the course of the feasibility investigation, the Social Well-Being Account (and the *Manual*) has largely indirect utility in this ultimate stage of the planning process.

Figure 1. *Outline for the Preparation of the Social Well-Being Account*

1. The Water Resources Context and the Alternative Plans
   - A. History of Water Needs
   - B. Brief Descriptions of the Alternative Plans–Their Activities, Functions, Impact Areas, and Schedule
     - 1) No Plan
     - 2) National Economic Development Emphasis Plan
     - 3) Environmental Quality Emphasis Plan
     - 4) Alternative Plans
     - 5) Recommended Plan
2. The Planning Area To Be Affected
   - A. History of the Area
   - B. Present-Day Characteristics and Social Profile
   - C. The Life Style of the Area
3. The Future Social Impacts Attributable to Each Alternative Plan
   - A. The Future with No Plan
   - B. The Future with the National Economic Development Plan
   - C. The Future with the Environmental Quality Plan
   - D. The Future with the Alternative Plan(s)
   - E. The Future with the Recommended Plan
4. The Comparative Future Beneficial and Adverse Social Effects of the Alternative Plans
   - A. The Individual, Personal Effects
   - B. The Community, Institutional Effects
   - C. The Area, Socioeconomic Effects
   - D. The National, Emergency Preparedness Effects
   - E. The Aggregate Social Effects
   - F. Various Trade-offs Among Effects
   - G. A Summary Comparison of the Plans
5. Recommendation–Selection of the Plan with the Optimum Future Social Well-Being Effects on the Plan Area

3
The Function of the Social Well-Being Account

General Statement of Purpose

The fundamental objective of the Social Well-Being (SWB) Account is *to forecast the probable future impacts which are likely to occur as a result of implementing a given water development plan (i.e., NED, EQ, or alternative plan), or as a result of not implementing any such plan, and to then assess the beneficial and adverse social effects upon people and their communities.*

This definition highlights certain features of the Social Well-Being Account:

1. A distinction is made between changes which will occur, referred to as *impacts,* and their social meaning, which is referred to as "beneficial and adverse social *effects.*"
2. The impacts of direct concern are *social.* These are rated as to their beneficial and adverse social effects.
3. The impacts of concern are those which will occur in the future. The major comparison of interest is with respect to the comparison of alternative *futures,* not with present vs. future.
4. The impacts of concern are those which *result from plan*

implementation. The SWB Account is not interested in social changes in the future which are *not* associated, directly or indirectly, with the plan, other than the extent to which such "trends" may interact with plan implementation. In short, the SWB Account does not look at man's social futures in general.

The Effects Displayed in the Social Well-Being Account

Impacts and Effects

When we speak of the *impacts* of a plan, we are referring to *changes* which will be brought about (in the future) by the implementation of a plan. To really understand the impacts of a plan, however, we must also consider what changes would have occurred without the implementation of any plan whatsoever. We have already noted that some changes (i.e., impacts) will take place even in the absence of any plan. The impacts due to the implementation of a plan, therefore, will be the changes which would not have occurred without any plan. Let us give a simple example. Suppose that at the present time there are 100 jobs in a given area in one industry. If no plan at all is implemented, it is anticipated that twenty years from now the number of jobs in that industry will fall to eighty because the area is expected to undergo slow stagnation. *With* the plan, however, it is anticipated that twenty years from now there will be 200 jobs. The impact of the plan, therefore, is an increase of 120 in the number of jobs. If it had been anticipated that the industry would gain fifty jobs, even without the implementation of any plan, then the impact due to the plan would have been an increase of fifty jobs.

We use the word *effect* when we *evaluate* the impacts of a plan. If it is felt that the increase of 120 jobs is good for the community, then we would say that the plan has a positive effect on the plan area. Whether or not a change due to a plan is beneficial or adverse is something that has to be evaluated in terms of the needs of those affected by the impact (individual, institutional, etc.) and by the local situation. An increase in jobs, which may be a positive effect in one area (where there is poverty and unemployment), may be a negative effect in another area and for other persons (where there is overcrowding, pollution, and insufficiency of public services). Completion of the SWB Account requires forecasting attributable social impacts and assessing their social meaning or *effects*.

Types of Effects

Basically there are two types of effects which are to be displayed in the Social Well-Being Account: beneficial effects and adverse effects.

> Beneficial effects on social well-being are contributions to the equitable distribution of real income and employment and to other social opportunities. . . . Adverse effects of a plan on social well-being have detrimental impacts on the equitable distribution of real income and employment or otherwise diminish or detract from the attainment of other social opportunities (U.S. WRC, *Principles and Standards*, 1973, p. 81).

As the *Principles and Standards* notes, adverse effects include not only clearly detrimental ("bad") effects; they also include missed beneficial ("good") effects. If the opportunity for good effects to occur was denied by the plan, then the absence of such a good effect is itself a bad or adverse effect.

Another idea worth noting is that the Social Well-Being Account, unlike the other three accounts, must consider not only the future effects of a plan but must also concern itself with the *process* by which the effects occur or are permitted to occur. The concern by which decisions about social well-being are made is itself a social effect and has a positive or negative effect, depending on how it is handled. To provide a simple example, the implementation of a plan may have what appears to be some very real beneficial effects on a part of the population in the plan area. If, however, the persons affected are not consulted and involved in the decision-making process, then those persons will likely suffer from a sense of powerlessness over their own lives; their feelings toward the government may deteriorate, even though the effects that later will accrue to them are positive.

Parameters of Impacts

Impacts may also be categorized according to other parameters, which will be discussed in detail in Part 1, pp. 60-64. Here we will just briefly note some of the other ways in which effects may be grouped.

Impacts may be direct or indirect. *Direct* impacts are those which are caused directly by the implementation of the plan, while *indirect* impacts occur through the intermediating causality of some other direct impact (often a change in the real income of persons). Impacts may also be either long-term or short-term. Most *short-term* impacts will tend to be due to construction impacts (noise, pollution, and the like), while *long-term* impacts are those due to the plan implementation itself. Impacts will also be distributed differently in different *geographic areas.* Some areas will be impacted more than others, and some areas will receive beneficial effects, while other areas will receive adverse effects. Impacts may also be distributed differently among different *groups.* For example, implementation of a plan may have different impacts on high income and on low income persons, leading, of course, to questions about the equity of such a distribution. The effects to be displayed in the Social Well-Being Account also differ according to what area of human life they affect. The implementation of a plan will affect an individual's attitudes and values, family life, institutions, and communities. This list is not exhaustive. It does make clear, however, that the implementation of a plan affects different *levels:* some of these effects will be felt by persons, others by the community, still others by an entire region, and some by the nation as a whole.

An Overview of the Structure of the Social Well-Being Account

The Social Well-Being Account as presented in this book incorporates both the Bureau's guidelines as set forth in the *Yellow Book* and the Water Resources Council's *Principles and Standards* but expands upon them considerably in terms of both content (as discussed in Chapter 4) and organization. The following basic structure for the Social Well-Being Account has been developed to enable the planner to consider a broad range of social impacts and their effects from various perspectives. At the same time, this structure is parsimonious and easy to work with:

Social Well-Being Effects by Type of Concern and Level of Analysis	*Component Impacts by Unit of Measure and Level of Analysis*
Personal	Individual
Community	Institutional
Area	Socioeconomic
National	Emergency Preparedness
Aggregate	Social

Based upon this structure, the Social Well-Being Account is organized into five *components.* In turn, each component is composed of a number of *evaluation categories.* The components are the basic units of analysis for assessing the *social effects* of various water development plans. The *evaluation categories* provide the actual data on *forecasted impacts* upon which such effects are assessed. The SWB Account is presented in its basic order and content in Figure 2.

It is important to note that a major objective of this account is to achieve a comprehensive, balanced understanding of the likely beneficial and adverse social effects of implementing alternative plans. Like the economic and environmental accounts, social phenomena are complex, interrelated, and capable of being viewed in many ways, as described in Chapter 4. The purpose of a moderately tight structure is to make such assessments both logical and feasible. While overlaps between components have been minimized as much as possible in the SWB Account, obviously, interactions exist between some of the evaluation categories. Therefore, a fifth component called "aggregate social effects" has been constructed to measure social effects across the other components.

Figure 2. *Structure of the Social Well-Being Account*

Components	Evaluation Categories
I. Individual, Personal Effects	A. Life, Protection, and Safety B. Health C. Family and Individual D. Attitudes E. Environmental Considerations F. Other (specify)
II. Community, Institutional Effects	A. Demographic B. Education C. Government Operations and Services D. Housing and Neighborhood E. Law and Justice F. Social Services G. Religion H. Culture I. Recreation J. Informal Organizational Groups K. Community and Institutional Viability L. Other (specify)
III. Area, Socioeconomic Effects	A. Employment and Real Income B. Welfare and Financial Compensation C. Communications D. Transportation E. Economic Base F. Planning G. Construction H. Other (specify)
IV. National, Emergency Preparedness Effects	A. Water Supplies B. Food Production C. Power Supplies D. Water Transportation E. Scarce Fuels F. Population Dispersion G. Industrial Dispersion H. Military Preparedness I. International Treaty Obligations J. Other (specify)
V. Aggregate Social Effects	A. Quality of Life B. Relative Social Position C. Social Well-Being D. Other (specify)

The rationale for the contents of the components (i.e., their categories) is presented in Chapter 4, pp. 32-48, and the structure of the components is presented in more detail in Chapter 5. Full discussion of the evaluation categories and their data is reserved for Chapter 7.

Products of the Social Assessment

The social assessment may be used as a document in its own right. As such, it displays all the various beneficial and adverse effects under a number of components in the Social Well-Being Account. This document may be included as an appendix to the larger Feasibility Report for a given plan or may be used as a supporting file. Second, the social assessment will provide data for the various chapters of the Feasibility Report. Third, the social assessment has applications in other investigations. Most important of these probably is the preparation of the Environmental Impact Statement which is required for some projects by the National Environmental Policy Act (P.L. 91-190, 42 U.S.C. 4321 *et seq.*). Although the social assessment is prepared primarily in order to display the social account for planning purposes (at the level of the Feasibility Study), the data collected and analyzed in order to display the account will obviously also be of value in the Environmental Impact Statement, insofar as that statement is concerned with social factors. The SWB Account can also be augmented in various ways in the completion of any future implementation report requirements.

4

Theoretical and Methodological Basis for a Social Well-Being Account

Any assessment which purports to be "social" in its character must deal with man in social terms. A meaningful assessment must refer not only to economic indicators but also to questions of man's social relationships, personal life-style, and the culture in which she or he lives. It is imperative to recognize the social, cultural, and psychological needs of people, their families, institutions, and communities. The identification of social concerns does not, surprisingly enough, rule out the considerable use of secondary data in answering questions about social impact. It does, however, demand a conceptual framework to convert "data" into truly useful and appropriate "social information."

The following statement from the *Yellow Book* speaks to a number of these points:

> It should be emphasized that an analysis of social factors is and must be primarily, although not exclusively, non-monetary in character. While economic factors are involved in analyses of social factors, they are, for this account, subsidiary to attitudes, values, beliefs, and expectations of individuals, groups, and

> communities of people impacted directly and indirectly by the development of water resources.
>
> This does not mean, however, that social factors are, or should be, primarily nonquantitative in nature. There will, of necessity, be a mixture of quantitative and qualitative evaluations made. Techniques and procedures for making quantitative assessments of attitudes, values, beliefs, and expectations, and the relationships between these and various forms of social behavior have been well developed in social psychology and sociology. While these concepts and methods have rarely been applied directly to water planning in the past, as techniques are developed, they will be added to these guidelines (p. 6-2).

A sound approach to social assessment includes the concept that whatever social good occurs from a public investment, it must, in part, be expressed in terms of how individual people are affected. A social assessment also includes the idea that people live in communities and that the institutions and cultures of these communities have a great deal to do with how various changes are "valued." Another critical aspect of any social assessment is an understanding of who benefits and who loses; i.e., the distribution of impact. Finally, social assessment must provide a sense of the "trade-offs" associated with a public investment; i.e., what benefits are obtained in the presence of what adverse effects?

This chapter treats a number of fundamental issues concerning development of a social well-being account, including:

- The type of model it requires
- The concept of a causal agent
- The nature of the area being affected
- The various types and levels of social effects, including:
  Individual
  Community

Area
National
Aggregate

- The important conceptual dimensions of social assessment
- The important measurement dimensions

The Dynamic Systems Model

It is important to have a general model of the process by which plans lead to social impacts. The model should take into account the complexity of interactions which exist over time between the present-day community context and the ultimate implementation of a plan.

The simplest model of cause and effect states that a given action produces an equal and opposite reaction. This model describes a direct transfer of energy in which there is no particular interest in what is being acted upon. Another model states that a stimulus is applied to an organism which, in turn, responds to it. This model is more complex in the sense that it introduces the object being acted upon as a variable; thus, *different* responses are possible. However, it also assumes that the organism remains the same and that only its response changes. Any model of analysis utilized in social assessment, however, must take into account that in responding to a stimulus (such as a major water development project), the character of the organism (e.g., a community or the quality of life of its residents) may also undergo significant change.

To illustrate the complexity involved, let us examine a sequence of events which might be set into motion with the implementation of a water resources plan. When a plan is actually implemented, it affects a complex system over a period of time by setting into motion a variety of cause–effect–cause chains.

1. The project alters water availability.
2. New economic and environmental conditions are developed.
3. Changes in economic opportunities affect existing population groups differently and attract new residents.
4. New residents bring new values which may conflict with

those of the present population.
5. New people demand more and perhaps different services.
6. Institutions must respond in new ways.
7. Changes occur in the quality of life and in community attitudes and values.
8. Changed conditions, in turn, may attract new outside investments, and so forth.

The social assessment is effective to the extent that it takes into account not only the more immediate and "direct" social impacts on the community (in population, economy, etc.), but also the extent to which it forecasts the changes in the social processes, values, resources, and the quality of life of the people which emerge over a period of time.

The approach most useful in thinking about the process of effects and of changes can be labeled the "dynamic systems model." This model has the following properties:

1. Such a model allows for consideration of various influences "acting" upon a system. Plans for alternative water development projects are examples.
2. This approach also allows one to consider other sources of influence upon the system, such as changes in the resources and values of the larger society, which may interact with the implementation of the plan.
3. The approach allows one to conceptualize the system—its communities and residents—in terms of a complex of present-day characteristics. This implies, in part, that the effects of a plan are contingent upon the nature of the community being affected.
4. Changes taking place in the system are viewed in terms of distribution over space, over time, among many groups, and of being valued differently by different people.
5. Changes are viewed as both a direct and an indirect result of the plan implementation. This occurs as a result of interactions set into motion among persons, groups, organizations, and new demands placed upon institutions. These are complex and involve many "cause-effect-cause" chains over time.
6. Changes which occur will, in fact, encompass a variety of

beneficial and adverse effects, and the ultimate recommendation of a given plan will involve judgements about the value of a variety of trade-offs of "good" and "bad" effects.

7. In turn, there will be a variety of non-social factors (such as economic, environmental, technical, etc.) which must be taken into account before making any final decision. This logic is illustrated in Figure 3.

Figure 3. *Diagram of the Dynamic Systems Model*

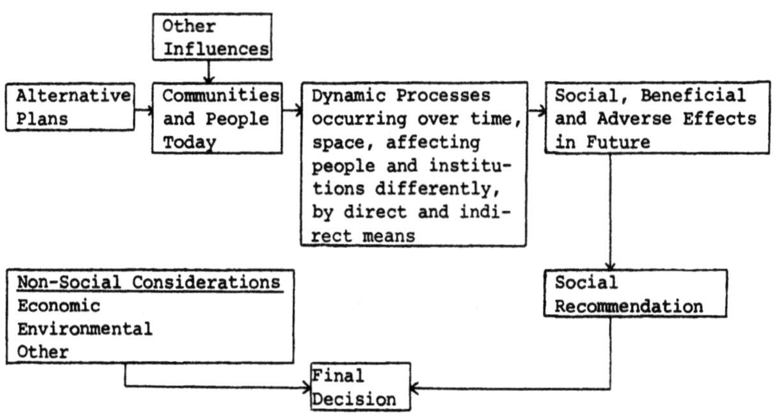

Implementation of a Plan as a Causal Agent

In the language of social research, each of the various alternatives (NED, EQ, or Alternate Plans) constitutes an *independent variable.* If one alters the present situation by implementation of any of the plans (or chooses to leave the present situation as is), what will be the subsequent and corollary effects of that decision with respect to social impacts? In research language, the impacts of the implementation are considered to be the *dependent variables.* These are such effects as change in income, life-style, etc. Finally, certain conditions may tend to influence how the plans have an impact. These include such conditions as population, economic base, existing services, and are referred to as *mediating variables* in the design. Thus, the first step in the social assessment is to identify the plans as the key independent variables.

In more general terms, each of the plans presents a different approach to affecting water and its related land development for an area. Different *activities* associated with each plan (e.g., combinations of dams and multipurpose reservoirs, power interties, canals, trans-mountain diversions, wilderness areas, wild and scenic river reaches, etc.) will, in turn, serve various *functions* (e.g., irrigation, industrial and community water supply, power production, recreation, ecological support, etc.). The first step in social assessment entails stating clearly the precise functions served by implementing any plan. It is from these differences (and the possibility of not implementing any plan) that different types of social impacts and effects may be expected to take place. Specific details of this step are discussed in Chapter 7 of this book.

The Present-Day Community Affected by Implementation of Alternative Plans

A second major consideration in social assessment involves the communities in the geographic area of the implemented plan—those which are acted on by the plan. Just as it is vital to have a clear understanding of the nature of the alternative plans, so, too, must the planner have a clear picture of what and who is being affected. There are two separate aspects of social response to the plans. First, one must understand the area affected in order to determine if a given effect is socially beneficial or adverse. Second, different types of data are required to achieve such understanding.

Present-day (and historical) *community characteristics* provide a basis upon which future effects can be assessed. For example, let us assume that a particular plan emphasizing NED will provide conditions which are ideal for a variety of new industries to enter the planning area and to begin construction. If the present-day area has a limited population, which is largely employed in the agriculture sector, two changes are likely to occur. First, more people will be drawn into that area to fill the newly created, industrial jobs. Second, while the area at present is composed of agricultural (and presumably rurally acculturated) citizens, the individuals coming to the communities are likely to be more urban-oriented (in connection with their job training and aspirations). Thus, population size expands, and the background of new arrivals is likely to be somewhat different from those citizens presently in the area. So far, we have been speaking of impacts; no judgement has been made about their relative social effects, *per se.*

In order to examine social effect, let us expand the preceding NED plan and community scenario. Assume that, in fact, there are two communities, relatively similar in composition, which will be affected in a similar manner; i.e., more urban-oriented, industrial job seekers arrive in the area. In one community, residents are seeking to expand their community and to increase its diversity and opportunities. The prospect of expanding employment is welcomed, indeed sought after. In this case, the social effect (barring severe, unanticipated consequences) of the expanding, diversifying population can be assessed as "good"; that is, it contributes to important social goals and aspirations of the citizens for their community. Let us assume, however, that a second community fails to share the enthusiasm over such growth, that citizens in this present-day community value the rural way of life and the fact that there is a uniform set of values held by a relatively small population. For this community, the same projected effects upon the population size and composition are viewed as a disaster; the social effect of an identical impact would thus be rated as quite negative, at least from the perspective of present-day residents.

In order to assess the current social characteristics of the area, a clear boundary must be identified so that data are collected for comparable groups of persons across plans. A rough operational definition is that the area being assessed corresponds to the furthest outer boundaries of each of the plans being considered, *across plans;* i.e., the furthest boundary in each geographic direction of any given plan becomes the boundary for assessments of all the plans. This is also, by definition, the boundary for the plan assessment. It is possible to look at certain social effects on communities beyond this boundary for selected considerations (e.g., recreation, transportation, etc.) where such effects are not of primary importance to those individuals who neither work nor reside in the area, but there is little advantage in going to distant cities for interviews to provide data; it is sufficient to be aware of the presence of existing and external demand for such access.

There are *three types of information* that can be reported which broadly characterize present-day community life. The first kind of information is *historical and descriptive.* Such information is usually narrative in character, describing when the area was settled, by whom, and with what economic and social characteristics. Growth trends and significant patterns of the last ten to fifteen years (e.g., migration, economic base, community values) are identified. The second type of information is more statistical and may be referred to as a *social profile.* Information on selected social variables such as population size, composition, and characteristics, and on employment, housing, and schools, can be displayed on tables for all communities in the planning area. Usually, accompanying narrative is required, as well as maps depicting the plan area. Finally, it is important to have a larger sense of what the *community life-style* is really like; i.e., the ethnic composition of the community, rural characteristics vs. urban characteristics, values held by various groups, typical patterns of community life, conflict resolution procedures, cooperation among various parties, etc. The reader should be able to gain a sense of what the kind of environment the community would be like to live and work in. By understanding the communities in the planning area in these three ways, the social impacts of implementing various plans can be rated from the perspective of the communities being affected. It is now appropriate to consider what types of social impacts should be examined, and the level at which they are likely to be occurring.

Social Effects at the Individual and Family Level

At the most basic level, beneficial and adverse social effects derive from a plan's success or failure to meet the social needs of the *family* and the *individual.* There are many ways of approaching the study of the behavior and needs of individuals and families. A particularly useful way of thinking of human behavior has been set forth by Abraham Maslow (1954). Maslow organizes fundamental human needs into a hierarchy. He maintains a person must first satisfy fundamental needs before satisfying higher needs. When a person's life is characterized by reasonable satisfaction at one level, this level becomes less important, and the higher levels of need become more important. Maslow's hierarchy can be summarized as follows:

1. *Basic survival and physiological needs.* At this level, the individual copes with basic needs for food, water, clothing, shelter, sleep, air, warmth, reproduction, elimination, etc. This state involves scarcity and extreme poverty or age. Survival is all important and little else counts.
2. *Security and self-sufficiency needs.* Here, the individual seeks protection from various types of harm, whether natural or man-made, and tries to protect basic family needs by maintaining a sense of basic security.
3. *Social and belongingness needs.* At this level, the individual focuses his concerns on his social relationships to other groups in the community and satisfies needs for belonging and for living under the values which appeal to him.
4. *Esteem.* This category focuses on needs for the achievement of independence, self-esteem, deserved respect of peers, and recognition of accomplishments.
5. *Growth or self-actualization.* The final and topmost level includes needs of self-fulfillment, achievement of full capacity as a person, the acceptance of new challenges, and the view of the world as a place which can be improved through human action.

This approach emphasizes several concepts about human behavior. First, when an individual experiences a need, especially at the lower end of the continuum, this may block concern over resolution of higher order needs. Second, the achievement of higher economic standards may motivate behavior up to a point, but beyond that point, quality of life may require non-monetary improvements. In short, a higher standard of living does not necessarily mean that people will be happier. As standards of living rise, the needs at levels three through five may become more important, and demand for various amenities (e.g., cultural, aesthetic, and environmental) may rise. Third, it is important to identify individuals and families in the planning area whose standard of living is below the general poverty line and whose need levels are at the lower end of the hierarchy, both because they are most in need and because helping these individuals may be an especially significant social contribution. Conversely, harming them may be an especially serious matter, for they have the least capacity to bear additional costs.

Just as individual needs are complex, so too are the kinds of social concerns associated with family life, which has an interpersonal quality. These concerns are focused on the qualities and services found in a community which directly facilitate sound family structure. Programs which displace families or jeopardize their economic survival are likely to cause severe problems, especially in families with a low income and whose members are poorly educated. Severe economic hardship is considered by many specialists in family life to be a major cause of marital and child-related problems. Conversely, plans whose implementation will bring added economic relief to an impoverished area may be of significant benefit to families. Addition of various services for families' needs (e.g., health, education, housing, etc.) may also benefit family life. Family services are discussed in more detail on pp. 36-39.

It is important to recognize that a similar impact can have different meaning for the individual, depending upon his family role. Perhaps the most serious problems are those associated with displacement from one's home. In this situation, different family members can face very different problems, as the following illustrations suggest. The aged may fear resettlement because of reasons of health, the availability of needed services, and location of new friends, particularly if the move is to a distant place. Living on a fixed income may also make associated financial costs a serious problem. For the middle-aged farmer, starting a new farm presents difficulties in getting to know the land, developing irrigation procedures, choosing crop mixes, and so forth. Housewives frequently face many problems simultaneously in preparing youngsters for new schools, establishing new patterns of home maintenance, locating new services, etc. Youngsters adjusting to new schools can also undergo a strain. While the implementation of a plan might introduce problems in family life, the family is also a resource which may be helpful in coping with the new changes.

Another area of special concern in the measurement of social impacts has to do with the *attitudes* held by individuals and how the plans are related to them. Attitudes are complex and have various dimensions—emotional, intellectual, ethical, etc. They vary markedly according to the groups to which one belongs, one's personal views about life, experiences, goals, and the extent to which one acts upon her or his position. Of special interest to the planner is the extent to which the attitudes and values held by residents of the area are consistent with effects the plans are likely to have upon the communities. Thus, attitudes about the type of community (e.g., rural vs. urban), the type of people one chooses to live with (of similar or varied backgrounds), the characteristics of the community one seeks (e.g., highly stable, growing, or declining) can all result in different *responses* to a given plan. Some families may value preservation of the natural environment, while others seek greater economic development. An important consideration, then, will be the correspondence of the impacts of the various plans and the attitudes residents have toward their community.

Finally, in the category of individual and family effects, it is important to consider the fundamental concern of the relationship of the individual to his or her natural environment. Many families are especially concerned that they are able to live in a clean, accessible, and attractive area. Pollution, in addition to legal and economic costs, has social costs. It is important to gain a sense of how the quality of the environment will be affected in the plan area.

Social Effects from the Perspective of Groups and the Community

The community level of social concern is different from that of the individual. At this level, the focus is on institutions and values which tie people together and which allow for cooperative efforts and the development of collective action for the "greater good." Social impacts are considered in terms of how they affect groups of people and the institutions of the community which serve them; e.g., how social impacts affect supply and demand factors which, in turn, affect the number and diversity of community services. The concern also includes effects upon the informal groups which make up the community, and the general composition and character of the "future community" as it corresponds to what people today hope for and work toward.

Sociologist Robert Merton (1957) has identified a number of concerns which are relevant at this level, three of which are of particular importance here: (1) the *opportunities* available to people enabling them to participate in their communities; (2) the *stability and enhancement* of community values and norms; (3) *the nature of social organization and control* in the community.

The idea that individuals, irrespective of age, sex, race, ethnic background, etc., have an equal opportunity to participate in the public institutions of their community is viewed as a major (and constitutionally directed) responsibility of communities. A special concern in social assessment is the way in which beneficial and adverse effects are distributed throughout the community.

The basic concern in the stability and enhancement of community values and norms is how drastic the changes introduced by the plans will be in light of the present-day values and norms of the communities. For example, do future effects complement and extend the values and norms of the residents of the area, or are they likely to bring about radical changes in the community? How is a predominantly rural community, with its associated values and established relationships among key groups, affected by the emergence of a whole new set of values which are associated with the increase of urban-dominated, economic activities and with very different types of people coming into the area? Radical changes in community composition can lead to a real sense of estrangement from the emerging community character by present-day residents, a phenomenon referred to as "anomie" and which is associated with feelings of alienation, powerlessness, estrangement, feelings of control by external forces, frustration, and sometimes despair. Any plan that either offsets the presence of such attitudes or does not inadvertently induce them for significant segments of the population is making a social contribution. Since this phenomenon is likely to happen to groups of individuals in the community who lack a sense of identity with the larger community, it is handled as a problem within the community context.

The focus of concern on the nature of social organization and control in the community is on those social institutions which provide important services and controls in the communities. A major change in the demographic composition of the community, for example, can not only produce some of the problems described above, but it can significantly alter the capacity of the community to respond to legitimate needs in education, social services, cultural expression, and many other governmental services. From the opposite perspective, the institutions themselves can be severely overtaxed in their efforts to respond to the needs of their constituents.

It is not unusual, for example, to hear about significant problems faced by law enforcement agencies in trying to cope with rapidly expanding populations, especially where new arrivals come with values and expectations different from those of the local population. The introduction of severe strains on the informal group and institutional fiber of the community would be considered a severe social cost to the area. Conversely, changes in population which reduce conditions of crowding, general social unrest, or overtaxing of the physical, economic, and social resources of the communities, and which further the maintenance of family and group ties in the community, are examples of the benefits which might be generated by implementation of some of the plans.

Another major question is how do changes in the population affect the institutions of a community? There are various ways in which community institutions can be impaired in their operations. Most of these stem from a combination of a severe increase in demands from services with that of shortage of budgetary and staff resources. Impaired operations include overload, bottlenecks, unavailability of the right types of services, and delays in the provision of services. When operations are impaired, residents lose needed services and they begin to distrust the institutions; the institutions may respond inappropriately to service demands, may become outmoded, and may no longer be sought out for services.

Another level of the community which may experience impacts from a plan are the various groups and processes in the community which are not part of the more formal service-providing mechanisms of the community. These may involve informal settings such as local fraternal orders, special interests groups, and small neighborhood or ethnic groups which play a vital role in community life. One concern of social assessment is the extent to which these less formal structures will be affected by changes in population, value systems, and resources in the community.

In analyzing the characteristics of local social impacts, it is also useful to examine the present-day characteristics of groups in the planning area, the nature and structure of these groups, extent of cooperation and conflict within and among the groups, the types of activities (home, work, and leisure) which are important to the community, and the attainment of important goals. Examination of present-day characteristics of informal groups is useful for two reasons. First, to a considerable degree the quality of life of many persons is tied to the presence of meaningful contacts with informal group situations. Any radical change which affects such community ties and organization will change the character of the community. Second, in many communities, behind the more formal organization structures are networks of informal contacts and decision-making structures which usually relate in one way or another to many community operations. In short, community well-being involves both the formal and the informal aspects of group life and institutions.

The Larger Picture of Socioeconomic Effects in the Area

In the previous section, the focus of attention was on the local community level and its various aspects of groups and institutions. Certain other phenomena, while sometimes wholly contained within a given community, may also be viewed in a broader context, often providing continuity across a number of communities in a plan area. We are concerned here with the nature of the economic base of the area and its implications in employment, basic communications and transportation characteristics of the area, and with the effects of the planning process and construction on the area. Implementation of a plan may affect not only communities within the plan area, but those outside of it as well. A community which experiences economic development due to the implementation of a plan may attract new development to the greater region. Rural communities which have sufficient population and local resources for a sound economic base (including favorable conditions for certain types of agriculture or industries) are called "growth centers" by political geographers and economists (Borts, 1960). They serve as magnets to other communities for shopping, employment, services, etc. Implementation of water development plans may make a given community or area of communities into a growth center, thus affecting not only the particular community, but many others in the area as well. As described in central place theory (Haggett, 1966), the presence of economic, geographic, and political phenomena reinforce development of a given area. As these changes take place, major social changes in the communities can be expected to follow.

Many studies have documented the integral relationship between changes in the local economy and social impacts. As illustrations, shifts from labor intensive to capital intensive farming results in a loss of jobs for unskilled farm employees (frequently minority group members). Shifts in the economic base either from farm to industrial or from a few industries to a broader range of service and commercial jobs likewise can have important social effects. Different types of jobs mean different sets of skills, and this can attract new members to a community. While such changes in population can be a boost to the local economy, they can also bring conflicts between newer and older residents, between rural- and urban-oriented families. Even where such problems do not emerge, new populations can radically alter the demands for services such as education, health, fire protection, police, and housing. The interest of the SWB Account is *not* with the economic changes *per se*, but rather with how the economic changes alter the character of the community, place new demands on local institutions, affect the lives and finances of different groups of people in the community, and complement or contradict the important values and folkways of the area.

With economic changes come changes in the employment characteristics of the area. Some people, especially those near retirement age, may become structurally unemployable (i.e., lack the skills to fill available jobs), and unless they leave the area, they may end up permanently on the welfare rolls. Aside from costs to the community, this can have a drastic effect on self-confidence, feelings of self-worth, and family stability. On the positive side, when a plan implementation boosts the economic strength of a rural area, new job opportunities for local youth can stem the tide of migration to the cities. Thus, plan implementation provides the necessary ingredient to make dying rural communities viable again.

Significant changes in population generated through new employment opportunities are likely to increase population and as this occurs, new transportation networks and new media may be established in the community (local radio, TV, and newspapers). Existing facilities and services may expand, diversify, and improve. From a social standpoint, these events can be quite significant in altering life styles (e.g., commuting patterns, shopping, leisure activities), and changing the nature of media exposure (e.g., through cable TV, greater contact with outside world through local press, a more diverse local political process), all of which may or may not complement existing values and institutions.

The planning process itself can also have important consequences. Local communities, aware that changes may be coming, may be stimulated to new plans for development, or in some cases, may be seriously constrained in the planning because of uncertainty. Local municipal improvements, bond issues, tax questions, and the like may all be delayed pending resolution of the decision to implement a plan; the credit ratings of the communities in the area can also be affected. Individuals likewise may be uncertain as to whether to improve their homes or to invest in development of a particular career line, etc. Thus, while careful planning is critical, protracted uncertainty during this period can clearly have damaging social costs.

Finally, there are numerous examples of social problems associated with construction once a given plan is implemented. When a significant work force is associated with construction activities, there can be the following types of problems: drastic increases in local prices for goods, services, and housing; strain upon a variety of local services such as schools, hospitals, social services; increases in local conflicts involving police and courts; and a general change in the character and quality of life to which local residents are accustomed. Local merchants may do a "land-office" business, but the larger community can undergo severe strain. In part, the situation is influenced by the extent to which an indigenous vs. a large, outside labor force is employed in the activities. Different problems can be anticipated based upon the length of time of the construction period and the volume of outside manpower required during construction.

To summarize, the concerns of this area of social impact are with the employment, welfare, transportation, and communications patterns of the local economy and infrastructure, all of which cause important social changes in communities and services of the area.

Contributions to the National Good

To this point the social assessment has dealt with important social effects relevant to the individual locality. An important part of the mandate of the Water Resources Council is to consider the ways in which the changes proposed in the plan may have selected national impacts. While these changes may not "trade-off" against local considerations, they can form an important part of the decision-making process.

A major concern of social assessment is how plan implementation would contribute to national viability in a variety of ways; e.g., significant increases in local agricultural productivity or in the potential for agricultural development are important at the national level. Expanded crop production is important both for domestic consumption and for international distribution or sale of food and fibers. In a similar sense, the altered capacity of water supply can be important in its own right. Greater stability of water availability, especially through transmountain exchange, can help meet emergencies through various emergency contingency plans. Plans which will enhance electric power supplies and increase the nation's capacity to support new populations and industries or which will assist directly or indirectly in the preservation of scarce fuels are other examples of plans which help to support national goals. Finally, plans which comply with national laws and international treaties pertaining to water utilization are important from the national perspective. In some cases, it is just such external criteria which may determine the outcome of a recommendation when, from the local perspective, two plans appear to be roughly equal in their social effects.

Aggregate Social Effects

All of the preceding components have been limited to a particular aspect of social effects. It is also desirable to consider the more general social characteristics of the impacts. Three types of effects, called "aggregate social effects," have been chosen for this purpose. They are: (1) effects on the general quality of the life of the people; (2) effects on the relative social position of groups of people; and (3) effects upon the social well-being of communities and their social institutions.

Quality of Life

Quality of life refers to the overall nature of impacts on the individual and his or her family and to the effects which such changes, in turn, may have on the individual's perception of the opportunities for personal and family development. A recent national study conducted by the Environmental Protection Agency in connection with work on the meaning of quality of life suggested that a variety of social goals exist for individuals and families which can be important in the quality of life. Among these are: good health, opportunity for a reasonable income and a reasonable standard of living, healthy development of children, happy family life, decent home and neighborhood, peace of mind and emotional maturity, recreation, community stability, and so forth. An individual's stage of life, the overall economic security of his or her situation, and his or her present location in the community are all relevant in the assessment of an individual's quality of life. It must be remembered that the purpose of the assessment is to measure the effects of implementation of a water development plan on an individual's quality of life, rather than to describe the individual's quality of life in general.

It is useful to identify some of the current knowledge which is available on the concept of quality of life. The following findings are documented in Rabel J. Burdge's *A Summary of Sociological Studies of Water Resources Dealing with Social Goals and the "Quality of Life"* (1973).

- Quality of life impacts will be different if one is displaced vs. not displaced.
- Quality of life impacts will be different depending upon who is involved and what they value (e.g., younger people may value recreation, farmers the certainty of crop development, the elderly a sense of security).
- Quality of life impacts will be different if one is in a position of strength (e.g., economically, in terms of age, legally) rather than a position of weakness (e.g., poor,

elderly, unable to secure legal help).

- Quality of life impacts will be different if one is able to maintain one's sense of community and have neighbors who share one's beliefs, as compared with a situation where one is thrust into a new community, especially if that community has a new life style (e.g., rural to urban, comfortable economic circumstances to marginal existence).
- Quality of life impacts will be different if one is leaving a situation with which one has only marginal attachment rather than leaving a place where one has strong roots and deep attachments.
- Quality of life impacts will be different depending on whether one is anticipating a favorable future in his or her new circumstance or whether one is anticipating a personal or family crisis in a new situation.

In a more psychological sense, quality of life can include concern over stability in family relationships, friendships, and love and companionship. Figure 4 (from Burdge, 1973) reflects the diversity of elements which can be considered in this aggregated social concept. However, since the factors shown have, in large measure, been reflected upon in the other components (pp. 32-42), we are mainly concerned here with how the individual is likely to react to these impacts in the aggregate and how they affect one's expectations for his or her future life. We are interested in how protracted, how painful, and how resented experiences associated with the plan implementation might be; the extent of uncertainty introduced into people's lives; increases in the interest in community life and local institutions; and in general, the sense of pride a person feels as a member of the community, especially as it relates to the development of a new future in the community. Short-term costs and long-term benefits, which are dealt with in more detail under Relative Social Position, may be expected to trade off against one another in various ways.

Relative Social Position

It is important to distinguish between the assistance provided to an area which is depressed and that which is provided to

Figure 4. *The Quality of Life Index*[a]

Weights			*Quality of Life Dimensions*
.10			1. Psychological Well-Being
			1) Love, companionship
			2) Self respect
			3) Peace of mind
			4) Stimulation, challenge
			5) Other: popularity, accomplishment, individuality, sexual satisfaction, involvement, comfort, novelty, dominance, privacy, etc.
.90			2. Situational Descriptors
	.40		*Economic*
		.50	6) Standard of living (income per capita, discretionary income)
		.10	7) Unemployment
		.10	8) Financial dependency (welfare, dependency ratio)
		.20	9) Housing (persons per room, home ownership, percent substandard)
		.05	10) Supply and distribution bottlenecks (food, fuel, commodity, etc. shortages)
		.05	11) Transportation convenience (including commuting time)
	.25		*Social*
		.17	12) Family relations
		.13	13) Friendships
		.20	14) Job satisfaction
		.05	15) Crime and violence (crime index and exposure to civil strife and political violence)
		.35	16) Health, safety and nourishment (calorie and protein consumption, infant mortality, disability rate, life expectancy)
		.20	17) Education (reading achievement, enrollment ratios, graduation rates)
	.20		*Leisure*
		.30	18) Media entertainment (radio, TV, movies)
		.15	19) Entertainment: other (spectator sports, "night life," live programs)
		.15	20) Cultural opportunities (performing arts, art objects, reading, museums, historical sights)
		.20	21) Recreational facilities and areas (sports, strolling, play, picnics, etc.)
		.10	22) Areas of natural beauty (access to park lands, landscapes, etc.)
		.10	23) Exposure to pollution (air, water, radiation, noise)
	.15		*Political*
		.15	24) Political participation (voting, campaigning, activism)
		.15	25) News coverage
		.30	26) Freedoms and civil rights
		.15	27) Government responsiveness
		.05	28) Public services (shortages, blackouts, interruptions, unavailability)
		.20	29) Equality (income, opportunity, justice)

[a]From Burdge, 1973.

individuals who are poor or disadvantaged. It is possible to help the first without having much effect on the second; i.e., those people already in a reasonably good position in a community may further benefit from assistance to an area while poor families and individuals may not. By *relative social position* we mean the extent to which the various beneficial and adverse social effects of implementing a plan would be equitably distributed among various members of the community. We are also interested in the capacity of different groups of people to bear such costs. It may well be that in some areas, the position of a group of individuals is so bad that the group is unable to bear any cost; i.e., in the case of extreme poverty or social isolation. Special attention would have to be given to such a group in the event of the implementation of a plan.

In order to assess the equity of the distribution of plan effects, it is useful to identify the groups of individuals who will be affected. In some cases, these groups will be fairly formal, such as ethnic groups, income groups, education groups, groups by geographic location, and so forth. In other cases, there may be an informal grouping of people, such as people living in a small cluster of poverty or an informal association of farmers or local businessmen. Landowners and large business owners make up similar informal groupings.

Various measures are used in assessing equity of distribution; these include the changes in the distribution of income, job opportunities, services provided by formal agencies to residents, housing availability, employment available outside the community, educational opportunities, recreation opportunities, etc. Again, different groups may benefit or lose differently from implementation of a plan.

Finally, the real opportunities in the future for various groups are also a concern in the area of relative social position.

Social Well-Being

While quality of life is an expression of the degree to which individuals and families enjoy their lives in good health, in economic security, and in general peace of mind about the present and future, *social well-being* can be evaluated at a higher level of aggregation; i.e., the level of the community and its constituent groups. Social well-being *contributes* to the quality of life. The effects of impacts are assessed on formal institutions (such as schools, churches, and local government) and informal groups of people (such as farmers, fraternal orders, local leisure groups, and special interest groups) that collectively reflect the values, goals, and life activities of people in the community. Most important, the future capacity of the community to sustain itself in a character consistent with the desires of its residents and institutions must be assessed.

The following are some of the evaluation categories of social well-being.

- The viability and stability of organizations and institutions such as schools, churches, clubs, colleges, and the like, especially as they contribute to the quality of life of individuals
- Improvement of conditions associated with the achievement of economic stability and improved personal income
- Achievement of a desirable population distribution in terms of male/female balance in various age groups, reasonable dependency ratios of elderly to work-age population, continuity of values such as rural or urban orientation, and avoidance of severe problems associated with high density
- Enhancement of security of life and health through a reduction in the risk of floods, drought, or other water-related disasters by better water management and control
- Improved stability of local government operations
- Improvements in national, emergency preparedness which make a contribution to the nation's collective security

While these categories have necessarily diverse characteristics, their frame of reference remains constant: the community and its overall viability. For example, a generally declining population can have a major influence on all the institutions in a particular area; the social future for a community or area which suffers a continued migration of its youth is usually bleak. Alternatively, an influx of a proportionately large number of new residents can, as indicated earlier, cause social havoc. The function of this aggregate measure is to assess, on balance, the probable future character and viability of the community and its institutions.

Some Other Dimensions of Assessing Social Effects

A variety of considerations influence how to most effectively organize a social assessment in such a way as to achieve a responsible and useful Social Well-Being Account. In this section, the general orientation of the social scientist toward social assessment is briefly discussed. The trade-offs between "breadth vs. depth" are identified. The nature of forecasting is reviewed, and selected parameters of forecasting are identified. Finally, certain limitations in the procedure are set forth.

The Social Science Orientation—Substance and Method

One of the most important caveats in social assessment is the fact that social scientists, depending upon their field and interests, have a variety of orientations. Psychologists study motivation, perception, emotional development, language, attitudes, interpersonal relations, etc. Sociologists have interests in the relationship between social values of the society and those of individuals and groups. Anthropologists explore the ways in which the inculcation and reinforcement of cultural norms and values occur. There are also differences within disciplines. For example, some sociologists are interested in the behavior of institutions or of large population groups, while others are more interested in social action.

Because of limitations of time, money and integrating theory, not all social science fields of interest are present in the *Social Assessment Manual;* i.e., at one end of a continuum from individual to social concerns, there is not a "psychoanalytic" conceptualization of human behavior incorporated into the design. While these aspects of social science are recognized as important, it is believed that the SWB Account does not have the capability or mandate to analyze the impacts at this level of individualization. At the other extreme, the SWB Account does not question what types of society are optimal, since this is largely a matter of political decision-making (e.g., voting) and not of social assessment. Within these somewhat extreme boundaries, however, the SWB Account still covers a broad range of concerns.

The most direct way of describing the substantive approaches being employed is that they combine elements of orientation from the fields of sociology, social psychology, and to a lesser degree, anthropology. These interests of the various fields of social science appropriately dominate the orientation of the social assessment; we are examining people, institutions, groups, values and the like. However, the relationship of the methodology of the social assessment to social science research is more complex. The research studies of sociology generally begin with a theory or concept, then formulate hypotheses, gather data, conduct formal analyses, and arrive at conclusions concerning hypotheses and theory. In its simplest form, this is a relatively deductive research method. A less deductive method of research is to gather data and, through successive iterations, move toward the development of theory; this is often referred to as the "grounded theory" approach. On the more inductive end of the continuum, the field of anthropology has pioneered in the development of ethnographic research. The anthropologist frequently enters a community with no preconceived notions of what to study (in terms of predefined data categories) and lets the experience of interaction with local residents and institutions determine what questions and issues ought to be dealt with. The ethnographic method can be a highly effective approach to research; it is similar to the use of naturalistic observations in some of the life sciences. While these descriptions of methodology are over-simplified, they serve to point out that different traditions have contributed to the orientation of the social assessment. The strength of the sociological method is that it centers on the precise delineation of data necessary to answer specific questions. Its weakness lies in the fact that it may not always ask the questions which are important for a given community. The ethnographic approach finds its strength in the fact that it lets the data guide the researcher to important issues. Its weakness, for purposes here, is that it may fail to get information that is needed for various policy decisions. The sound assessment leans to the more deductive approach, but has elements of the inductive method of inquiry in it as well. As will be seen in Part 2, a variety of specific variables are identified for consideration. In addition, attitudinal and informal group data allow for issues not specified elsewhere, but which are deemed important by the local community, to emerge and be dealt with.

Assessment of Social Effects from a Broad Perspective vs. Selected, In-depth Assessment

For many years, social scientists have been concerned that investments made in the name of the public good have been evaluated from far too narrow a perspective. Technology development, economic progress, and change for the sake of change have often seemed to dominate the value systems of agencies. In some cases, the frequently unanticipated consequences of plans have been quite severe. The limitations of this one-sided view of assessment have been increasingly recognized. With these considerations in mind, the social scientist is faced with a trade-off of considerable importance: Does he confine himself to deep understanding of a few phenomena or does he attempt to gain a broader perspective of social impact, albeit somewhat less precise? Each approach, breadth vs. depth, has its merits.

The *Principles and Standards* is clearly concerned with a range of social effects. Studying only a few areas of impacts in depth (e.g., culture, individuals, institutions), while quite valuable, might be as "one-sided" as the earlier approaches have been. In contrast, the broader approach, though it lacks some of the depth of an intensive one-point investigation, has the virtue of gaining an overall perspective on a range of social impacts of different types and at various levels (i.e., individuals, communities, larger areas). If plan implementation will have a significant social effect, then this orientation is quite likely to identify it. Moreover, this approach facilitates the identification of social impacts which may be associated with one plan but not with another. Finally, if a particular problem area is identified as a part of the Feasibility Report SWB Account, this could then be explored in greater depth during the final stages of the Definite

Plan Report assessment (or under a social impact assessment conducted as part of the preparation of an environmental impact statement). Thus, the broader approach considers many possible alternative social outcomes and points to further investigations which can be pursued when a given plan comes closer to actual implementation.

The Use of Hard vs. Soft Data

If the SWB Account uses a broad approach in assessing the social impacts associated with various water plans, an important question is raised with respect to the type of data it will be able to use: Does one gather information which is only highly quantified in its characteristics and thus limited in the information that can be assessed, or does one allow somewhat softer data to be presented which provides non-uniform measures but gives additional information? Since the SWB Account explores a variety of areas of social impacts, it, in fact, requires both quantified and non-quantified information.

The SWB Account utilizes a variety of types of data, varying from population data and morbidity statistics to data on attitudes and values. To not include this range of data would be to deny the account access to very useful, frequently reliable information which is critical in gaining a social perspective. While non-quantifiable data present problems of non-uniform measures across the components, there is no absolute virtue in being able to "add everything up," and there is clear value in being able to consider a variety of social impacts. The objective is to assess the impacts of various effects, whether or not they are easily quantifiable. In fact, the effects need not be readily quantifiable in order to be valuable to the assessment. The uses of various types of data to forecast social effects are discussed in somewhat more detail on pp. 64-74.

The "Art" of Forecasting—Causality and Change

On pp. 27-29 the concept of the community as a dynamic system was described. One implication of this concept is that the planning area is in a process of constant change, whether or not a particular plan is ever implemented. For this reason, the changes which are forecast are not those which compare present-day characteristics with future characteristics related to a water development plan. Rather, the changes which are forecast are those which compare future characteristics related to a water development plan with the area as it would exist in the future without any plan. In a simplified sense, this can be stated as:

Change Value of a Given Water Plan for Community X = Present-Day Status + Future Status With Plan - Future Status Without Plan

The function of the future status without a plan is critical to the process of forecasting the impacts attributable to a plan. It is possible that a community will remain constant with respect to a given variable and that any changes are simply directly attributable to whatever plan is under study. More likely, however, changes will occur without any plan. If a variable is forecasted to decrease without any plan, then the true, attributable change of implementing a given plan is the sum of the amount added to the present value, plus the amount it would have decreased without the plan. Similarly, if a variable will increase, the change attributable to the plan is the amount added, *minus* the amount it would have gained without the plan.

Let us look at the possible future effects of four alternative futures for a given variable for the same community, under the possibility of implementing different plans (Figure 5).

Figure 5. *Examples of Alternative Employment Effects of Alternative Planning Futures for Community X*

Plan	Present-day Employment (+)	Future Employment With Plan (-)	Future Employment Without Plan (=)	Change in Employment Attributable to Plan
No Plan	10,000	N.A.	12,000	0
NED	10,000	18,000	12,000	6,000
Alt.	10,000	12,000	12,000	0
EQ	10,000	10,000	12,000	-2,000

In Figure 5 we see in row 1 that there is a forecasted increase in employment *without* any plan whatsoever of 2,000 persons. However, since no plan is implemented, this change is *not* attributed to water planning. In row 2, when the NED plan is implemented (perhaps providing more water to industry), there is an increase in future employment of 8,000 persons. However, since without the plan there is an expected addition of 2,000, the amount of 6,000 new employees is "attributed" to the plan. In row 3, the change in employment with the plan remains the same as without any plan, so no employment is attributed to the plan. This is an important example, for real employment actually increases from 10,000 to 12,000, but it is not attributable to the plan. Finally, the EQ plan (perhaps diverting present community waters for environmental purposes) is shown to be associated with employment at the same level as it is today. Again, however, since employment would have been expected to increase without any plan, the net attributable employment effect of this plan is -2,000 employees, who otherwise would have been employed in the absence of the plan.

Discussing forecasting logic in terms of the employment variable is relatively straightforward. Employment uses a quantifiable, familiar unit of measure: the number of persons employed. Employment was chosen as an example in order to clearly explain the concept of forecasting. However, forecasting is not always this simple and frequently presents several problems. First, not all forecasts concern variables which are so tangible and familiar to the planner. Second, the methods used in forecasting are, in reality, more of an art than a science. While the planner may, in fact, be able to use some sophisticated forecasting techniques for some variables, generally most variables lend themselves more readily to forecasts which are imperfect, though reasonable.

Different types of forecasting present different problems. The easiest variables to work with are those which, barring some unforeseen disaster, will behave in a predictable manner over a reasonable period of time in accordance with known principles. The most accurate forecasts concerning human behaviors are found in actuarials, as used by insurance companies. These forecasts deal with very specific events based upon statistical extrapolations; they are not readily applied to most of the concerns which a responsible social assessment must deal with. Even with demographic statistics there are six or seven forecasting techniques, and demographers are often surprised by reversals in trends which, after the fact, are often explainable through a complex of social and economic considerations, either local or regional. Another kind of forecasting is found in a variety of economic research. These different kinds of forecasting, which utilize different variables, have two characteristics in common. First, the forecasting is generally at a fairly macro level (either in terms of behaviors or size of population). Second, all three fields have a fair amount of theory and empirical experience associated with their forecasts. Even in these circumstances, forecasting is still considered difficult and is still referred to as an "art."

A number of variables in the social assessment benefit from previously constructed forecasting techniques. These variables are affected by economic and demographic changes which can be forecasted with some reasonable probabilities. These variables include such items as the number of jobs, the number of housing units, highway access to an area, number of hospital beds or school classrooms, etc. In forecasting the social impact on these variables, we know that an increase in the number of people will usually increase demand and thus strain existing facilities. We also know that if sufficient private capital or taxes are added to the economic base, there will be a resulting increase in investments to add, for example, new houses, facilities, and service jobs to satisfy the demand. In fact, it is precisely this logic whereby most forecasts, in one way or another, are made. Often they are reasonably accurate for our purposes within a "band of probability." Essentially, these forecasts can be worked out in the presence of certain knowledge. Local expert informants (e.g., in a local employment office, local key industries, real estate planners, school superintendents) typically have rather precise information on the present-day characteristics of a specific variable such as employment. Various agencies (such as the telephone company, retail outlets for products such as gasoline, etc.) often make forecasts on local population for the coming years in order to anticipate service demands. Interviews with such experts, or reviews of annual reports (e.g., of school districts), can provide the planner with valuable information concerning the future trends of the planning area in the absence of any plan. Obviously, most of these forecasts do *not* assume an NED or EQ plan being implemented.

There are two specific kinds of impacts which are absolutely critical in forecasting other impacts under a given plan (e.g., NED, EQ, and an alternative plan). The first type of forecasting concerns the likely impact of plan implementation upon the *local economy.* The second type of forecasting is concerned with the likely relationship between the economy and the present-day *local population.* For example, if the capacity for various types of industry will increase, in forecasting its effect, one determines the extent to which these industries are labor or capital intensive and how this quality relates to the present employment situation. Loss of farm jobs through increases in capital-intensive production will reduce farm jobs where there are labor-intensive agriculture operations. Labor-intensive industry arriving in an area with little or no such labor available will usually act as a magnet to attract new employees. Moreover, different types of employers (agriculture, industry, commerce, government, etc.) have been known to have multiplier effects; i.e., they create "support" employment in local service industries.

The development of a reasonable forecast includes an understanding of the present situation. When one is interested in "forecasting" the employment impacts of a dam on an area, certain data can be brought together under the following questions: What is the present number of people in the labor force? What do they do? Who are they? What is their employment context? This information is very useful, for if one knows that with the establishment of new water conditions, new industries or agriculture will be supported and others will die out, then logical projections can be made. In some cases, individuals currently employed by dying industries can be transferred to new industries, while in other cases, this is not possible; these people will either leave the area to find new employment or will remain in the area with little or no prospect for employment. The fact that new industries often must attract new employees is useful information for forecasting population growth, which is somewhat constrained by the extent of new jobs opening up. New jobs, in turn, will create increased demands for various services (schools, fire and police protection, local retail outlets) and so there is also some multiplier effect of new jobs. Different industries have different multiplier effects. Therefore, by determining the number of jobs created both directly and through multiplier effects, one has a basis for estimating possible rises (or declines) in population. In addition, different jobs draw different people; some jobs will need engineers, while others will need service operators. The composition of the work force will affect the composition of the community; as these changes take place, the character of the communities in the impact area may be expected to change. For example, a change in the character of the population from one primarily engaged in agricultural production to one more diverse in its employment and thus also more diverse in educational characteristics can affect the values, attitudes, consumption behaviors, service demands, etc., of the community. Thus, when one speaks of forecasting, what is really meant is the logical extrapolation of likely impacts that will occur based upon known associations among different social phenomena. Thus, an important part of forecasting the many social impacts of a plan will stem from an understanding of what the plan is likely to do for the local economy, and the ability of the area to draw new population or its likelihood of losing it.

Aside from using local demographic forecasts (e.g., obtained from local demographers or other sources), one can also make use of the Office of Business and Economic Research and Statistics (OBERS) projections to determine the future size and characteristics of the population (U.S. Water Resources Council, 1972). Projections of population change in a study area provide an important element of the foundation upon which the subsequent structure of social effects associated with alternative plans will be built. By combining knowledge of future population characteristics with an understanding of the changing character of the labor situation in the area, many social impacts can, in turn, be assessed. Thus, forecasting of this sort entails logically extrapolating the likely effect from known associations among different phenomena and making use of individuals experienced in a particular area of community life (e.g., local specialists) to help in calculating the likely effects. This procedure essentially represents a step-by-step analysis of likely impacts which will be occurring for some identifiable reasons. The types of social impacts which can be calculated for individual social areas is the subject of the second part of the *Social Assessment Manual.* For example, it will be shown that the direct impact of an increase in population can have the indirect impact of drastically altering the values and life-style of the community, an equally important social consequence to the increase in population itself.

There are many variables which are not as straightforward in character. These variables include such concerns as the changes in people's attitudes, the satisfaction people will feel with their communities, the changes in equal opportunity to benefit from the changes which are coming, etc. A variety of such variables will be detailed in Part 2. We turn our attention here to describing briefly some of the forecasting techniques available for dealing with some of these variables.[1]

Two types of forecasting can be carried out, both of which use the same methods. First, one can forecast the likely change in a variable; e.g., types of employment likely to be introduced into an area such as farm, industrial, and commercial. Second, one can forecast, for example, who is likely to obtain the jobs. In one case, the diversity of characteristics of an institution are forecast. In the second case, the distribution of the changes by sub-groups of the population is forecast. The SWB Account calls for both types of forecasts. (The nature of differences among types of variables is dealt with in more detail on pp. 66-68.) At least six different approaches to forecasting might be employed in the social assessment. The following are brief descriptions of each.

1. Detailed discussion of forecasting logic and techniques may be found in Box and Jenkins, 1970.

Trend extrapolation is perhaps the most widely used technique for forecasting. Using this method, one plots a curve over a number of years (yearly, bi-yearly, or for 5- or 10-year periods) for a given variable, and then extends the trend line into the future. External constraints are often placed on the upside or downside extrapolation of the curve, based upon limitations that are known about the population, changing consumer patterns and the like. Such a curve might be constructed for the future without any plan: in this way, how the implementation of other plans is likely to interrupt the projected characteristics may be determined. Such changes can, in turn, be related to various sub-groups in the population (e.g., farmers, youth, and minorities) in terms of their distribution among the groups. The development of trend extrapolation is greatly facilitated by the use of secondary data sources, which are readily available to planners, in most cases, from local sources such as libraries, or state and county offices of the various federal agencies.

A second, closely allied approach to forecasting is the use of *discussions with expert informants* who can help generate expected characteristics for a given variable. This method is both inexpensive and very valuable in terms of making use of locally available, knowledgeable persons. Since the interviewees live in the area, it has the added advantage of enabling citizen participation in the planning process. Local public health officials, school district staff, welfare officials, private agency personnel, and local businessmen and farmers are invaluable sources of information on past, present, and possible future social characteristics of their community. Doctors are aware of health problems both in general and for specific groups. Employment agencies generally know what types of jobs are filled and who typically has trouble finding work. This is perhaps the most informed and cost effective approach to forecasting.

A third approach to forecasting is that of *contingency trees.* This method of forecasting, which has been used both in business and government as a technique for planning, utilizes a graphic display of different outcomes, usually beginning with a higher order impact and working toward different "branches" for lower order impacts. A similar tree can be constructed for a time period to indicate consequent impacts of earlier decisions or events. The technique can be used to indicate not only the directions or branches of social impacts but can also be used to assign probabilities to these events. Assigning probabilities to social impacts is usually accomplished by techniques such as expert opinion, conducting surveys, brain-storming, or using other sources of data; e.g., knowing the multiplier effects of different industries would allow one to show the probable increase in types of jobs in sectors other than those which have been forecasted to expand as a direct result of plan implementation.

The fourth technique of forecasting involves conducting *surveys* (Rosenberg, 1968) in order to obtain actual distributions of anticipated resident behaviors (e.g., employment, migration, and attitudes) in response to the implementation of plans. Based upon such surveys, actual data are used to help develop forecasts. This technique requires the collection of primary, as distinct from secondary, data and presents certain costs in dollars and labor which need to be weighed in light of the added value of the information.

A fifth technique of forecasting is the use of the *Delphi Technique* (Helmer, 1966). This is a fairly well established approach to forecasting; it begins with obtaining the opinions of experts on a given outcome, then returning with a second iteration in which each person sees how and why each forecast was made, and then making a second projection. A distribution of final forecasts is then obtained. The approach has proven quite useful in dealing with fairly complex forecasts. A variation of this method involves the use of Bayesian probabilities (Morgan, 1968), which also can make use of small surveys of experts who assign probability values to alternative futures which are then dealt with in a specific statistical treatment.

A sixth technique of forecasting is that of *scenario generation.* In this technique, planners develop brief stories about the different types of futures which are foreseen under each of the alternative plans (e.g., three economic futures under the NED plan); these scenarios are reviewed by experts to determine the likelihood of their occurrence given present internal and external realities of the planning area. Various cause-effect hypotheses are set forth in the scenarios as the basis for such forecasts.

These techniques, then, constitute some of the main approaches which have been used to forecast impacts. However, it is also important to recognize that there are a variety of parameters which are important in making such forecasts. As indicated before, forecasts can be broken down in various ways; we now turn to some of these parameters.

Parameters of Impacts

While it is possible to determine what is going to happen as a result of plan implementation, it is frequently necessary to also specify whether the impact is direct or indirect, when it is going to happen, where, and to whom.

Direct versus indirect impacts. Any impacts which are caused by the implementation of a given plan, such as changes in water availability, are obviously direct impacts. However, there are other equally direct social impacts (such as the disruption in life-style caused by the process of plan implementation and the changes in the future characteristics of the planning area) which are directly a function of the change in water characteristics. If new industries or farms are established in an area as a function of the change in water characteristics and thus provide jobs and draw people to the area, these are termed direct social impacts. The types of direct impacts are described below.

Mere knowledge of the fact that a project is being planned sets into motion *disruption impacts*—with people taking sides, debating issues, experiencing conflicts, and feeling anxiety over what will happen to jobs, homes, schools, and so on. State and local agencies may have to spend considerable time and money constructing plans just on the basis of the possibility that a project is planned for the area. Subsequent construction has obvious direct impacts—especially when people are forced to move. Other obvious direct impacts of construction include blocked highways and noise and air pollution.

Second, direct *demographic impacts* can be both short- and long-term. Construction workers swell the population for some period with attendant consequences in cash flow, services, and civil activities. After implementation of a plan is completed, new citizens may arrive in the area, affecting the size, characteristics and composition of the area's population.

Finally, *economic impacts,* which draw persons to an area or increase revenues of capital-intensive industry and agriculture, are directly attributable to the quantity, quality, and supply characteristics of a plan.

These direct impacts are reasonably straightforward. They don't tend to be overlooked; rather it is the consequences which these impacts, in turn, have on various aspects of family and community life which are often unforeseen. It is in the very nature of social phenomena that there are a variety of *indirect impacts* which are critical in assessing the true social effects of plan implementation. As population changes and the nature of employment changes, many other impacts, in turn, begin to occur.

These indirect impacts are many and varied. They can be found in many areas of community and family life—impacts on health, education, attitudes, family life, and the social structure of communities. As illustrations, new types of jobs in the community which draw in new populations can, in turn, lead to:

- A different composition of groups making up a community (different income levels, ethnic characteristics, attitudes toward community institutions, etc.)
- Different levels of demand for important (and frequently expensive) services such as schooling, medical care, and types of housing
- Different expectations from local government institutions relating to sanitation, law enforcement, recreation, etc.
- Increased diversity and capacity of services provided as a result of a larger economic base
- Important changes in the character of community life (e.g., rural to urban life-style) and the values of different groups now living in the community
- Changes in the equality of opportunity of different groups of citizens to benefit from and participate in community activities

Since these impacts are due to changes in population and

economic characteristics which were, in turn, due to plan implementation, they are termed indirect.

Short-term vs. long-term impacts. Impacts also vary according to the time frame in which they occur. Certain impacts are likely to be short-term and very noticeable, especially when uncertainty is introduced into the planning area by the consideration of the "alternative futures." Even more striking can be the impact of heavy and especially large-scale construction. Changes in population and service needs for a period of from three to five years can be very significant. Long-term changes in population, employment, values, community life, though of immense importance, may be anywhere from five to twenty years away. For these reasons, the data in a social assessment can usually be qualified by the time a given impact is likely to occur. Generally, the ability to forecast other than general types of impacts over a longer period of time (e.g., twenty years) is quite difficult. For example, in 1955, who would have forecast the attitudes and values of Americans with respect to concerns about minority group rights, attitudes toward sex, employment prospects for college-educated youth, etc., as they turned out to be in 1975?

Geographic location. Another fundamental characteristic of impacts is where they will occur; i.e., their geographic location. The geographic location of persons often determines whether or not they will be affected by implementation of alternative plans. In the most obvious instance, where individuals live in an area in which there will be a flood pool, they will be most directly affected in the short run; they will have to seek new homes or farmland. In other parts of the planning area, there may be significant increases in employment, and in still other areas new recreation facilities may be added. Some areas may receive little or no benefit, and even some areas outside of the planning area may be affected by implementation of a plan. It is important that the social impacts be described in terms of their aggregate distribution over geographic areas within which the beneficial and adverse social impacts of the plans may fall and, while it may not be worthwhile to research in depth the possible impacts of plan implementation outside the area, that these also be considered. In sum, certain areas will benefit markedly under a given plan, while others may be seriously and adversely affected. A good understanding of present-day geographic characteristics of the area facilitates forecasting inequitable distributions. Geographic inequities will usually translate into other types of inequities in terms of who is affected.

The recipients of impacts. Who the recipients of the impact are, is our final concern in this section. We may find that persons living in one of the areas affected by the proposed plan will be forced to relocate, while those in another area will be beneficiaries of new jobs, better schools, etc. However, there are distinctions other than geographic which must be considered. The following sets of categories demonstrate the different groups of people who may be impacted:

- Demographic groups:
  - Age: the very young, youth, young adults, the middle-aged, and the elderly
  - Minority Status: Western, Eastern, or Southern Europeans, Spanish-Americans, Afro-Americans, Indians, Orientals, and others
  - Religious Status: Catholic, Jewish, Mormon, Protestant, etc.
  - Sex
  - Marital Status
- Occupational groups: professionals, managers and administrators, sales workers, clerical and kindred workers, craftsmen, operatives, farm managers, farm laborers, service workers
- Economic groups:
  - Income level: high, medium, or low
  - Property ownership: homeowners or non-homeowners
  - Business ownership: large business owners, small business owners, industrial owners, non-business/industrial owners

Benefits and costs may affect various "combinations" of these categories. When one is looking at the combined benefits and costs associated with the implementation of a water plan, patterns should be identified in terms of whether one group is significantly benefiting, while another group is paying dearly in many different ways.

Trade-offs Among Effects

All of these types of impacts involve a phenomenon quite familiar to the economist, that of "trade-offs"; i.e., certain social concerns may be operating in a contradictory manner, thus complicating the decision-making process. Implementation of a water development plan may simultaneously generate good and bad social effects. For example, implementation of a plan may simultaneously enhance recreational opportunities for local residents (generally perceived as "good") and also attract many outside tourists who inundate the area for weekends (seen as both "good" and "bad" depending upon the perspective). Similarly, increases in employment opportunities for youth may also produce an increase in high school dropout rates. Preservation of natural environment under strict federal codes may also result in a plant closing, with a consequent drop in employment and income security for local residents. A sound social assessment must take into account that a combination of good and bad effects will arise from the implementation of a plan or the decision to not implement any plan. Frequently, these trade-offs do not affect the same people; some people will benefit while others will lose.

Dealing with the Measurement of Social Well-Being

Measurement and the Causal Agent

Measuring the data concerning each plan usually involves a straightforward transfer of information from the description of each plan. Materials are obtained concerning the activities (e.g., channels, powerlines, dams, multi-purpose reservoirs, proposed wild and scenic river reaches, and open or green spaces) associated with each plan and then the functions which will be performed under each activity (e.g., irrigation, water supply for industry, ecological supports) and their location in the plan area are indicated. The future without any plan must be similarly analyzed in terms of the present water infrastructure and functions in the area. A general history of the development of water resources in the planning area is also helpful, but no measurement activities are associated with this step in the process.

Measurement and the Present-day Community

Three types of information have been indicated as useful in describing the present-day community: historical information, a social profile, and general descriptive information. To compile such information, no measurement activities *per se* are actually involved. Statistics on the historical and present-day characteristics of the area are needed, but they are primarily used for descriptive purposes. Historical data, including age of community, settlement patterns, natural features of the area, and more recent trends in population are all handled in narrative form with accompanying maps and tables as appropriate. The social profile involves display of data rather than measurement, and therefore it is dealt with in Chapter 8 rather than here. Materials describing the life-styles and values of the community complete the presentation.

There is, however, one distinct measurement activity associated with preparation of this section; i.e., the determination of how *typical* or *atypical* some of the present-day features described in the profile are. Essentially, the characteristics of the planning area communities must be rated in terms of their similarities and differences *in comparison to either other areas in the region or, where appropriate, to national averages.* For example, a 9% unemployment rate would appear to be unusually high unless the surrounding area is generally experiencing unemployment in the vicinity of 17%. Similarly, if in one community there are presently a total of six doctors serving 4,500 persons, it is important to compare this ratio with national averages in order to determine whether the local population is benefiting from an adequate supply of doctors or suffering from an inadequate supply of doctors. Thus, this measurement activity involves *assigning a value* to the various present-day characteristics in comparison with an appropriate regional or national reference group. Three different ratings may be assigned:

AA - Above Average
A - Average
BA - Below Average

An important distinction must be made here between this type of measurement and one described below which evaluates changes in community impacts in terms of their social effects. The measurement here is concerned with the "goodness" or "badness" of the community characteristics in terms of contemporary norms from an appropriate *reference group*. In other words, the measurement is a statement of the relative adequacy of the present-day characteristics *compared with another set of communities at the same point in time*. In contrast, the social assessment of future impacts and effects uses the present-day characteristics of the community as the baseline to compare future characteristics across different plans in terms of today's situation. In this second measurement, the community serves as its own frame of reference. As we shall see, one of the values of this dual approach is that it allows us to compare future social effects of the plans with the relative present-day adequacy of the social characteristics. For example, communities which are already comparatively well-off in terms of one social characteristic may need positive social effects less in that area than they do in areas where they are, in comparison to other communities, doing very poorly. In short, this procedure allows us to identify where the communities are experiencing problems and to then ask whether a plan is positively affecting the areas of need which require little improvement.

Use of Omnibus Data Categories to Assure Continuity of Approach in Assessing Social Effects in Various Areas

Many, although not all, social effects which are being studied have certain generic similarities, irrespective of the area of effect in question. For this reason, in addition to considering each social effect area for various indigenous characteristics (e.g., dropout rates in education; morbidity rates in health), it is useful to have some standard types of items which can be considered for purposes of social effects measurement. Generally, most of the evaluation categories of the SWB components described in Part 2 will have three types of data concerns. First, they will examine certain variables describing the characterization of people with respect to the area being studied; these are referred to as *state variables*. A second group of measures deals with *relevant conditions* or important community characteristics which have a bearing on the operation of a system (e.g., population) but which would not formally be considered as a statistic for that area. Finally, certain variables describing the institutional characteristics of the area are examined; these are referred to as *system variables*. Included are measures of quantity, function, and quality of operation of the system. In order to make these distinctions clear, the following lists all of the types of variables included in the three omnibus categories:

- Change in State Variables
  Specific to each component of the Well-Being Account: employment rates; school attendance rates; morbidity rates; occupancy of sub-standard housing; etc.
- Change in Relevant Conditions Variables
  Population, transportation, economic base, etc., as they apply to both supply characteristics of institutions and demand characteristics of the population
- Change in Systems Variables
  Quantity and structure of local institutions: number, units, level, size of facilities and staff, organization, administration, and location
  Function and purpose of local institutions: composition of programs, staff types, services, diversity of operations, and coordination
  Quality and character of local institutions: accessibility, frequency of use, hours open, distribution of services, equality of opportunity to benefit (by age, sex, ethnicity, income, occupation, geographic location, membership, etc.), efficiency, effectiveness, satisfaction, cooperation, and conflict

It is not necessary to use all measures for all components in the social assessment. Rather, the intent is to have a systematic way to obtain data for these areas of social concerns, as appropriate, *across* components. The actual variables chosen then provide the categories from which forecasts are made of the social effects associated with the alternative plans. This basic model states that there are alterations of the present situation which affect institutions, relevant conditions, and people, and that these are inter-related in terms of the ultimate social impacts.

Assessing the Impacts in Terms of Their Social Effects

As discussed on pp. 30-32, in order to rate an impact as good or bad, something must be known about present-day characteristics of the communities themselves. For example, in one community, the more urban one, residents value growth highly. They desire more industry and new people to expand the community and its capacity to support more services. For this community the effect of more industrial employment can be rated as quite *positive.* In the second community, residents are very rural-oriented in their values and life-styles and wish no growth of this type. From the perspective of this community, the same impact, the rise in industrial employment, can be rated as a *negative* effect. The following five values can be assigned to a given social effect:

++ Very Positive
+ Positive
0 Neutral
- Negative
-- Very Negative

Using this rating system, one deals with two generic issues simultaneously: the direction of impact and the magnitude of impact. However, a given impact can, in fact, have more than one value assigned to it. We have noted that forecasted impacts may, in fact, be rated differently according to who is affected, how they are affected, where they are located, and so forth. The schema is ordinal in that, for example, a value of ++ represents a greater positive effect than a value of +. It is not a ratio scale, however, in that we do not say it is twice as great, but rather that it is relatively greater. Therefore, one might have the following effects and assessment for a given variable:

Rise in overall income for area	++
Decrease in income for minority labor force in area with low education	--

The extent of the magnitude of a rating, i.e., magnitude, must be measured *from the perspective of the community in question.* In the second rating area, if there are only 70 individuals out of 14,000 who face loss of work, the impact might be assigned a negative rating (-), whereas if 20% of the labor force faced loss of work, the impact would be assigned the more extreme rating of very negative (--). The rating depends on various factors, including:

- who is going to suffer disproportionate costs and their capacity to bear the cost;
- the types of costs that will be suffered;
- the presence of both short-term (e.g., displacement) and long-term (e.g., self-support) costs;
- the character of the costs (e.g., health, legal, self-support, education);
- the distribution of the costs (numbers of people, types of problems, etc.);
- the number of persons affected.

These ratings are *not* viewed as additive across evaluation categories. They do, however, provide an important and direct way of comparing social impacts for the same variable *across plans.* The information on the characteristics and values of the present-day communities should be useful in judging which rating to assign to a given impact on the community.

Use of Table 1 for Arraying Impacts Under Alternative Plans

Table 1 of the SWB Account allows the planner to display data on all of the likely social impacts identified for each plan. This table indicates the plan in question, the item forecasted, the extent of change, and then calls for a value statement to be made about the social "goodness" or "badness" effects of the plan (i.e., ++ to --). Each plan is examined in its own right, using the same table.

Table 1 (sample). *Beneficial and Adverse Effects on Social Well-Being Under the Plan for* ________________

Items in Evaluation Categories	Measures of Impact	Effects ++,+,0,-,--

Use of Table 2 for Comparisons of Social Benefits and Adverse Effects Across Plans

Table 2 uses the values assigned from Table 1 for each plan and arrays them, item by item, across the plans. This table is different from Table 1 in that it no longer presents the data, but rather the projected social meaning of the data. This table also compares one plan against another as to their respective social merit. In addition, where possible, data from present-day community characteristics are rated (AA, A, or BA) for comparison with future areas where effects are forecast.

Table 2 (sample). *A Summary Comparison of the Benefits and Adverse Effects of the Alternative Plans for the Social Well-Being Account*

Items in Evaluation Categories	Present Conditions	Beneficial & Adverse Effects of Plans					
		No Plan	NED Plan	EQ Plan	ALT "X"	ALT "Y"	RECCO Plan

•Conditions (Above to below Average: AA,A,BA); Effects (Beneficial to Adverse: ++,+,0,-,--).

Types of Analysis Performed in the SWB Account: The Question of a "Uniform" Measure

There are six different types of analyses in the process of completing the SWB Account. These include:

1. *Rating the present-day community characteristics* found in the planning area as they are compared with either other communities in the region or with national norms. These are expressed in terms of being above average, average, or below average by comparison to an external reference group.
2. *Developing "impact forecasts" for each plan* on a variety of items found in the various evaluation categories of the components of the SWB Account. These are expressed in various forms, such as dollars, number of people, staff size, etc.
3. *Assessing the beneficial and adverse social effects of the impacts of each plan as found in the evaluation categories,* based upon the relationship between the impact and the present-day community characteristics and aspirations. These are expressed as being anywhere from very positive (++) to very negative(−−).
4. *Comparing the effect ratings of these impacts across the various plans* to ascertain their "comparative" beneficial and adverse social effects. The ratings of ++ through −− are used here rather than the impact data themselves.
5. *Comparing the positive and negative effects* (Item 4) *to the present-day community characteristics* (Item 1) to ascertain the extent to which individual plans provide benefits where they are needed, and avoid further costs when problems already exist.
6. *Breaking down the distribution of beneficial and adverse effects* by various groups, time frames, and geographic areas in order to ascertain their relative equity and distribution.

The maximum extent of uniformity of measure achieved in this account is the positive to negative social effects rating across plans. While it is true that these represent a variety of data, some hard and some soft, even the hard data vary in the way in which they are measured (dollars, number of persons, number of jobs, number of facilities). In short, uniformity of measures is absent.

This raises an important question: Why not convert these social effects to dollar values; i.e., monetize them? There are various ways of monetizing social outcomes. One way is to measure the creation of social goods in terms of assigned monetary values, so that the worth of a given phenomenon (accessibility to service providers, the value of an hour's hunting and fishing, etc.) can be expressed in dollar terms. Increases in monetized value are equated with social benefits. Another way utilizes the concept of value hierarchies. For example, by taking into account protection from flood control, drought, access to community service, etc., one can generate a proxy measure of "security" which has a high social value. This, in a sense, is a social metaphor for the economists' aggregation approach.

But while it may be advantageous to use dollar amounts as units of measure (especially since the user is familiar with them), dollar amounts are not representative of the range of values contained in the Social Well-Being Account. Another reason for not monetizing social effects is that it may not be appropriate. The experience of job satisfaction, of enjoyment of time with the family, or of visiting a natural wilderness area varies between different people, and while individuals will allocate income or make decisions which have dollar implications, many social experiences will not be assigned the same dollar values by different individuals.

A further problem is that while one might be able to assign dollar values to social effects, it is difficult to add the value of these effects across areas of social good. For example, one can add $1,000 in increased per capita health benefits to $800 in increased per capita enjoyment of the out-of-doors, but it is not clear just what the $1,800 per capita gain really means. Moreover, it is not clear what it means to trade off a dollar of family security against a dollar of pollution-free air. The SWB Account does not take a strong position against efforts to develop such a system. Rather, it takes the position that clear, but non-uniform measures which are explicit in their nature can be used to provide a more useful decision-making tool to the policy maker than will uniform dollar measures whose aggregated meaning is unclear.

Making Recommendations

Based upon the overall comparative social merit of the individual plans, the plan which seems to achieve the best balance between social good and ill in terms of how the effects of the plan are distributed among people in the area or who are likely to come into the area must be selected. This judgment is to be made solely on social criteria; it may or may not agree with ratings made by other accounts. The purpose of this rating of social effects is not to reach the final decision about which plan to implement, but rather to make sure that the social effects of the plans are equally considered along with information displayed in the other three accounts.

A simplified format for a two-step decision process is presented in Figure 6. First the planner must determine if the implementation of the plans in general would have more beneficial effects than if no plan were implemented. If this is clearly the case, the individual plans can be compared with one another in order to reach a decision concerning the plan which would cause the most beneficial effects if it were implemented.

Basically, a plan is recommended based upon the criteria of who benefits or loses, the types of costs and benefits absorbed, the duration of effects, their magnitude, and their relationship to present-day needs. This is further discussed in Chapter 11.

Figure 6. *Social Assessment Decision Logic*[a]

FUTURE WITH VS. FUTURE WITHOUT PLANS	
CONDITION	DECISION
Plans' social benefits are greater and costs lower than with no plan.	A plan should be implemented.
Plans' social benefits are lower and cost higher than with no plan.	Reject plans.
Plans' benefits are higher, but plans' costs are also higher than with no plan.	Trade-offs require a decision based on whether higher costs are offset by higher benefits or vice versa. Decision could go either way.
PLAN A VS. PLAN B	
CONDITION	DECISION
Plan A has higher social benefits and lower social costs than B.	Implement A.
Converse of above.	Implement B.
Plan A has higher social benefits but also higher social costs than Plan B.	Implement A or B, depending upon which, in the final analysis, is most acceptable—losing the benefits sought or accepting the costs.
Plan A has social benefits and costs which are neither higher nor lower in the same ways than Plan B. That is, they both have social benefits and both have social costs, but they are not comparable.	Build A or B, depending on which benefits are most desirable and/or which costs are most tolerable (or intolerable).

[a]Note: This logic applies specifically to the *social* assessment of plans. In the total planning context, other factors such as economic, engineering, or environmental feasibility may override decisions made exclusively on social grounds.

5
The Structure and Organization of the Social Well-Being Account

The Components of the SWB Account, and Their Evaluation Categories

As discussed on pp. 20-23, the Social Well-Being Account is made up of five components. Each of the components will now be described briefly in terms of its general scope of concern and evaluation categories. In each case, a flow chart will be presented along with the text to indicate the kinds of variables included in each component and how the overall component fits into the larger social assessment picture. A final flow chart shows the entire SWB Account, with all components and their evaluation categories, as it exists in the context of the Feasibility Study planning level.

Component I: Individual, Personal Effects

The social effects of implementing each of the plans are assessed first from the point of view of the individual and his or her family. In all, six evaluation categories are provided:

A. Life, Protection, and Safety
B. Health
C. Family and Individual

D. Attitudes
E. Environmental Considerations
F. Other

Each of these evaluation categories is fully described and the data categories for them are suggested in Part 2 of this volume. Only certain features need to be stressed here. First of all, the individual or family is the unit of measure. For example, floods take the lives of individuals; decreases in pollution can improve the health of individuals; attitudes about the value of different community futures are held by individuals, and so forth. In this component, impacts of the various plans on a variety of the measures of the evaluation categories are assessed and in turn rated as to their beneficial or adverse effects on the individual and the family. The flow chart in Figure 7 depicts the progression from the implementation of alternative plans, the context of the present-day community, the types of beneficial and adverse effects upon individuals, and, finally, the Individual, Personal Effects Component.

Component II: Community, Institutional Effects

The beneficial and adverse social effects of a given plan implementation will also affect the community or communities located within the planning area (and possibly beyond) in a variety of ways. While these impacts have important effects on the lives of individuals, in this component the benefits and costs are examined as they affect larger groups of individuals, usually in carrying out various aspects of their lives within the community. Because we are concerned here with the functioning of individuals in formal and informal groups and with many community-related considerations, the measures of social effects are focused on the institutional aspects of community life. The following twelve evaluation categories are included in this component:

A. Demographic
B. Education
C. Government Operations and Services
D. Housing and Neighborhood

Figure 7. *The SWB Individual, Personal Effects Component, Its Evaluation Categories and Impacts*

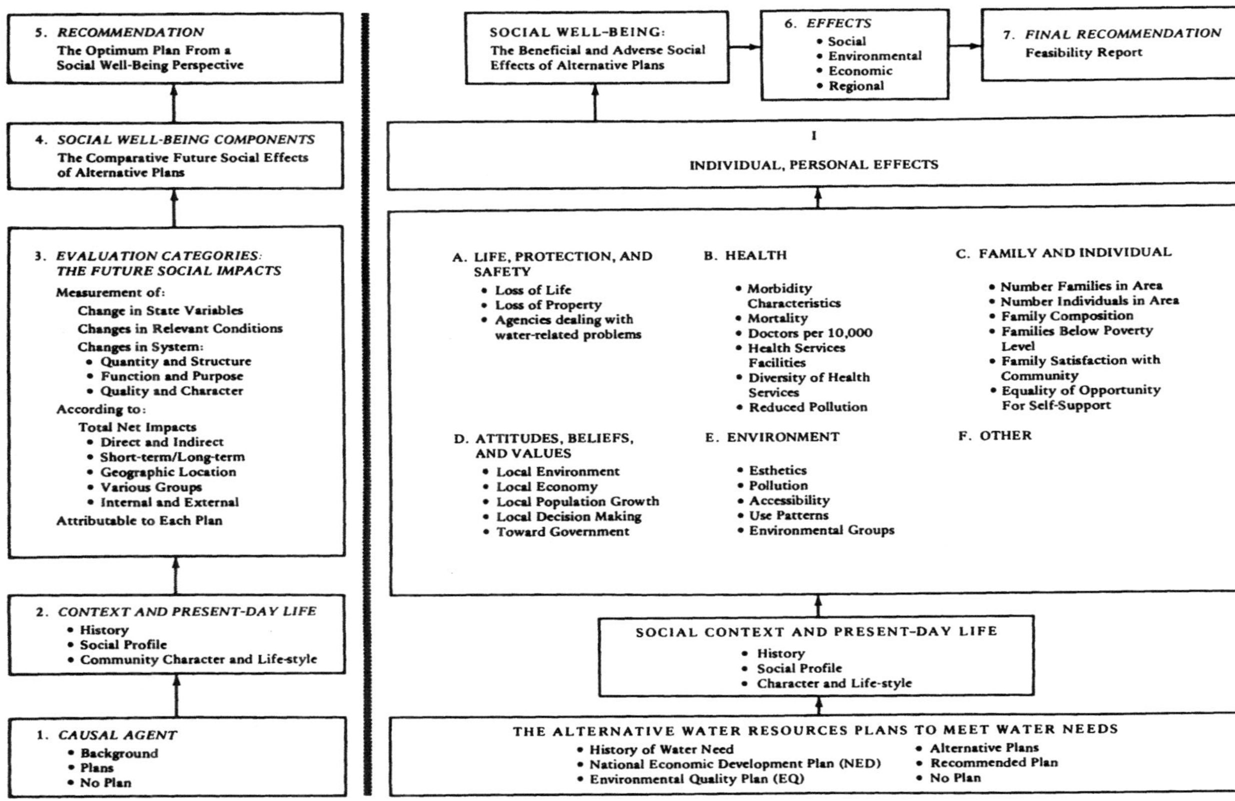

E. Law and Justice
F. Social Services
G. Religion
H. Culture
I. Recreation
J. Informal Organizational Groups
K. Community and Institutional Viability
L. Other (specify)

In this component, the future effects on the structure of the population, the demands for education, housing, various social services, and informal group structures, and in general, the community, are explored.

Figure 8 displays an overview of the account within the entire plan framework.

Component III: Area, Socioeconomic Effects

Certain types of beneficial and adverse effects are more efficiently understood from the perspective of a number of communities, counties, or on more regional bases. People commute to jobs from one community to another, and receive benefits or incur costs from larger economic forces operating in the area, many of which transcend the individual community. In all, eight evaluation categories are set forth under this component, including:

A. Employment and Real Income
B. Welfare and Financial Compensation
C. Communications
D. Transportation
E. Economic Base
F. Planning Effects
G. Construction
H. Other (specify)

The plans, by virtue of their having impacts on population and economic characteristics, are likely to generate effects on these more regional characteristics.

A complete overview of this component and its evaluation categories is presented in Figure 9.

Figure 8. *The SWB Community, Institutional Effects Component, Its Evaluation Categories and Impacts*

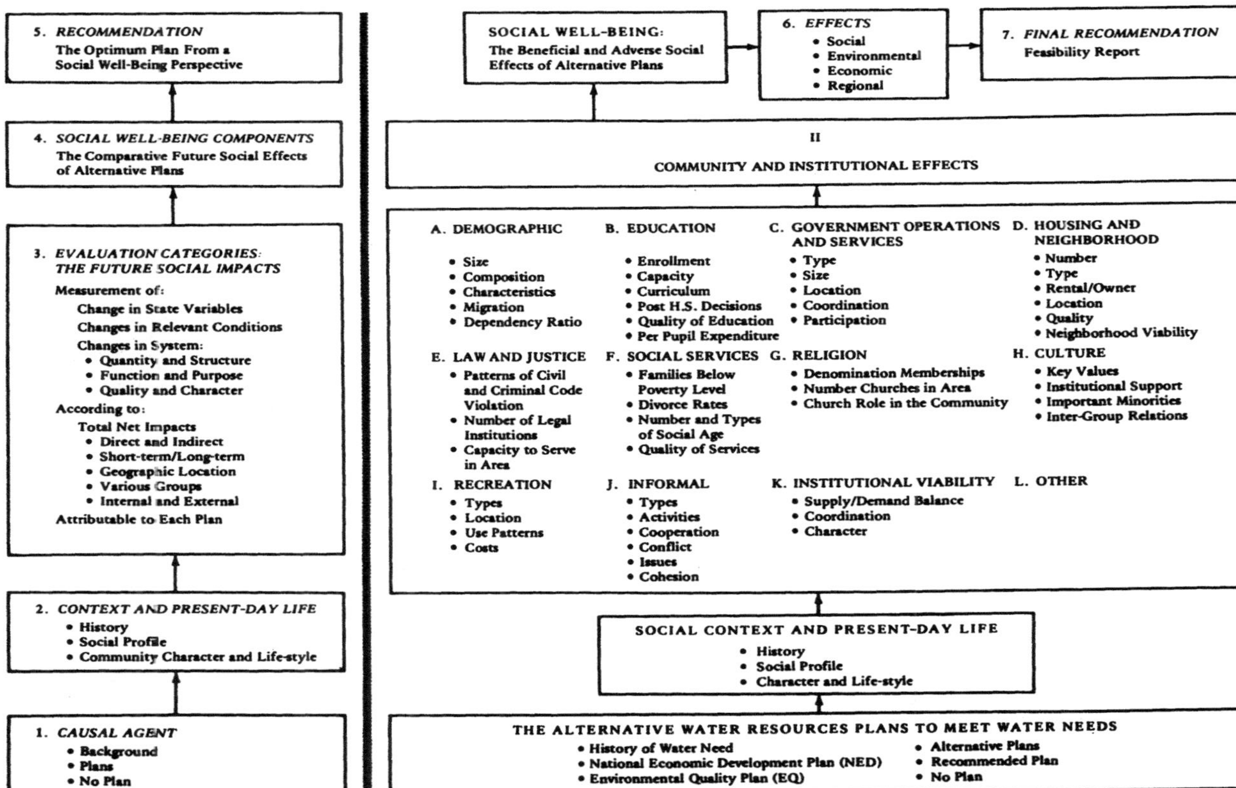

Figure 9. *The SWB Area, Socioeconomic Effects Component, Its Evaluation Categories and Impacts*

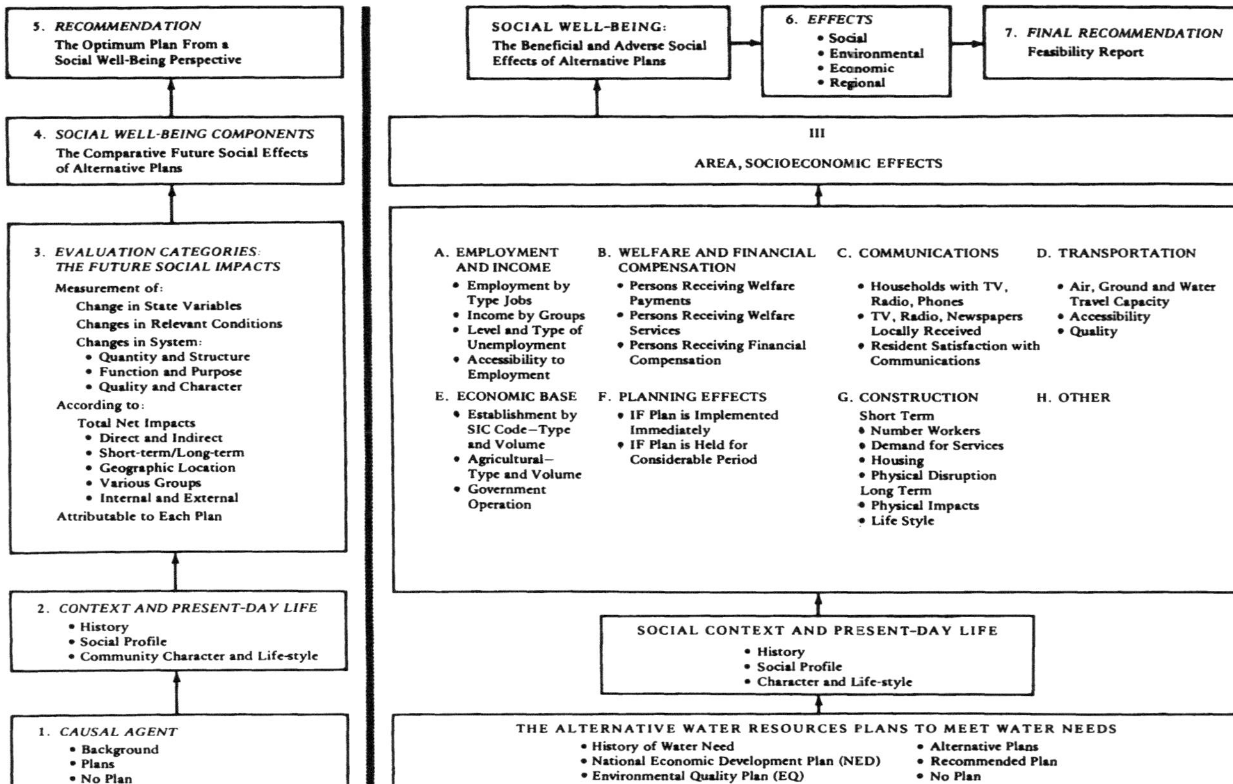

Component IV: National, Emergency Preparedness Effects

One social impact area of the SWB Account is concerned with the larger social good of the nation rather than the local area of the plan implementation. The plans are assessed in terms of the ways in which the presence of alternative plans will better prepare the nation in coping with the possibility of future emergencies. In a sense, this presents a form of contingency planning, providing greater options to the nation in times of natural or man-made crises. In all, ten evaluation categories are established to assess social contributions to national emergency preparedness. These include:

A. Water Supplies
B. Food Production
C. Power Supplies
D. Water Transportation
E. Scarce Fuels
F. Population Dispersion
G. Industrial Dispersion
H. Military Preparedness
I. International Treaty Obligations
J. Other (specify)

It is not necessary that each of the plans makes major contributions to any one of these areas, since that is not their primary purpose. However, for national reasons, these types of contributions if made by the plan are important to identify. In Figure 10 a flow chart details some of the types of contributions which are identified in connection with these evaluation categories.

Component V: Aggregate Social Effects

Up to this point, the beneficial and adverse social effects have been dealt with in the context of specific aspects of social life: i.e., they are related to external sets of concerns. It is important, however, to try to develop a better picture of what this means in a "bottom line" sense. Three sets of aggregate evaluation categories for this component are identified. These include:

A. Quality of Life
B. Relative Social Position

Figure 10. *The SWB National, Emergency Preparedness Effects Component, Its Evaluation Categories and Impacts*

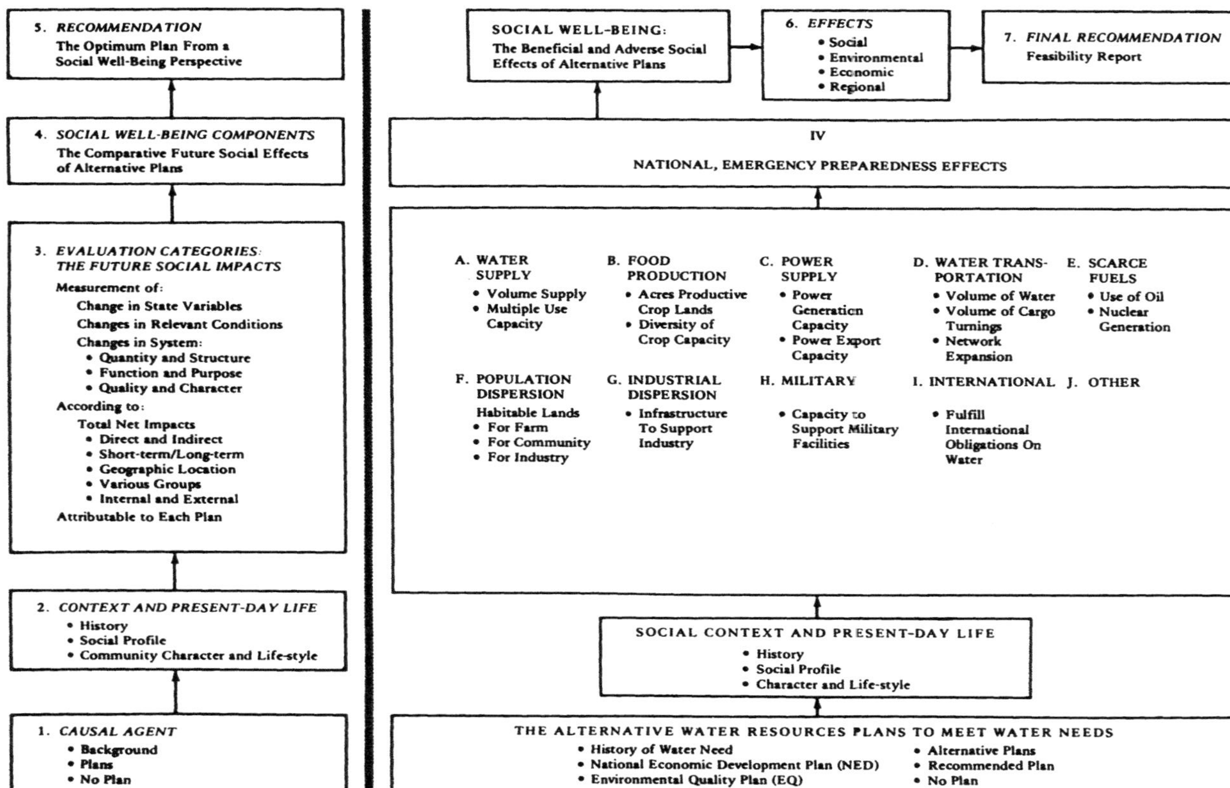

C. Social Well-Being
D. Other (specify)

The quality of life for the individual and the family can be assessed as affected, in the aggregate, not only by the individual measures, but also indirectly by changes in the other accounts as well. The same is true for the quality of life of various groups of the community and for the overall viability of communities in the planning area. The evaluation categories with some of their measures are shown in Figure 11.

The Overview of the Social Well-Being Account

The five components together make up the entire SWB Account. All follow a similar progression, moving from the measures which establish likely future impacts under alternative plans, through aggregate social effects, to a final statement of the beneficial and adverse social effects of each plan. Collectively, they provide a basis of determining impact on overall social well-being. This is portrayed in Figure 12.

The logical progression upward from the plans, through context, to impacts, to comparative effects, and finally to recommendations is also clear.

Organization of the Social Well-Being Account

Completion of the SWB Account entails five separate but related steps. These form the basis for the chapter structure of Part 2 and include the following concerns:

1. A description is prepared of the historical context of the water needs and problems of the area which motivate development of alternative plans for the area. Then each of the plans is briefly described in terms of its activities and functions. These descriptions provide the basis for understanding the reasons why social impacts are ultimately expected, and how they may differ under alternative plans or with no plan implementation.
2. A description of the historical context, social profile, and general characteristics of life in the area is prepared. The area is then compared with regional or national

Figure 11. *The SWB Aggregate, Social Effects Component, Its Evaluation Categories and Impacts*

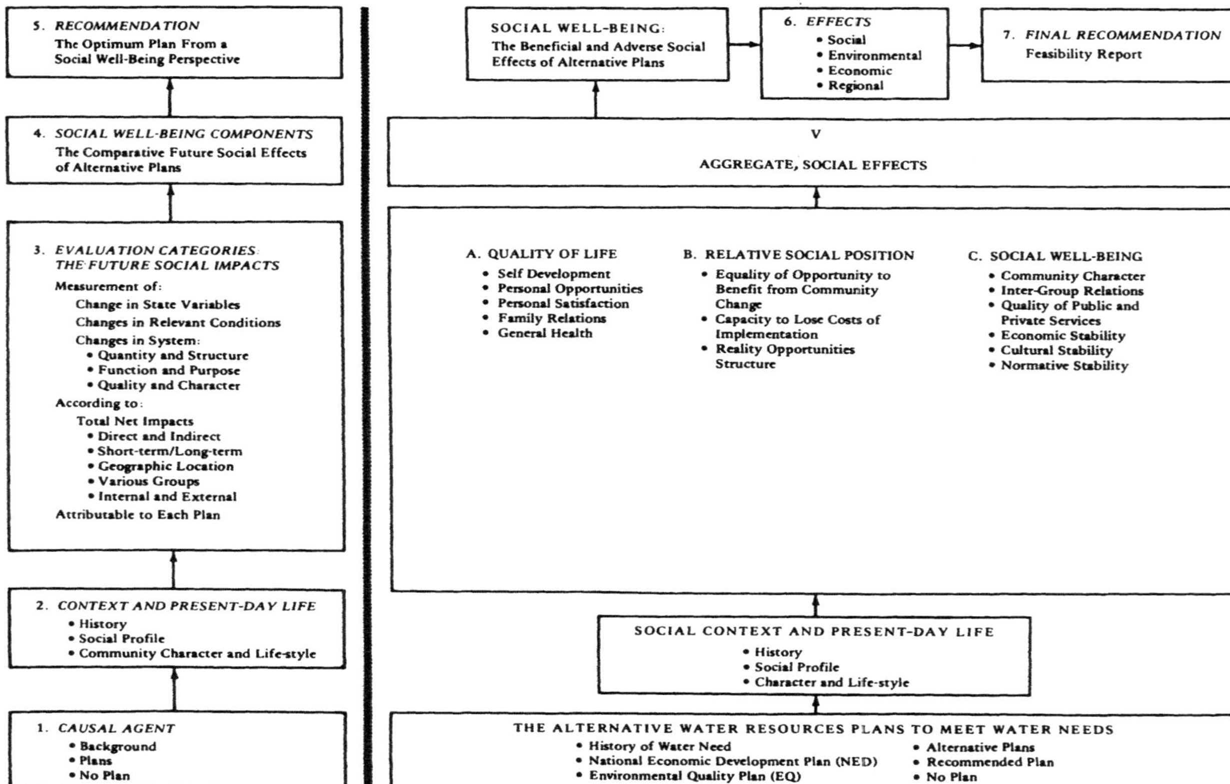

Figure 12. *An Overview of the Social Well-Being Account, Its Components and Their Evaluation Categories*

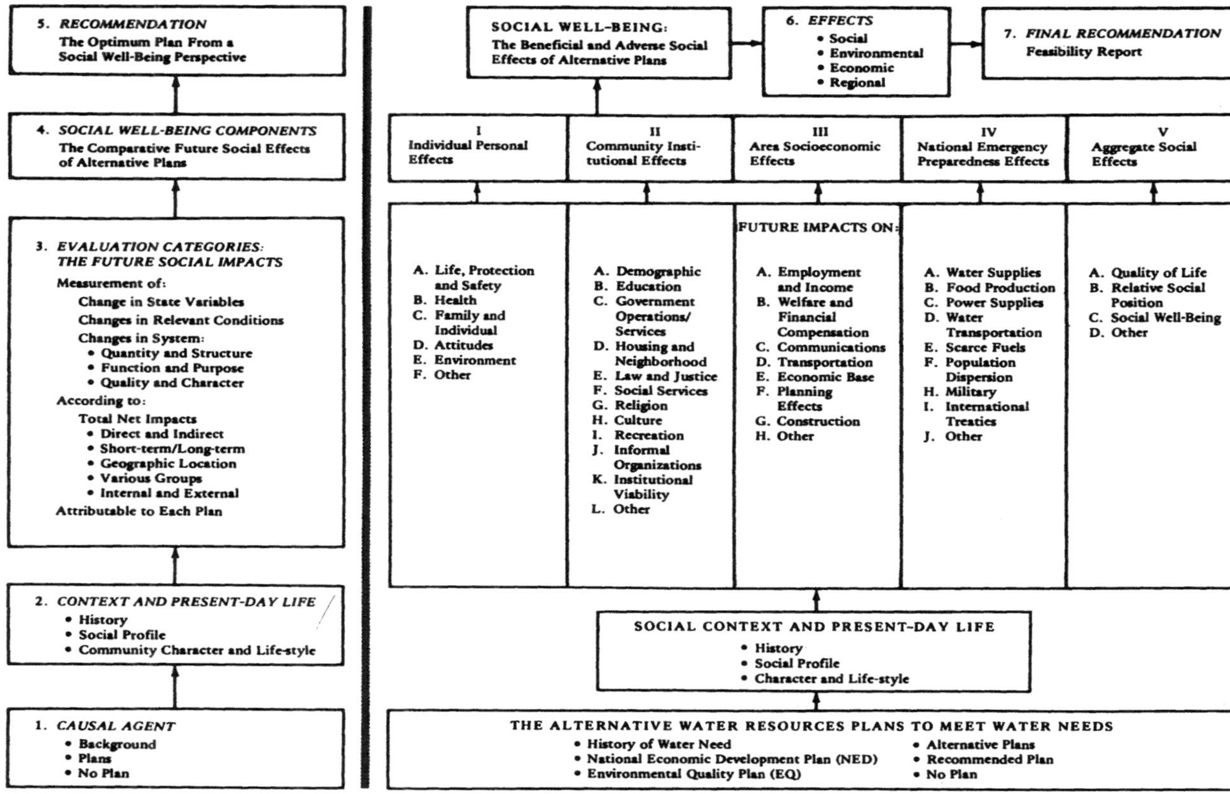

characteristics in terms of whether it is above average, average, or below average. This corresponds to the needs of the Feasibility Report as contained in the chapter of that document which describes the planning setting.

3. Each of the plans is examined in order to forecast the likely social impacts of its implementation according to the components of the SWB Account. Actual data forecasts are first made, and then these impacts are assessed for their beneficial and adverse social effects.
4. A comparison across the plans is made in terms of the relative social effects of different plans. In addition, the relationship to areas of need is examined to ascertain correspondence between problem areas and the "solutions" of the plans. Further breakdown is made according to the distribution of these effects. Trade-offs among plans are identified.
5. The best plan from the perspective of the beneficial and adverse social effects is selected and the recommendation made in the larger Feasibility Report context.

Part 2
Instructions for the Preparation of the Social Assessment

6
Organizing the Preparation of the Social Assessment

The social assessment, when completed, will provide data and information enabling the Social Well-Being Account to be set up and displayed, as required by the *Principles and Standards* promulgated by the Water Resources Council.

> These Principles are established for planning the use of the water and related . . . resources of the United States. . . .
>
> Plans for the use of the Nation's water and land resources will be directed to improvement in the quality of life through contributions to the objectives of national economic development and environmental quality. The beneficial and adverse effects on each of these objectives will be displayed in separate accounts with other accounts for the beneficial and adverse effects on regional development and *social well-being.* Planning for the use of water and land resources in terms of these objectives will aid in identifying alternative courses of action and will provide the type of information needed to improve

the public decision-making process (U.S. WRC, *Principles and Standards,* 1973, p. 5, emphasis added).

Part 1 of this book provided the general orientation for the social assessment; Part 2 gives specific instruction for the preparation of the social assessment. In Chapter 7, there are instructions on how to describe the history that has led up to the present plan generation, followed by instructions on how to prepare the descriptions for the various plans that are called for under the *Principles and Standards.* Chapter 8 deals with the social characteristics of the planning area. Chapter 9 gives instructions for forecasting the social impacts associated with the various plans and then rating their future beneficial and adverse social effects. Chapter 10 deals with how to assemble the ratings into a Social Well-Being Account in order to assess their comparative social effects. Chapter 11 discusses how to make a recommendation from the social assessment and the completed Social Well-Being Account. In Figure 13, a summary of the Social Well-Being Account preparation process is presented. (See also Figure 1, in Chapter 2, for the formal chapter headings of this Account.)

Organizing the Social Well-Being Task Group

In order that the Plan Formulation Task Group (PFTG) can formulate and evaluate different plans, a Social Well-Being Task Group (SWBTG) needs to be formed. This latter task group will be charged with conducting (or having conducted on its behalf) the social assessment and preparing the Social Well-Being Account. The SWBTG will be only one of several task groups set up, such as the Resource Base Task Group and the Public Involvement Task Group. The SWBTG may also employ a professional writer to prepare narrative for the social assessment.

The work for the preparation described in Chapter 7 should be done by the staff of the Social Well-Being Task Group. The tasks described in Chapter 8 will have to be done either by the staff of the SWBTG or by outside consultants. If data for the description of present-day characteristics are readily available through secondary sources, this task can be handled by staff (see

Figure 13. *A Schematic Presentation of the Social Well-Being Account Preparation Process*

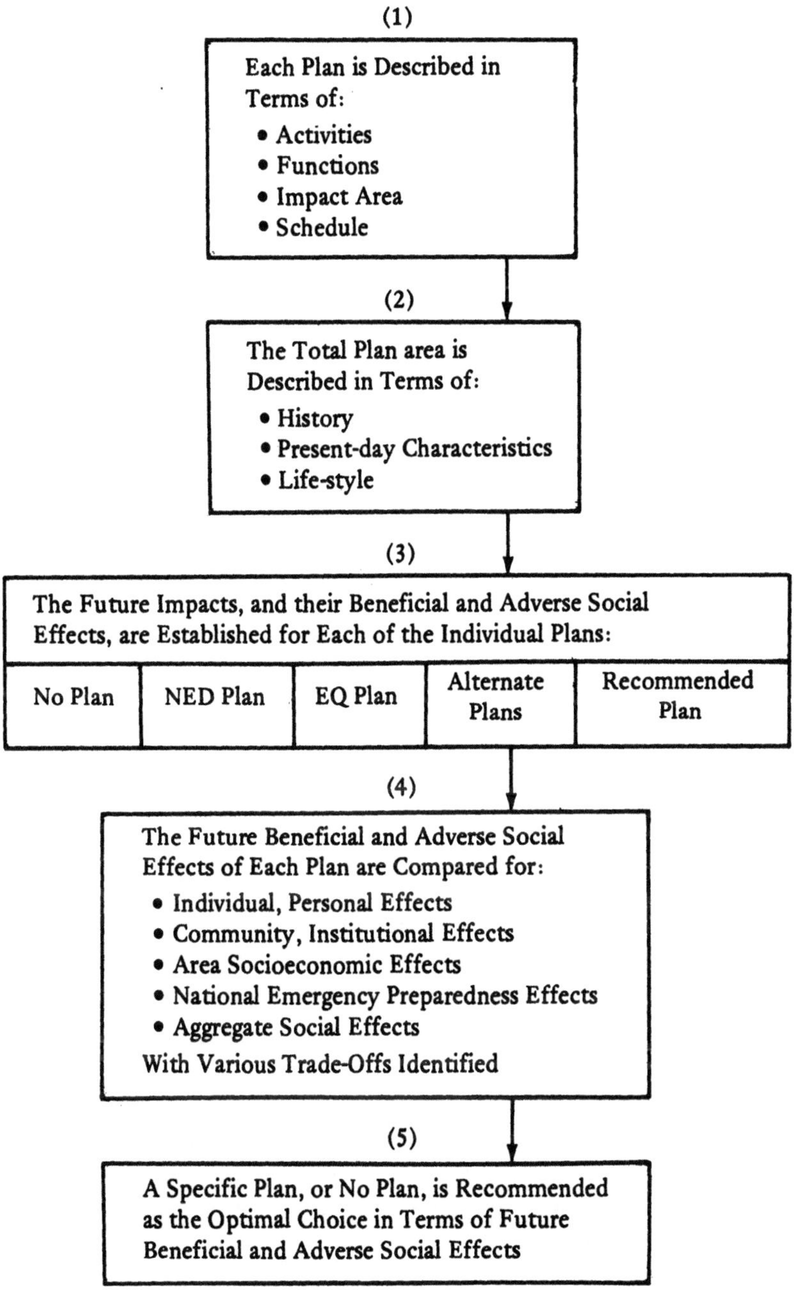

Chapter 8, pp. 113-117, on gathering secondary data); if, however, the planning area is such that secondary data are difficult to obtain and if the features of the plans are such that many primary data must be collected (see Chapter 9. pp. 121-128), it may be necessary to contract this portion of the work, either to an individual who is knowledgeable about the area (say, a local demographer) or to a firm that is equipped to collect primary data by means of surveys and interviews.

Listing the beneficial and adverse effects is one major task required in the preparation of the Social Well-Being Account. The SWBTG needs to take full responsibility for this task, although it will depend on its staff or on outside consultants for the data collection. Many of the data will, of course, be available from the various plans themselves; e.g., an NED plan will indicate what the anticipated impacts on economic factors are and so will deal with many of the evaluation categories of the components. Once future impacts have been identified, the SWBTG then evaluates their beneficial and adverse social effects. Summarizing the social impacts across plans and aggregating them can only be done by the SWBTG itself, as is also the case with the fifth task, making recommendations. It is for the sake of the latter task, of course, that the entire plan-by-objective and four-account system is set up.

The Social Well-Being Task Group could include among its members a sociologist, a social psychologist, an economist, and perhaps other social scientists, such as a demographer, a specialist in social services, and an environmentalist, as well as planning engineers and other planners.

Because the *process* of social planning is itself one of the social effects of a plan (Chapter 3, pp. 19-20), it is particularly important that the Social Well-Being Task Group interface consciously, consistently, and continuously with the Public Involvement Task Group.

The SWBTG must also interact with the Plan Formulation Task Group (PFTG). Usually the PFTG will decide upon the population projections which will be used in formulating the alternative plans. The Social Well-Being Task Group (SWBTG) needs information about which projections are being used

(OBERS and/or some combination of state, council of governments, or local projections), if different projections are being used for different alternatives, or a range of projections is being used.

The SWBTG should provide preliminary descriptions of the social consequences of different population growth units as early as possible to the PFTG. It is also essential for the SWBTG to be aware of the rationale which guided the PFTG in its choice of projections so that any salient social impacts of different choices may be fed back to the PFTG as early in plan formulation as possible. In this way, the PFTG will be alerted to adverse social effects of different projection levels and will thereby be able to make any necessary changes in the plans being formulated.

The Social Well-Being Task Group must also have available for its work a staff who can collect necessary data and conduct the actual social assessment.

Preparation Sequence

It is recommended that the Social Well-Being Account be prepared according to the sequence outlined in Figure 13 by filling in the information in this sequence. The planner will find that she or he is accumulating the information called for in the chapters of the typical Feasibility Report and that she or he is able to fill out the various entries of the Social Well-Being Account and its components, first for each of the plans (NED, EQ, or other) and then for the large table (corresponding to Table 6 described in the *Principles and Standards,* 1973, pp. 137-139). In addition, the report writer will be able to prepare the narrative sections of the Feasibility Report dealing with the Social Well-Being Account, which will explain the data used, the impacts identified, the measurement techniques used for the impacts, and the trade-offs made between effects in order to arrive at a recommended plan (from the social well-being point of view).

7
Basic Water Development Context and the Various Plans

Two separate but related activities are associated with completing this chapter of the Social Well-Being Account. First, the SWBTG prepares a brief statement on the historical context of water needs and previous development activities which have taken place within the planning area. These should be related to the present-day initiatives which motivate the current alternative water plans. Second, the SWBTG, working with information available from the statement of the plans (NED, EQ, etc.), should prepare concise, clear statements about the nature of each of the plans, describing its various activities (e.g., dams, reservoirs, power stations), the functions which will be provided under the plans (e.g., irrigation, industrial water supply, conservation), the impact area findings, and the Plan Implementation Schedule.

Historical Factors Leading to Plan Generation

Before the various plans can be described, it is first necessary to describe the history that has led up to the formulation of the plans which have been designed to meet different national objectives (NED, EQ, and others). The setting of the plan area and the past, present, and future water needs should be described.

Without such an understanding of the historical context within which the water planning is taking place it will be difficult, if not impossible, to conduct a social assessment. Social needs (including the needs of the individual, the community, the region, and the nation) will be among the factors that have caused water resource plans to be developed. However, the historical interest here is with water needs, rather than the general social context, which is the subject of Chapter 8.

Most likely, the description of the planning area and its water needs will be included as part of the general Feasibility Study. Thus, it may not be necessary for the Social Well-Being Task Group by itself to generate a description of the history of the plan area and its water needs. Not only the Social Well-Being Account, but the other three accounts as well (National Economic Development, Environmental Quality, and Regional Development) will require the description of the history of the area, its setting, and its water needs. Briefly, the statement of the historical factors leading to plan generation should cover the following items. It should deal with the general water characteristics of the area. It should also include facts concerning annual rainfall (also times of heaviest and least precipitation), ground water table, number of wells, and present water sources (including reservoirs, both publicly and privately owned).

Problems with the water supply in the past, such as droughts, floods, and lowering water table, should be noted. There should also be an indication as to what has been done in the past to try to deal with those problems which would include public and private construction of dams, reservoirs, dikes, relocation of river beds, drainage canals, and so on. It is important to note legal aspects of the situation: What (if any) are the local laws and regulations governing water supply in a period of shortage? Who is responsible for preventing damage from excess water (county, state, flood control district)? Have there been any efforts in the past to ameliorate some or all of these identified problems? What was the result?

Other questions to be covered include: When did the present

plans first begin to be thought about? What has been the history so far of the plans? Note local support or opposition and any factors that have tended to change local opinion, such as a big flood, a drought, changing employment patterns, or the election of a certain person or party.

The Water Development Plans

For any development of water resources, there will be various plans to consider; usually, there will be a plan emphasizing National Economic Development (NED), one emphasizing Environmental Quality (EQ), a No Plan condition, and, often, a Recommended Plan. In addition, there may be several other alternative plans which emphasize to a greater or lesser degree either the NED or the EQ objectives.

The NED plan will have the same general objectives of increasing goods, services and efficiency of production. The EQ plan, on the other hand, will seek to protect and enhance natural, cultural and ecological systems. *How* these objectives are to be achieved, however, will differ from plan to plan as one considers NED and EQ plans for different planning areas. NED and EQ objectives (and the objectives of alternative plans) will be implemented through particular water resource development projects, involving particular water *activities* and *functions.* The diverse activities which may be included when a plan is implemented are listed in Figure 14. However, social effects come to be not by virtue of water activities as such, but rather by virtue of the functions which are performed by the activities. These functions have impacts on individuals or communities because they affect such functions as farming, ecological balance, and industrial processes. Figure 15 provides a listing of such functions and what they generally include.

As was noted in the previous section, the general description of the various plans is *not* the duty of the SWBTG alone. One important part of the Feasibility Report will be chapters which describe the National Economic Development Plan, the Environmental Quality Plan, the No Plan, and any other alternative plans that may be being considered by the Plan Formulation Task Group. The SWBTG need only prepare a brief statement

Figure 14. *Water Resource Development Mechanism*

1. Development Activities

   A. Construction Activities

      - Dams and Reservoirs
      - Water Transport Systems
      - Flood Control Facilities
      - Navigation Facilities
      - Power Plants
      - Transmission Lines
      - Desalting Plants
      - Drainage Systems
      - Wastewater Collection/ Recycling
      - Geothermal Wells
      - Recreation Facilities
      - Fish and Wildlife Facilities
      - Groundwater Development

   B. Managerial Actions

      - Operational/Efficiency Programs
      - Weather Modification
      - Legal and Institutional Arrangements
      - Environmental Management
      - Operation and Maintenance
      - Phreatophyte Control

2. Utilization Activities

   A. Municipal and Industrial

      - Household
      - Industrial
      - Community

   B. Other

      - Irrigation
      - Navigation
      - Hydroelectric
      - Recreation
      - Fish and Wildlife
      - Flood Control
      - Environmental Enhancement (including water quality)
      - Land Stabilization
      - Streamflow Maintenance
      - Land Acquisition
      - Relocation

Figure 15. *Functions of Water Development Projects Having Social Impacts*

Ecology maintenance and control: including activities generally designed to maintain and protect the ecosystems of the earth and its species

Life support: specifically tailored to support the life of man and wildlife

Security: designed to protect man from periodic man-made or natural disasters

Available and predictable supply: including activities to maintain sufficient quantities of water

Available and predictable distribution: including activities to move water from point A to point B on regular and controllable bases

Land use: including activities to utilize water-related lands in such a way as to maintain necessary water characteristics

Energy recovery: including uses of water for the generation of power

Production in agriculture: including water development activities designed to support land, crops, and livestock for national consumption (including amount, nutritive value, diversity, and supply maintenance)

Community functions: including activities designed to maintain community operations such as sewage, fire protection, and parks

Industrial functions: including activities designed to maintain sufficient supply and distribution of waters specifically as required for industrial production and operation

Interdependence and transportation functions: including activities designed to support all forms of navigation making trade and travel between communities feasible, and insuring the maintenance and protection of a national network of water transportation

Recreation functions: including all water and land-related activities such as swimming, fishing, and boating

Construction functions: including all activities to construct and maintain water and power infrastructure for the above thirteen functions

concerning the activities and functions of each plan.

These summary descriptions will tell what activities and functions are included in the plan, their location, intended area of impact, and the manner and schedule in which each plan is to be implemented. The descriptions should probably be no more than a few pages long; they will serve as a guide during the social assessment as to what the details of each plan are. They will be useful to the SWBTG, its staff, and to expert informants and other persons living in the plan area who may be interviewed about likely future effects of the plans.

For each plan, the summary description will state what is planned in terms of physical facilities such as dams, reservoirs, power stations, recreational facilities, and preservation areas. Different activities will be anticipated for different plans. Thus different functions such as irrigation, industrial water supplies, and ecology preservation will be emphasized under different plans which emphasize different national objectives. The summary description for No Plan will be a description of the physical characteristics of the planning area, together with whatever future changes are anticipated due to existing trends and causal forces. If possible, the descriptions should also be accompanied by a map which shows all the plan areas of possible implementation.

After the plans have been described not only in terms of their generalized objectives but also in terms of the form which their implementation will take, they will be compared as to their effect on national economic development, on environmental quality, on regional development and on social well-being; i.e., in terms of the four-account system described in Chapter 2. (It is for the sake of this comparison that the social assessment is undertaken, since it provides the planners with the Social Well-Being Account.) A recommendation will then be made as to which of the plans or mixtures of plans best meets the various objectives with the greatest overall benefits and the least overall costs.

8

The General History, Social Profile, and Community Characteristics of the Planning Area

This chapter of the social assessment is to be made up of three separate but related sections. First, there should be a brief historical statement of the basic development patterns which have led to the community and social characteristics of the area as it exists today. Second, there should be a social profile of the area which describes its characteristics on selected variables. Finally, a description should be provided of the important groups and institutions which make up the area, the contemporary values which dominate it, important minority group presence in the area, and a description of the aspirations (sometimes conflicting) which residents have for the future of their area. These should provide the basis for a general narrative of the community which can be used as support materials for selected sections of the Feasibility Report, and selected data should also be compared with relevant regional or national norms. These materials are vital to the requirements of the Feasibility Report.

The historical information, the social profile, and the community characteristics are required in the chapter of the Feasibility Report containing information on the setting. This part of the Feasibility Report includes specific information on the historical and present-day population, economy, social structure, and cultural patterns of the area. In addition, it calls for information of the type contained in social profiles pertaining to such matters as employment, education, communications, transportation, community facilities, and population trends. Another part of the Feasibility Report deals with problems and needs of the area and calls for information concerning a variety of social data, including demographic and economic projections and various social and cultural needs of the area (for services, resolution of conflicts, maintenance of various values, etc.). Still another part is concerned with the presence of important human resources which can be used in solving social problems in the area; i.e., the people, groups, and institutions which can make a contribution in improving life in the communities. Finally, one part of the Feasibility Report compares the needs and resources of the community; it pays special attention to such matters as population distribution, education and cultural opportunities, and individual growth.

Development of a Historical Statement of the Characteristics of the Planning Area

There are various reasons for collecting historical data on the communities in the plan area. The information helps to explain why the community exists as it does today. It helps to identify trends which would not be apparent were one to look only at a present-day profile of the community. It also gives insight into the ways in which the community relates to the outside world. It may help to explain possible future trends in the community and what influence the community will have on the development of plans in the area. Perhaps of greatest significance, it provides an important basis for assessing a range of variables (presented in Chapter 9) in terms of whether or not certain types of changes will be socially beneficial or adverse for the community. Finally, such information helps the planner to obtain a general sense of how well the community is doing in relation to other communities outside the planning area or to the nation, in terms of selected comparison characteristics. While history is not a harbinger of the future, it can point to significant causal forces operating in a community, and it can provide a basis for assessing the effect of the implementation of a plan on an area.

The following categories are some of the types of issues which can be described in such a history. It is not necessary to include all items nor to follow the precise format presented here. *The planner should select out those features which will be most appropriate to the planning area in question,* and which will directly relate to the materials being developed for the larger Feasibility Report.

- Basic Facts

  Name of communities in planning area, county, state; elevation; square mile area; most recent population census; date first settled; date of formal incorporation; location expressed in longitude/latitude, and in miles and direction to nearest large city(ies).

- Basic Geography, Geology, and Ecology of Planning Area

  General description of the countryside (e.g., plains, rolling hills, mountainous country, wooded hills, oceans, rivers, large lakes).

  Topographical features of land affecting community development (e.g., confined by hills, rivers, or unusual land features).

  Unusual resources of scenic beauty, climate conducive to health, etc.

  Pictures of countryside.

  Major mineral deposits or other natural resources.

  Soil conditions and how land is used (e.g., farming, mining, forestry, agriculture).

  Natural wildlife, waterfowl, fish, and birds found in vicinity.

  Average temperature range for the various seasons.

  Any major changes which have taken place in the natural and local environment over the years due to natural or human cause.

  Major influence of these characteristics on community life and economics.

- Early Settlement of the Planning Area—the First Twenty to Thirty Years

  Circumstances under which initial settlement took place. Westward movement, logging, cattle, etc. Why people chose this location.

  The first settlers. Who were they? Any stories about the period of arrival? How many came? Ethnic, racial, and religious groups?

  Dominant values of early settlers.

  Economics of settlement. Sources of finance for economic activities and the nature of early occupations.

  Early growth rates. How rapidly, during the first ten to twenty years, did the population grow? Who came after the first settlers? General age distribution, presence of families, and so on.

  Major events in early settlement, such as: formation of local government, establishment of law and order, development of land ownership, emergence of local business, breakdown of law and order, involvement in war, evidence of starvation and/or disasters, arrival of "foreign" cultural patterns, arrival of railroads, beginnings of mail delivery.

  Sources of general influence from outside of the community during early settlement period. County or state government, prevailing regional culture, religious missionaries, cultural assimilation with natives of area, nearest big city, economic influences.

  Emerging economic structure. Agriculture, forestry, fishing commerce, light or heavy industry, services, banking. Outside economic factors (railroads; county and state government; federal support of Indians, Eskimos; army installation; reclamation; etc.).

  Emerging social stratification. Aspects of "class" distinction—ownership, occupational, ethnic, religious, neighborhood or locality. Early sources of cooperation and conflict. General institutions which assumed leadership role (business, church, associations).

  Significant shifts in values which emerged after initial settlement. Traditions which began.

As planning area began to form, *how rapid was development, and what were key areas of community life established?* Local government; citizen involvement; early institutions such as churches, schools, clinics, law offices, and cattlemen's associations; first newspaper; development of schools.

- General Development of the Community up through the Early 1960s

Demographic characteristics. Over the course of the years, what was the pattern of population growth (or decline) and were there particular periods of rapid change? Changes in various aspects of population composition (age, sex, ethnic groups, marital status). Patterns of immigration and emigration, birth rates, and events which influenced population level.

General development of the planning area. Major events of significance over the years. Outside events (Civil War, World War I, Depression, railroad, etc.) that had marked effect on community. Any marked changes in physical environment, relations to state government, or significant external influences upon the community.

Economic picture. Major development or shifts in the economic base of communities (e.g., from agriculture to industry), arrival of new industry, "boom" or "bust" eras, new infrastructure (dams, irrigation, hydroelectric power, interstate highway, railroad), new sources of funding (banks, state or federal grants), welfare, food commodities, or provision of other amenities.

Cultural and traditions. What emerged as the dominant values of the area as a whole, or various subgroups (e.g., honesty, work, spirituality, family, community, material possessions, patriotism, rural life, as well as negative values —prejudice, hostility toward "outsiders," mutual distrust, criminal behavior, etc.)? Were certain traditions established (e.g., special festivals, honors, religious practices, ways of doing things, etc.)?

Political. Form of government which emerged, and how and why it emerged. Representativeness of government.

Citizen participation according to various subgroups. General enforcement of community norms and values through formal mechanisms. Operations of courts and other government functions.

Education. Type of school system which emerged. Characteristics of education content and process. Community role in school system. Typical patterns of education for various groups in community. Leadership in the schools. Where students went after graduating from school (i.e., employment, army, college, etc.).

The historical information presented in the preceding outline will be very useful in the development of a narrative. The length of the narrative should be kept in proportion to the rest of the social assessment; the narrative should be documented as to source of facts and written to provide the reader with an understanding of the development of the planning area.

Information sources, which are numerous, include:

1. *Public records,* e.g., census, public school records, town records, county archives, surveyors' notes, and various state and regional documents.
2. *Privately-owned records,* e.g., town library collections, newspapers, local historical documents, special studies, family histories and biographies, directories, maps, anniversary addresses, and local church and fraternal records. Older local residents may be an excellent source of information.

The information contained in these categories is fully adequate to cover the historical requirements of the Feasibility Report. Various parts can be omitted, combined with other parts, or expanded according to the specific planning context. It should be kept in mind that it is through the development of the narrative that the requirements for social matters in the Feasibility Report are fulfilled.

Coordination with other task groups developing similar information is especially important at this stage of planning. Duplication of effort can be avoided with such coordination.

Preparing a Social Profile of the Present-Day Community

The Profile

The fundamental reason for developing a social profile is to have baseline information on the community as it exists before a plan is implemented, so that the probable effects are understood in light of the nature of the communities in the planning area. The profile is developed for all the communities which fall within the boundary of the planning area. The purpose of the social profile is to depict a clear, concise, easy to understand summary of the social features of the study area as compared with the regional, state, or national averages, or other baseline data, as appropriate. Data for the social profile will tend to be cross-sectional, although some trend data, usually population, can be included as well. Generally, the most efficient way to present the profile is through the use of appropriate tables and figures accompanied by a narrative.

Narrative in the profile should first describe the information depicted in the tables, graphs, and figures of the social profile and associated data. This part of the narrative should be objective and factual in tone and interpretation.

In Figure 16 a hypothetical social profile is presented which illustrates a simple, effective format. It can, of course, be refined to show separate data on communities in the planning area if necessary.

The items used in this section can be selected by the planner either from those items in Figure 16, or those described on pp. 112-13 or in Chapter 9, under the various evaluation categories of the components. Typically, the planner will select items for which there is a readily available source of secondary data (sometimes in the library) or which can be obtained by a visit to a local employment agency, a public health center, etc. The data for the "base planning year" should be entered in the measurement column labeled "Area," and the appropriate baseline comparison data are then entered in the column marked regional and national. In the final column, the planner makes a judgement as to the extent to which a disparity exists between

Figure 16. *A Hypothetical Social Profile*

Topics and Items	Measure		Rating AA/A/BA
	Planning Area	Regional or National Norm	
POPULATION			
Density Per Sq. Mile			
% Minority Population			
Dependency Ratio			
Male/Female Ratio			
Migration Rate			
Net Growth in Past Decade			
ETHNIC COMPOSITION			
% Native Parentage			
% Foreign Stock			
ECONOMIC BASE			
Total Agricultural Prediction			
Total Establishments by SIC Code Category			
Net Change in Establishments 1960-1970			
Total County Tax Base			
EMPLOYMENT			
Total Employed Persons as % of Total Population			
Unemployment Rate for Base Year			
Total Employed Persons Receiving Wages or Salary as % of Total Workforce			
Total Self-Employed Persons as % of Total Workforce			
Total Persons Receiving Farm Income as % of Total Workforce			
Total Persons Receiving Non-Farm Income as % of Total Workforce			
INCOME			
Average Income Per Capita			
% of Families Earning ≤ $2,999			

Figure 16 *(cont'd.)*

Topics and Items	Measure		Rating AA/A/BA
	Planning Area	Regional or National Norm	
INCOME (cont'd.)			
$\geq$ \$ 3,000 $\leq$ \$ 9,999			
$\geq$ \$10,000 $\leq$ \$24,999			
$\geq$ \$25,000 $\leq$ \$49,999			
$\geq$ \$50,000			
EDUCATION			
Average Education Level for Adults 25 Years or More			
% High School Dropout Rate			
% H.S. Seniors Going to College			
Average H.S. Senior Achievement Test Performance			
WELFARE			
% Population Receiving Welfare Payments			
% Population Receiving Welfare Services			
GOVERNMENT			
Local Gov't. Employees Per Capita			
Total Gov't. Budget			
% Adult Population Registered Voters			
LAW AND JUSTICE			
No. Reported Victims of Crime per 1,000			
Per Capita Loss Due to Crime			
No. Police Officers per 1,000 Persons			
HEALTH			
No. Deaths per 1,000 Live Births			
Average Age of Death			
Number Reported Cases per 1,000			
Streptococcal			
Sore Throat			
Scarlet Fever			
No. Doctors per 10,000			

Figure 16 *(cont'd.)*

Topics and Items	Measure		Rating AA/A/BA
	Planning Area	Regional or National Norm	
SOCIAL SERVICES			
No. Divorcees per 1,000			
No. Children in Adoption Homes per 1,000			
No. Juvenile Arrests per 1,000			
No. Trained Mental Health Professionals per 10,000			
RECREATION			
No. Recreation Establishments by Category			
Attendance Statistics for Key Recreation Facilities			
TRANSPORTATION			
Key Transportation Facilities in Area			
Miles Paved Road in Planning Area			
Automobile Ownership per Capita in Area			
COMMUNICATIONS			
No. Local Newspapers Serving Area			
No. TV Channels Received in Area			
HOUSING			
Percent Owner-Occupied Dwellings			
Average Number Persons per Room			
Median Value of Dwelling Units			
Percent of Total Dwelling with All Plumbing Facilities			
Vacancy Rate			
RELIGION			
Active Churches in Area by Denomination			
Percent Population Members of Church			

the data for the planning area and those for the region or nation and the extent to which this indicates that the planning area is average, above average, or below average for a particular trait.

This information is required for subsequent use in Chapter 10, where the social impacts of the plans are compared with one another on selected variables and then in relationship to the present-day status of communities in these areas.

A second type of display which will *summarize* these ratings (i.e., AA, A, or BA) can be constructed as follows:

Figure 17. *Hypothetical Social Profile Comparisons Across Areas of Life, with National and Regional Data*

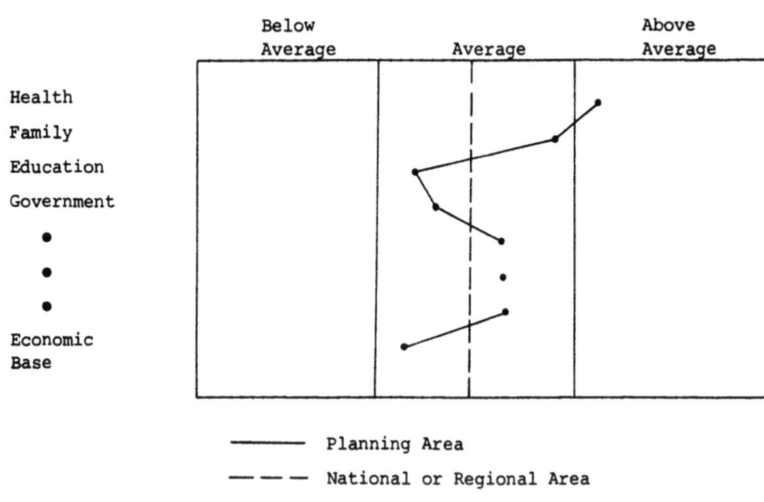

Finally, it will be useful to include various secondary data source graphs on population distribution by age and sex for the area. It is important to know if there are any anomalies in this aspect of community life, such as a high outmigration of a certain age range, or a large number of elderly in the population in proportion to the size of the work force.

Types of Data Called For

Comparable to the historical data, a variety of data can be gathered concerning contemporary life in the planning area. The following are examples of such data.

Demographic. Current population characteristics: number, age/sex distribution; ethnic-religious composition; migration trends at present time; any other relevant census breakouts.

General Considerations in Planning Area. Recent events of significance to entire community such as new newspaper, cable TV, new highway, federal grant for non-educational program, recent trends in youth behaviors, significant external influences upon the community.

Community Services. Health personnel and facilities; post-graduate facilities and curricula; transportation (ground, rail, air, freight, water); primary suppliers of power and fuel; religious institutions; clubs and organizations; recreational and entertainment activities and facilities; communications (telephone, postal, radio and TV, newspaper and library); water and sewerage; general housing ownership, supply and condition; financial institutions; sanitation; special human services programs; and other important services and facilities.

Economic Situation. Size and general composition and characteristics of labor force. The nature, size, and production levels of industry, agriculture, commerce, and services. The employment picture (level of employment and types of jobs held; level of unemployment, sub-employment, under-employment); external factors influencing economics of area today. Key leadership in economic development in area. New industries considering entry into the communities; and existing employment which may soon disappear. Economic trends in community today.

Social and Psychological. Is current social structure of the community similar to that described earlier or is it in a process of change? If so, who and toward what? Why? New institutions emerging in the community? Old ones dying out? Citizen satisfaction with life in the community and sense of self-fulfillment in community as it now is.

Values and Traditions. New or emerging values coming to the community. Stability of longer term values. Maintenance or abandonment of earlier traditions.

Gathering Secondary Data

In the context of this manual, secondary data are defined as those "hard" or objective data which may be obtained from publications of the U.S. Census agency reports, special governmental or private studies, etc. They can be used both for Chapter 8—on present-day community life—and in Chapter 9—to form the basis upon which changes, or impacts, are forecast. Fortunately, the United States is "data rich" in many respects. The best and most complete source of data is the decennial census. In addition, much information is gathered in relation to "categorical program areas" (e.g., housing data, and employment data). These data have been developed for many purposes, including analyzing progress in the nation toward specific policy objectives (such as reduction in unemployment or infant mortality rates); for federal subsidy of districts on a formula basis; for national planning of various types, etc. However, they are not usually collected with social assessment in mind. The data are often quite valuable (reliable, collected at various time intervals, standardized, and readily available). Usually, they have been developed with the support of one or more scientific disciplines (e.g., economics, medical research, biology). For this reason, indicators of important social phenomena exist for many areas of community life: descriptive statistics (e.g., employment rates), time series data (e.g., trends in the economic base), educational data (e.g., size of school systems), and so forth.

These secondary data are gathered in one of three ways. The first and best source of secondary data will probably be the various plans (NED, EQ, and alternative plans) themselves. In describing the plans and the extent to which each one meets the national objectives, data are provided which give information for the Social Well-Being Account. A second source of data are various reference sources available through a local public or federal agency library (as with Census and Industrial Code data). Third, data may be available at various local offices, where they may be obtained from the person responsible for record keeping (e.g., as with the U.S. Employment Service Office and the Public Health Service).

Use of Census Data

U.S. Census data should be used in describing the social characteristics which include the *demographic profile* of the people (i.e., age, sex, ethnic groups, migratory trends, education, and family economic characteristics). The Bureau of the Census publishes a "volume" (Volume I) called *Characteristics of the Population.* This "volume" actually has 58 parts. Part 1 is a summary for the entire United States; Parts 2 through 52 cover each of the 50 states plus the District of Columbia; Part 53 covers Puerto Rico. Parts 1 through 53 are bound separately (i.e., each looks like a separate volume); Parts 54 through 58, covering "Outlying Areas" (Guam, the Virgin Islands, American Samoa, the Canal Zone, and the Trust Territory of the Pacific), are bound together in one book.

In order to obtain the necessary data, the researcher will have to consult the part of Volume I that covers the state or states which are included in the water development plans. If the project is to be built in Montana, for example, he will consult Part 28. Each of the parts of Volume I is divided into four chapters, as follows:

Chapter A. Number of Inhabitants
Chapter B. General Population Characteristics
Chapter C. General Social and Economic Characteristics
Chapter D. Detailed Characteristics

Which tables in these chapters are consulted in order to present statistics depends somewhat on the kind of activities and functions under consideration. However, the following statistics are typically used in social descriptions:

- Persons by age and sex
- Persons of foreign stock by nativity and country of origin
- Native persons by state of birth
- Persons by the year they moved into housing unit

- Persons three years old and over enrolled in school by level and sex
- Persons three to thirty-four years old enrolled in school by age
- Persons twenty-five years old and over by years of school completed and sex
- Persons sixteen years old and over in the labor force by age and sex
- Families by family income
- Families by ratio of family income to poverty level

For some demographic profiles, the researcher may also want to consult the U.S. Census of Housing, which is divided into separate volumes along the same lines as the Census of Population.

It is important to note some of the caveats about the various publications of the U.S. Bureau of the Census. Although one of these, *County Business Patterns,* is published annually, the Censuses of Population from the other sources will be of decreasing utility as the decade progresses. The data collector should check to see whether any special censuses or data collection projects have been conducted in the area since the last official U.S. Census. In using such special censuses, however, it is important to keep in mind that different geographical bases might have been covered (e.g., school districts, U.S. Public Health districts), and that data from these special censuses may therefore not be comparable to one another or to other data, such as those from the U.S. Census. In such a case, the data will have to be manipulated to some extent to ensure a close match among geographical areas.

Another problem which might be encountered in using the U.S. Census figures relates to the fact that many of the items in the publications are collected only for geopolitical divisions with relatively large populations (states, counties, SMSA's, cities with populations of 10,000 or more). The U.S. Census of the Population contains some summary data for areas with 2,500 or more residents, and the Census of Housing has summary data for areas with 1,000 or more. However, even these breakdowns may not be viable in sparsely settled rural areas. Since it is not unusual to have such geographic units in the water planning areas, it may be quite useful to check with the various state agencies to determine if alternative, state collected statistics are available. In addition, there are various special commissions such as the Four Corners Regional Commission, various river basin commissions, etc., which may have useful statistics on population. Local universities, especially in the sociology and political science departments, may also have demographers or other specialists with useful information. Finally, where there is a particular population with a federal government program serving the area (e.g., the Bureau of Indian Affairs, OEO Community Action Agencies), these can also be contacted for possible data. A word of caution is in order, however, in that data from so many varied sources will vary in reliability; not all agencies follow precise census practices in obtaining and analyzing such data. For this reason, appropriate caveats should be presented where such data are likely to be used.

Expert Informants

Information in the census publications and other reference works may very well not be specific to the particular impact area in which the researcher is interested. Therefore, some of the secondary data will have to be obtained from local experts. For example, employment may be given for a whole county when what is needed are employment data for two or three villages or towns. Again, school enrollment data may be given for a large consolidated school district when what is needed are enrollment data for two elementary schools.

To get site-specific data like these, it will often be necessary to interview local experts, like the director of the Employment Security Office or the principal of a school. One must consider, therefore, which experts to consult and how to draw a sample of experts which gives reasonable certainty of obtaining relevant information for generalization.

It is important to remember that one is not surveying the experts in order to get a representative sample of their opinions. Rather, one of the major reasons one turns to experts is to get secondary data on those evaluation categories of the component where site-specific information cannot be found in existing reference books. Before deciding, therefore, which experts to interview, the researcher must be aware of which data are missing and what needs to be obtained from the experts. If the data are school data, the researcher will then go to school personnel and try to obtain them. If what is wanted are enrollment data for a particular school, then once those data have been obtained from a source that is reliable (such as a principal or someone in the school administration's office whose job it is to have enrollment and attendance figures), there is, in principle, no need to interview any more people. However, even experts sometimes make mistakes, forget, or are not as well informed as they should be. Since an expert is also unlikely to admit that any of these things could apply to him or her, it is best to check the validity of information even from an expert. The obvious way of doing this is to consult more than one expert and to compare their information. By going to two or three school people, the researcher should be able to get a reasonably accurate picture, for example, of enrollment. If there are large discrepancies between what one expert says and another, it is clear that more investigations must be made—either yet another person must be consulted or it must be determined whether the two original experts answered the same question. It is good always to check the validity of information received—even data that are written down suffer from errors, omissions and inconsistencies. Sometimes no reliable data of any kind exist; for example, it may be almost impossible to determine a meaningful drop-out rate, because different schools and different agencies define dropping out differently and because there is considerable resistance on the part of some educators to admit that their school has a high dropout rate.

The Description of Life in the Community

The final part of this section deals with life in the community. This should provide a word picture of the social world, including the general features of life-style, customs, attitudes, values, and typical behavior patterns which currently characterize the area. It should be in sufficient detail that the reader obtains an overview and understanding of contemporary life in the community.

The description should be economic in length, objective in

approach, and sensitive in style. Ideally, the planner should be able to show the result to a member of the community and have him or her say, "Yes, that is a good summary of life around here. It doesn't cover everything, but it has the important things." The following are illustrations of the kind of materials to be included in such a section:

Descriptions of the various groups of people who make up the community;
The nature of the work and leisure life for the majority of the community;
Special variations in these patterns for other groups;
Important community patterns of social life;
Changes in the politics and institutions of the community;
General reactions to the various plans to the extent that these are a topic of community concern;
Aspirations for the future of the community.

In preparing the narrative for this section a variety of outlines are possible and different approaches may be used.

The planner should begin by identifying the boundaries of the total impact area (in terms of county lines, rivers, large cities just inside or outside the area, mountain ranges, etc.), giving a reasonably accurate estimate of the total square miles in the impact area.

The communities located in the impact area should then be identified, with an indication as to whether they are located in the impact area of each of the alternative plans.

Next, the investigator should briefly describe the communities in the planning area in terms of size, general economic characteristics, etc. Numerous aspects have been identified which will help to characterize the communities under consideration. Questions to which the researcher might address himself or herself concerning the community at present include (but are not necessarily limited to) the following:

- Is the community primarily urban or rural in character?
  What is the population per square mile in the community or area?
  Is the economy of the area based primarily on small businesses and/or agriculture or are there large industries located in the area?

What is the distance from the community to the nearest large metropolitan area or Standard Metropolitan Statistical Area (as defined by the U.S. Census)?

- What is the basic demographic composition of the community?

  Composition (age, race, sex, ethnicity).

  Characteristics (education, income, housing, etc.).

  Major social groupings of the community.

- Is the community primarily agricultural or industrial in character?

  How many farms (large or small) are located within a fifty-mile radius of the community?

  What was the total value of farm products in the community during the past year? Of this total, what percentage came from crops; from livestock; from poultry? from dairy products?

  What is the nature of business and/or industry in the area?

  What percentages of the community's economic activities were devoted to mining? to construction? to manufacturing? to wholesale trade? to retail trade?

  How many people are employed overall in the community? How many live in the community but work outside (in another city, county)?

  What is the number of establishments by employment class size in the community (small = 1-19 persons; medium = 20-99 persons; large = 100 or more persons)?

  Is the community's economic base dominated by a single large industry (e.g., mining)?

- Have there been significant changes in the economic base of the communities over the past ten years?

  Has there been a perceived trend toward amalgamation of farms and toward corporate farming, or increases in external control of the agricultural sector?

  Have any large new industries entered the area recently?

- Are the communities growing or dying out?

  What has been the percent population change in the last 10 years?

  What do residents and expert informants perceive as the reasons for this change?

- Are the communities aging, remaining stable, or growing younger?
  What is the breakdown of inhabitants by age?
  How does this compare to ten years ago?
  What do residents and expert informants perceive as the reasons for this change?
- Are there significant cultural enclaves in the communities?
  What is the percentage of residents who are of native birth?
  Are there any large percentages of foreign-born, foreign language-speaking persons (or Indians) in the community?
  Do foreign-born, foreign language-speaking persons live in one particular section of the community? Do they work in one particular occupation?
- Are there especially important social value systems in the communities of the areas?
  What are the nature of these values?
  Which groups hold them?
  How do the various groups of the community relate to one another?
- What is the governmental structure in the community (mayor, city council, city manager)?
  What services are provided by government in the community (garbage removal, electricity, water, etc.)?
- Has the governmental structure changed in the last ten years? For what reasons?

Other pertinent facts include whether the community is a county seat, whether it is the trading center for a given area, whether or not it is incorporated (and, if not, where it obtains services such as police and fire protection).

Once each of the communities in question has been thus characterized, the investigator should compare them according to the above considerations. These comparisons should be brief, and should focus only on the most salient differences and similarities among the communities.

9
The Social Impacts and Effects of the Alternative Plans

The third step in completing the social assessment consists of preparing a forecast of the social impacts which each of the plans is likely to have, and in turn, rating these according to the direction and magnitude of their beneficial and adverse social effects.

This chapter is divided into four parts. First, procedures are described for gathering primary data useful in forecasting probable long-range impacts. Second, rating the NED, EQ, alternative, "recommended," and "no" plans is discussed. Third, procedures are outlined for completing a separated statement on the likely social impacts and effects of each of the plans. And fourth, the concern of each of the five SWB components and their evaluation categories is discussed, and examples are provided for rating the beneficial and adverse social effects of each evaluation category.

Gathering Primary Data to Forecast Probable Long-Range Impacts

Primary data will probably have to be gathered in order to obtain information relevant to the likely long-range impacts on the planning area, as called for in this chapter. Primary data are those that are collected not from secondary printed sources, but rather by means of personal interviews with various respondents. By definition, then, they can only be collected on site. Respondents for primary data interviews may be divided into two categories: expert informants and residents.

Expert informants are local officials, professionals, or agency employees who are responsible for such concerns as employment, housing, and education in their community. As has been mentioned previously, they will be able to provide the investigator with a good deal of secondary data; however, they will also be in a good position to offer valuable ideas on some of the likely consequences of the proposed plan on their specific areas of concern. For example, local school officials will be able to discuss the implications for the local school system of changes in population expected with a plan (increases or decreases in total number, change in age composition). Likewise, the local public health officer, who is familiar with the different medical needs of various age and income groups, can provide information on what such population changes imply for health service needs.

Some examples of the types of questions to be asked of various informants, given the availability of certain facts, are shown in Figure 18. However, it should be noted that these examples in no way constitute the total interview format for the various informants listed, nor do they indicate the types of questions which might be asked when fewer or different data are available or required. Questions addressed to expert informants should be "leading," designed to gather the largest amount of specific relevant information possible within a reasonable time period.

To some extent, the nature of each expert informant interview and the number and types of questions asked will depend on the amount of secondary information (see Chapter 8, pp. 113-114) which the researcher has been able to gather prior to the interview; i.e., if much secondary data in the informant's area has been unavailable beforehand, the researcher will probably want to begin the interview by asking questions relevant to the missing data. If, on the other hand, the researcher has already been able to compile a good amount of secondary information, she or he might want to focus the interview on the respondent's interpretation of the data which have been collected.

The second source of primary data is the residents of the planning area. Information from residents, unlike that from expert informants, is not primarily useful in forecasting the "actual" impact of a project, since few residents are in a position to make objective forecasts, for example, of school enrollment or health service changes required by a proposed plan. Rather, we are interested here in what residents do know something about—their own general attitudes toward the alternative plans and what they believe implementation of any of the plans will mean for their lives and for their community. By interviewing residents of different educational, occupational, and ethnic backgrounds, and from different age and income groups, it is possible to draw a profile of the relative desirability of the alternative plans from the perspectives of these different respondents. Different groups frequently see the same set of alternatives in very different ways. Young farmers, with most of their lives ahead of them, may perceive a new irrigation system as holding great opportunities for improving their land. On the other hand, older residents, especially those in lower income brackets who will be displaced by the implementation of a plan, may very accurately view the plan as having serious negative consequences for them. A move late in their life, especially when this move is a forced one, can be fraught with anxiety; problems of money, of establishing new friendships, and of learning how to use new services are all realities which may gravely affect the lives of older people. In a similar sense, local businessmen may look forward to new customers as the result of a proposed plan, while local farmhands who depend on labor-intensive farming may see the plan as promoting capital-intensive farming, a method which will no longer offer them jobs. Thus, interviews with different local residents will reveal which ones see themselves as benefiting from the various alternatives and which see themselves as absorbing unfair or serious costs.

Basically, the question which the interviewer must ask again and again of different interviewees, concerning different topics,

Figure 18. *Sample Questions for Interviewing Expert Informants*

INFORMANT	DATA/INFORMATION ALREADY AVAILABLE		EXAMPLES OF QUESTIONS TO BE ASKED
	Plan-Related	Community-Related	
Public Health Officer	Plan involves the influx of approximately fifty construction workers to the area over a two-year period, plus their families. The plan involves the construction of a water-pollution control facility on the local river which supplies most of the water for the community, as well as recreational facilities.	Community has one hospital with an inpatient capacity of twenty beds. There are nine full-time equivalent doctors and one full-time equivalent dentist within a fifty-mile radius of the population center of the community. There has been a relatively high, increasing incidence of hepatitis and gastro-intestinal disorders in the community over the past decade.	What has been the occupancy status of hospital beds in the past ten years? Do occupancy status trends indicate that the hospital will be able to extend services to an increased number of patients if necessary? Will the medical personnel (doctors/dentists) be able to handle an increased patient load over the next few years? Have any causes been attributed to the increasing incidence of hepatitis, etc.? Could it be related to water pollution? If so, what would be the effects of the pollution control facility? Do studies in other areas indicate that an influx of new people (e.g., construction workers) usually brings with it certain increases in incidence of certain types of diseases? of accidents? If so, will health facilities in the community be able to deal with such increases?
Transportation Director, Public School System	Plan involves the temporary (one-year) closing of a main street leading to community's one elementary school.	This year, 15% of children in elementary school walk to school; 10% are driven by parents; the remaining 75% go by school bus. A child's average one-way travel time by school bus is 20 minutes.	Will the fact that one of the main streets leading to the school will be closed mean that buses will have to be significantly rerouted? What will be the effect on children now using bus service? Will some be unable to do so after rerouting? What other provisions will be made for them? How much will rerouting increase/decrease the average travel time? What will be the effects of such an increase or decrease (less extra-curricular activity, e.g.)?

Director, County Department of Housing	Plan does not require the flooding or disruption of any residential areas. Plan involves the influx of approximately fifty construction workers to the area over a two-year period, plus their families.	Census data show seventy vacant year round houses in the area; of these, 50% are for sale and 50% are for rent. Of the houses for sale, 80% have been vacant for less than six months; of those for rent, 70% have been vacant for less than two months. There have been ten new housing starts within the past year in the community. Median monthly rent for occupied units according to census is $150. There is one mobile home park in the area, with space for five more homes.	The data provided are for the county in 1970. The community consists of two square miles in the northwest portion of the county. Can these 1970 county figures be used to estimate the number of vacant houses for rent in the community in 1975? Does the respondent have any newer or more relevant (to the community) figures? Do vacancy/occupancy trends over the past ten years in the community indicate that there will be sufficient housing for the construction workers? Are the construction workers likely to raise the cost of housing rentals for the community? Can the Department of Housing do anything to control this? What would be the effect on the community of more mobile homes in the area?
Director, Regional Recreation Commission	Plan requires the permanent closing of an area of the local river formerly used for boating and swimming facilities.	One private boat rental facility operated close to the plan's proposed project site. There are four stores in the community selling sporting goods and equipment, including one speedboat outlet.	Approximately how many people per year used the boating facilities in the area of the plan's proposed site? Where were these people from (the community, a nearby SMSA, etc.)? What is the nearest other water-related recreational facility in the area? How close is it from the population center of the community? How many people are employed in water recreation-related businesses in the area? Are there any areas within a twenty-mile radius of the project site which could be developed for water-related recreation? Have any recreational groups raised objections to the proposed plan (yacht clubs, etc.)?

and as regards different project alternatives is "What do you think will be the effects on you and the community if Plan A is implemented?" The answers to these questions must be recorded by the interviewer and constitute one source of basic data for the social assessment. The answers clearly will have a somewhat subjective cast. What residents *say* will be the effects of a water development plan will inevitably be influenced by what they *feel* about the plan (do they look forward to it because of economic benefits? dislike it because of environmental concerns?); conversely, however, how they feel about a plan will be influenced by what they perceive the future effects of the plan to be.

By interviewing residents who belong to different age groups, who live in different geographical areas, who have different socioeconomic status, and who belong to different advocacy groups, etc., the researcher should be able to detect trends in the effects that are anticipated by the residents as well as by experts who are not residents of the affected area.

The interviewer should begin by introducing himself or herself, stating whom she or he represents, the purpose of the interview, and why the study is being conducted. Inquiries should then be made as to how familiar the interviewee is with the proposed plans; in many cases, a brief description of each plan may have to be provided. A map should be carried, if possible, to show where activities connected with different plans will be located. Subjects should be asked what difference they think each condition would make to their community and in their lives; interviewees will probably identify several issues which they think are important and which should be pursued. If a subject cites three or four issues, for each issue the interviewer should ask the interviewee to describe the issue as she or he sees it. Depending on how detailed an answer is provided, the interviewee should then be questioned on various details (e.g., who would be affected the most, in what way) so that impact assessment can be handled later in terms of who will be affected, how, to what extent, and so forth.

The same strategy should be used if the respondent is being interviewed to obtain information on attitudes she or he personally has toward the plan alternatives or, if the respondent is an expert informant, so that the data later can be analyzed in a standardized and useful manner. The interviews will vary in length anywhere from fifteen minutes to over an hour, depending on the expertise and articulateness of the interviewee. It is likely that a standardized interview format ought to be employed. (See, for example, Miller, 1970.)

It is especially important to note that this inverviewing strategy differs in several ways from more traditional national sampling techniques. The concern of the assessment is with obtaining *relevant, accurate,* and *comprehensive* information on probable social effects; it is *not* with obtaining a "probabilistic sample." The objective of the study is not to be able to talk about the percentage of people who support the plan, but rather to draw some conclusion about the likely social effects of the projects. This distinction is important for two reasons. First, the extent to which a person believes something will happen is not necessarily related directly to its actual probability of occurrence. Second, by being able to match objective census data and other secondary data against a projected forecast, it becomes possible to determine the likelihood that a particular forecast will happen and what the magnitude of the impact will be. For example, a resident may feel that under a particular situation hundreds of persons will lose their jobs: that is a perfectly valid attitude, one which is, perhaps, representative of feelings of others. But it is important to know from objective data sources just how many people *could* lose their jobs; if only thirty people were employed in the area in question, the resident's estimate could not possibly come true. To summarize, the interview strategy is one designed to gain the maximum amount of relevant information on the range and likelihood of social impacts occurring (augmented with secondary data) and not to obtain a probabilistic sample of residents' forecasts.

If, because of the nature of the plans being considered and because of the nature of the planning area, it appears that a great many interviews with residents may have to be conducted in order to collect primary data, the SWBTG may want to consider employing an outside survey firm to conduct the interviews.

It is also important to be aware of the requirements of the Office of Management and Budget for clearance of interview forms and procedures. The chairperson of the SWBTG will be responsible for obtaining the necessary forms and initiating the clearance procedure through the Regional Office, Washington, and Denver. Since this procedure requires some time, it should be an early activity of the SWBTG.

A summary of the types of possible sources and examples of data needed to complete the Social Well-Being Account is presented in Figure 19.

Rating the NED, EQ, Alternative, "Recommended," and "No" Plans According to Their Beneficial and Adverse Effects

As discussed in Chapter 2, while the major focus of concern for the National Economic Development plan will be changes in the economic base of the planning area(s), economic effects do not occur in a vacuum, and it is clear that implementation of an NED plan will also result in a number of social (and perhaps environmental) changes as well. These effects must be taken into consideration in the Social Well-Being Account. Similarly, while the major focus of concern for the Environmental Quality plan will be changes in the environment of the planning area(s), the results of implementing an EQ plan are not likely to be limited to the environment; in assessing the EQ plan, its potential impact on the economy and society must also be given strong consideration.

As has been stated, in most cases the planner will not be limited to the consideration of only the NED and EQ plans. In the course of the planning, a number of other alternatives may be formulated which encompass both NED and EQ objectives in varying degrees and which might also incorporate what were previously known as "Regional Development" goals, as well as social well-being concerns. Essentially, then, the alternative plans represent compromises and, in some cases, innovations on the EQ and NED plans. In any event, alternative plans, like the basic NED and EQ plans, will have both direct and indirect beneficial and adverse effects which must be detailed and evaluated in the course of the overall plan assessment.

Figure 19. *Types and Selected Sources of Data with Illustrative Examples*

Type	Source	Illustrative Example
Historical Documents	Local Newspaper Files	Past controversies over water pollution abatement
	Local Governmental Records	Past local ordinances on water pollution abatement
	City or County Public Works Dept. Records	Local, often detailed, data on water use and planning
Secondary Sources	U.S. Bureau of the Census	
	a. *City and County Data Book*	Compilation of many demographic and social indicators
	b. 1st & 4th Count Census Publications	Wide range of detailed population breakdowns
	c. Housing Census	Detailed estimates of housing characteristics
	d. Agricultural and Industrial Census	Detailed estimates of elements of community's economic sector
	U.S. Department of Agriculture	Some data on crops and water consumption patterns available through county extension agents
Primary Sources	Local Residents	Subjective estimates of social impacts
	Local Business and Labor Leaders	Estimates of past and future economic effects
	Local Government Officials	Impacts of changes on social programs (i.e., unemployment campaigns to attract industry)
	Local Water-Related Agency Officials	Particulars of water-related activities

It may well be that, in the planning process which preceded the social assessment, one of the plans may be preferred or recommended based upon a variety of considerations. This recommended plan is then evaluated along with the NED, EQ, and alternative plans. (Obviously, if one of these plans with no modification is the recommended plan, only one assessment is necessary for the two.)

The labeling process is a little confusing, for the fact that there exists a favored plan which is entitled the "Recommended Plan" is not to be confused with the SWB Account's recommendations as to which plan is most desirable from the social assessment perspective. For example, if the "Recommended Plan" was a variation on the EQ plan, it is possible that the SWB Account would recommend acceptance of neither of these, but rather would state that the NED plan was, from the social point of view, the most desirable.

In the circumstance where the Recommended Plan is a combination of the elements of various other plans but not identical to them, an assessment of its beneficial and adverse social effects is completed in the same manner as for the other plans.

The decision to implement none of the alternative plans under consideration cannot be assumed to mean that, as a result, there will be no social changes in the plan area. Indeed, as discussed in Chapter 2, pp. 11-12, the effects may be far-reaching and of either a positive or negative nature. It should also be kept in mind that the present social characteristics of the area may undergo important changes independently of a decision to implement a plan or not to implement any plan.

Procedures for Completing a Separate Social Well-Being Beneficial and Adverse Effects Statement for Each Plan

The completion of the Social Well-Being components follows the description provided in Chapter 5. Each of the components is detailed later on in this chapter. The reader is provided with a description of the evaluation categories included under each component; e.g., the specific types of concern covered in the employment category. These descriptions are followed by a discussion of the types of data called for, and examples of data categories entries are provided. A few comments on each step are warranted.

1. *Concern of the Evaluation Category.* Each evaluation category plays a role in a component. In the aggregate, the component assessment is the end product of all the ratings made for each evaluation category. The reader is provided with a brief description of what can be learned from data in each evaluation category. Certain items in the evaluation categories may be more related to some planning areas than to others, and for some assessments, the planner may wish to add, drop, or modify them according to the unique characteristics of the communities of the area.

2. *Data for Each Evaluation Category.* One complete table (Table 1) is provided in Part 3 for each evaluation category, with a variety of data entries specified. Usually these data are categorized according to *state, relevant conditions,* and *system* variables as defined in Chapter 4, pp. 66-68.

3. *Entering Data on Effects.* For each item, Table 1 provides two columns. The center column concerns the amount of change, or the social *impact.* The planner may wish to construct sub-items to indicate that the social impact differs among various communities or groups in the area or that some other breakdown of the data is advisable. In this manner, distinctions can be made when the social impact is rated.

4. *Rating the Social Impacts as to Their Beneficial and Adverse Effects.* The planner is asked in the far right column of Table 1 to "rate" the impacts in terms of their social effects. As described in Chapter 4, each effect (or sub-effect by group) may be assigned a rating of from ++ to --. Examples of such ratings are described for each evaluation category. It will be remembered that the social effects rating is a function of the probable social value of a change for a plan area, given its present-day characteristics (see preceding chapter). In this manner, the social impacts are rated from the perspective of the affected communities.

5. *Preparing a Narrative.* Once Table 1 has been completed for each plan, it is necessary to prepare a concise narrative on the social impacts and effects in each of the five components

for each plan in the area. This narrative, along with Table 1, will be used in two places. First, the narrative and Table 1 will make up part of the SWB Appendix or supporting files, as the case may be, to the Feasibility Report. Second, the information can be used directly in the Feasibility Report itself.

6. *Later Use of the Social Impact Rating.* The rating prepared for each of the impacts will be used in the comparative assessment of the plans, which is the subject of Chapter 10.

The Social Well-Being Account: Its Components and their Evaluation Categories with Discussion of Concerns, Types of Data, and Assessment of Social Impacts

In this section, each of the five components is described in terms of its evaluation categories. For each evaluation category, there is a description of the general concerns to be dealt with. Following this, the reader is provided with illustrations of the types of future effects which can be forecasted and the basis upon which various social impact values can be assigned. All evaluation categories are included in the same order as they were displayed in Chapter 5.

The Individual, Personal Effects Component

The following section is devoted to a discussion of five evaluation categories of the "Individual, Personal Effects" component of the Social Well-Being Account. These five evaluation categories are concerned exclusively with the impacts of alternative plans as they are experienced at the most basic level of society, that of the individual and family; the component focuses on how each alternative plan will affect the personal health and well-being of members of the community and whether various aspects of the plan or its direct effects will contribute to or detract from the quality and stability of family life. Such concerns are, for the most part, qualitative in nature and less subject to aggregation than those in the remaining four components, although some quantitative measures can be applied: e.g., the size and capacity of health care facilities, or the potential number of lives lost due to natural disasters, and therefore the number of lives saved by the implementation of a plan which would diminish the effects of such disasters, and so forth. The five evaluation categories of this component are as follows:

Life, Protection, and Safety encompasses the effects of natural disasters on life and property and the possible diminution of such effects by alternative water resource plans.

Health encompasses both the health of individuals in the community and the services and facilities available to deal with health problems.

Family and Individual deals with the potential direct and indirect impacts of alternative water plans on the health, well-being and personal satisfaction of individuals in the community, and on the structure and stability of family life.

Attitudes, Values, and Beliefs discusses the attitudes of individuals in the community towards alternative water plans and the extent to which these plans affect people's attitudes towards other concerns, including their community, the environment, and government agencies.

Environmental Contributions deals with community members' interaction with their environment and the extent to which alternative plans may affect this interaction: e.g., by contributing to or detracting from individuals' enjoyment of their environment.

The complete tables listing the items of the evaluation categories in this component are presented on pp. 215-221 in Part 3.

Life, Protection, and Safety

Scope of concern. Life, protection, and safety, as they are considered here, refer not to the actual health of the populace (which is dealt with in another part of the account), but rather to protection from "natural disasters" which can drastically affect the economic and physical well-being of the residents of a given area. Such disasters include floods, droughts, and storms, which may seriously damage or destroy homes, crops, and businesses, as well as threaten the lives of the people.

A given water-related plan may affect not only the degree of damage and harm caused by such occurrences, but also the activities of organizations and institutions which deal with them.

For example, a planned flood control facility may offer the inhabitants of flood-prone areas increased protection from floods, and at the same time obviate the need for agencies formerly organized to deal with flood protection and relief in the area (e.g., Civil Defense and the Red Cross). While these agencies will remain valuable for other services which they provide, the scope of their activities in relation to flood control will be reduced. Conversely, insurance agencies which formerly refused to provide flood protection policies for farms, businesses, and homes in areas subject to frequent flooding might consider offering such policies once a flood control facility is operating in these areas. Similar impacts could result when a reservoir or irrigation system is planned for an area which formerly had been subject to severe droughts.

Rating the impacts and social effects of alternative plans. In Table 1, Section I, Part A, thirteen items are listed as indicators of possible changes which might occur as a result of a given plan on Life, Protection, and Safety. The planner will first check the present characteristic for a given item in the plan area. She or he might, for example, determine that as a result of flooding, presently, ten people lose their lives in an average year and property damage is $358,000. Then, by examining the No Plan situation, she or he determines that this is not likely to change much. However, if the NED plan includes a major improvement in flood control and an increase in agency capacity to deal with natural disasters, then the planner can forecast that the effect will be a reduction both in loss of life and of property under this alternative. Finally, in assessing the social impact it might be determined that, since under the NED plan a dam will protect only those persons in the western section of the area, the impact might be rated as positive for those residents protected and negative for those who continue to be exposed to threat of floods. Under this situation, the following entries would be appropriate on the table for the NED plan as shown on the following page. (See Part 3 for the full tables on Social Effects.)

Health

Scope of concern. Two factors are of prime consideration in

Examples of NED Plan Effects

Items in Evaluation Categories	Measures of Impact	Effects ++,+,0,–,––
2. Property loss due to water-related natural disasters	Expected reduction in loss of human life and property loss:	
3. Life loss due to water-related natural disasters	Western part of area: ten lives per year and $350,000 per year.	++
12. Accessibility of agencies which deal with natural disasters	Eastern part (above dam) no change in present levels.	––
	New office opened up in district as part of plan.	+

an analysis of plan(s) in relation to the health situation in a given area: the health of the residents of the area, and the health-related services which are provided to them either inside or outside of the area. The health of the residents at the time of plan analysis can be measured by a number of variables, including morbidity (e.g., disease) rates, mortality rates, etc. Other secondary variables may also be of interest, including pollution counts and sanitation facilities. Of interest in the area of health-related services are such factors as number and type (i.e., specialty) of health care personnel, and number and capacity of health care facilities, including clinics, hospitals, mental health agencies, etc.

Both the health of the residents and the services which are provided to them can be affected directly and/or indirectly by water-related plans. For example, the institution of a new pollution control facility on a river may have a direct beneficial effect on the residents who live nearby, if pollution has previously been serious enough to cause such diseases as hepatitis and dysentery. The creation of flood control devices might also have a direct effect on the health (i.e., safety) of the population. On the other hand, the decision to locate a large hydroelectric plant in a district, with the related necessity to relocate residents of that district, may have substantial deleterious effects, in terms of disruption and stress, on those residents' mental health; this might be particularly true in the case of the elderly and infirm. Indirect effects can also occur as a result of water-related plans. For example, a new dam in a particular area may, through increasing irrigation capacity and flood control possibilities, considerably increase the prosperity and standard of living in the area. This, in turn, could lead to the improvement of health facilities and services in the area. Conversely, if such a plan brought increased population into the area, the strain on the existing facilities and a concomitant reduction in the quality of health care could result.

Rating the impacts and social effects of alternative plans. In Table 1, Section I, Part B, twenty items are listed as indicators of possible changes in the overall health variables in an area which might occur as a result of a given water resource plan. The planner will first check the present characteristics for a given item in the plan area. It might be found, for example, that on an island, raw sewage dumped into the river by commercial establishments on the west and east sides of the island have added a high bacterial count to the water, making it dangerous to use the bathing beaches in those areas. The EQ plan under consideration involves the construction of a sewage treatment plant and sewer lines for the west side of the island, which would almost wholly eliminate the bacterial pollution from sewage on that side of the island and therefore reduce the number of reported cases of infectious hepatitis by approximately one-half for the island as a whole. However, since sewer lines are not planned to run to the eastern part of the island, sewage pollution and related problems of disease-carrying organisms for this part of the island will continue unabated. Thus the EQ plan would be given a high positive rating on the item relating to disease-carrying organisms for the western side of the island, but not for the eastern side. The rating for morbidity level would be positive, but not as positive as it might be if the sewage treatment facility served the whole island. Under these circumstances, the following entries would be appropriate in Table 1 as shown on the following page.

Family and Individual

Scope of concern. The family is made up of any number of

Examples of EQ Plan Effects

Items in Evaluation Categories	Measures of Impact	Effects ++,+,0,–,––
4. Number of disease-carrying organisms	Expected reduction in the number of disease-carrying organism:	
	Western side of the island: 100%.	++
	Eastern side of the island: no change in present levels.	--
1. Morbidity levels, by type of disease	Reduction in the number of reported cases of hepatitis: 50%.	+

persons, including children—brothers, sisters, stepchildren, foster children—and adults—mother, father, grandparents. Many unrelated persons living in groups such as communes also consider themselves to be families of a sort. Although recent decades have seen changes in the traditional concept of family structure, the family, however defined or constituted, continues as the primary organizational unit of our society; family life remains one of the most important forces in our society, shaping the attitudes and behaviors of family members. Thus, any assessment of a water-related plan must pay serious attention to the possible effects of the plan on families in the community. Also to be considered is the well-being of individuals as apart from the family structure; i.e., changes in the community, in jobs, in social activities, etc., which might occur as a direct or indirect result of the plan may considerably alter the individual's sense of personal satisfaction and happiness.

The effects of alternative plans will, of course, vary with their nature and with the nature of the community in which individuals and families live. Increased prosperity in the community which is brought about as a result of the plan may enable individuals and families in the area to enjoy new ease and luxuries which they formerly could not afford. The plan might also provide a job for a previously unemployed head of family, thus reducing tension in the family. Similar benefits might occur in an agricultural area where a new irrigation facility is constructed. If alternative plans involve the creation or improvement of recreational opportunities, this is likely to contribute to both individual and family enjoyment. For example, people may find themselves spending more time together in family-style pursuits such as picnicking, camping, and boating.

On the other hand, a forced move of a major place of employment from the area might increase unemployment for certain persons and therefore place a strain on families, as well as seriously altering individual life-styles. A change in the community brought about by an influx of new residents may also have an unsettling effect on individuals and families who value local institutions, neighbors, and "ways of doing things."

Rating the impacts and social effects of alternative plans. In Table 1, Section I, Part C, eighteen items are listed as indicators of possible changes which might occur in the area of Family and Individual Life as a result of a given water resource plan. Having reviewed the NED plan, the planner might have determined that this plan will increase the overall economic base of the area by increasing the productivity of the agricultural sector. At the same time, however, this increase in productivity is likely to encourage the possibilities for larger, capital intensive farming. Smaller, labor intensive farming will then be eventually squeezed out, eliminating jobs for approximately fifty workers now employed on smaller farms. If half of those workers do not leave the area, it is likely that they will be unable to find other employment and therefore their families will fall below poverty level. Tension caused by these circumstances has good potential for creating problems within the families, which in turn will place an added strain on the family service agencies and individual family counselors in the area. If more staff cannot be added to the agencies or if more counselors do not come into the area, the effects are likely to be considerably negative. Under these circumstances, the following entries in Table 1 would be appropriate for the NED plan as shown on the following page.

Attitudes

Scope of concern. As an individual repeatedly comes into contact with persons, situations, and other social concerns, she or he begins to form a set of cognitive impressions, emotional

Examples of EQ Plan Effects

Items in Evaluation Categories	Measures of Impact	Effects ++,+,0,–,––
9. Staff size of family-related service agencies	No immediate change in present staff size.	-
10. Number of family and personal counselors in the area (not in agencies)	No immediate change in present number of counselors.	-
4. Number of families below poverty level	Increase in number of families below poverty level: approx. twenty-five.	--
5. Number of persons unemployed as a percent of total labor force	Increase in number of persons unemployed: approx. 5%.	-

reactions, and dispositions to respond to situations in a certain way. These patterns are labeled attitudes and are usually distinguished from abilities, capacities, or intelligence. When an attitude is highly complex, with much emotional content, it may be referred to as basic value. When it is somewhat more intellectual and rational, or highly specific, it may be referred to as an opinion. How attitudes change depend upon many variables. It is obvious that some can be changed by experiences; for example, people who work together may change their attitudes towards one another. Other attitudes may change as a function of receiving new information which modified earlier ideas. Thus, in part, there is a direct relationship between the rational basis of an attitude and the extent to which new information can influence it. However, one thing is clear: many attitudes are not rational; i.e., they are not arrived at by a carefully thought-out process. As a consequence, the process of changing attitudes is frequently more complicated than merely supplying a direct message about the subject of the attitude.

It is of primary importance that the social account include indications of how residents feel the alternative plans will affect them and their families, and that the full range of these attitudes as well as their intensity be ascertained. It is equally necessary that the plans' impacts in changing people's attitudes towards other factors be considered. A particular plan can, depending on its nature, influence people's attitudes towards the local environment, the local economy, their community, and even the federal government. For example, a plan which is viewed as threatening to some aspect of a person's well-being (e.g., a plan which involves the relocation of a business and therefore the loss of the person's job) is likely to evoke a hostile attitude toward the plan's creator, whom the person might see as the federal government. Conversely, a plan which will change or improve the local environment in some way has the potential of increasing people's appreciation of their environment.

Rating the impacts and social effects of alternative plans. In Table 1, Section I, Part D, a set of items is presented to indicate what residents' expectations might be regarding the effects of a given plan, their attitudes towards these potential effects, and their resulting perceptions of the government agencies implementing the plan. Through either interviews with expert informants or a general population survey, the planner will have obtained information regarding resident perceptions of and attitudes about a given plan. For example, the NED plan might call for the construction of a multi-purpose reservoir on a river close to a given community; this plan will increase the attractiveness of the area for industry, since more water will be available for industrial operations, and there are some indications that a large manufacturer is already interested in locating a factory in the community if the plan is, in fact, implemented. Approximately 200 new jobs will be created, some of which can be filled by currently unemployed community residents. The new jobs and the increase in tax base brought about by new industry will have considerable positive effects on the local economy. Local residents are anxious for the plan to be implemented, and thus highly approving of the federal agency which is considering it. Under these circumstances, the following entries in Table 1 would by appropriate for the NED plan as shown on the following page.

Environmental Contributions

Scope of concern. The concerns associated with the impact of a water resource plan on the water, soil, climate, and plant and animal life of an area will be dealt with at length in the environmental impact statement accompanying the planning

Examples of NED Plan Effects

Items in Evaluation Categories	Measures of Impact	Effects ++,+,0,–,––
1. Resident expectations of what will be the effects of this plan, and their attitudes about the impact b. Local economy	Improvement in the local economy through: ±200 new jobs available; increased industrial tax base.	++
2. Resident perceptions of government agencies implementing this plan, and their reactions toward the agencies if the plan is implemented a. Federal agencies	High degree of resident approval of federal agency activity in regard to this plan.	++

report. The focus of interest in the social assessment should be on the *social effects* of environmental changes which might occur as a result of the proposed plan. These effects will relate, in most cases, to people's enjoyment of their surroundings, and the extent to which this enjoyment is altered, for better or for worse, by alternative plans.

Changes resulting from alternative water resource plans can be either positive or negative, depending on a number of circumstances. For example, a plan with recreational components might have a significant positive effect on people's enjoyment and appreciation of the surrounding environment. Likewise, a sewage treatment plan which decreases visual and bacterial pollution, as well as noxious odors, might add a great deal to people's appreciation of a formerly unattractive lake or river area. Conversely, a dam which blocks a river formerly used for canoeing, or a power plant which blocks a scenic view, might serve to detract from residents' enjoyment of their surroundings.

In considering the potential social effect of environmental-related aspects of a plan, detailed attention should be given to all possible changes which might add to or detract from people's enjoyment of the environment and therefore their general well-being and happiness. Visual and spatial effects on land and water should be studied, and any possible diminution or enhancement of areas of natural beauty (e.g., wilderness or primitive areas) should be carefully assessed.

Rating the impacts and social effects of alternative plans. In Table 1, Section I, Part E, a set of items is presented to indicate changes in the environment which might occur under a given water plan, the effects these changes might have on the physical and/or mental well-being of residents, and resulting changes in personal concern with environmental protection. In completing this part of the table for an EQ plan, for example, the planner might use information she or he has collected regarding the construction of an industrial waste treatment plant on a local lake. As a result of industrial pollution of the lake, the community has been plagued for several years by a high level of noxious odors when winds are blowing to the south-southeast (from the lake toward the community). Members of the community are therefore anxious for the plant to be built, and several groups have been formed to support the plan. However, the NED plan calls for the plant to be built on a scenic island in the middle of the lake, which would require the complete defoliation of this island. Other groups have been formed to opposed the NED plan as a result. Under these circumstances, the following entries in Table 1 would be appropriate for the NED plan.

Examples of NED Plan Effects

Items in Evaluation Categories	Measures of Impact	Effects ++,+,0,-,--
1. Changes in the environment as they affect residents' mental and physical well-being:		
a. Pollution levels (odor, land, water, etc.)	Decrease in the level of noxious odors: approximately 100%.	++
c. Accessibility to scenic or recreational sites	Decrease in accessibility to scenic island: approx. 100%.	--
2. Changes in personal concern with environmental protection:		
a. Number, existence of groups involved in environmental issues	Six new advocate groups formed: three for, three against EQ plan.	+
d. Conflict among environmental groups, between groups and other institutions (local, state, national)	Increased conflict among new and existing groups.	-

The Community, Institutional Effects Component

The following section discusses the eleven evaluation categories which make up the "Community, Institutional Effects" component of the Social Well-Being Account. These eleven categories are concerned with the impacts which might occur at a higher level of aggregation than those in the first component, but which are still limited to the confines of the community (or communities) which will potentially be affected by the alternative plans. Here the focus is on groups of people, their activities as members of different groups, the various aspects of the community which affect their lives, and the informal and formal institutions which serve them. Equally important is the nature of the community itself as an entity, its composition, its internal structure, etc. If one of the potential effects of the plan is to bring a large influx of population into the area, the resulting changes in the community in terms of size, ethnicity, age patterns, etc., are important, since they are likely to create further changes in numerous other social components at the individual and area levels as well as at the community level. The eleven evaluation categories which characterize the Community, Institutional Effects component of the Social Well-Being Account are as follows:

Demographic relates to the structure of the community in terms of size, ethnicity, marital status, age/sex distribution, etc.

Education deals with educational institutions within the community (primary, secondary, and post-secondary academic education as well as vocational training), and with their activities and capacity.

Government Operations and Services deals with the structure, size and complexity of local government and the services which government provides to members of the community.

Housing and Neighborhood concerns the quality and quantity of housing in the community, as well as the condition of its neighborhoods.

Law and Justice deals with the criminal justice system in the community and the possible impacts in terms of criminal and civil violations which might result, either directly or indirectly, from the implementation of a water resource plan.

Social Services concerns the public and private sector services available to various population groups within the community (e.g., children, youths, elderly persons, etc.).

Religion deals with the religious structure of the community and the extent to which religion affects the lives of community members.

Culture concerns the ethnic composition of the population and its associated values and folkways, as well as cultural "materials" (e.g., archeological sites, artifacts, etc.) found in or near the community.

Recreation relates to public recreational facilities and land and water areas in or near the community used for public recreation, and to changes in recreational uses which might occur as a result of the implementation of a water-related plan.

Informal Organizations and Groups discusses community groups which are not a part of the local governmental or institutional structure, including fraternal organizations, advocacy groups, religious or ethnic societies, and environmental groups.

Community and Institutional Viability focuses on the capacity of a community's institutions to meet demands for a range of services, on the inter-relationships among community institutions, and on the members' views of their community.

The complete table listing the items in the evaluation categories for this component is presented on pp. 221-235 in Part 3.

Demographics

Scope of concern. The term "demographics" refers to the sum of the characteristics of a population. In essence, studies of demographics can be broken down in three major categories: structure, composition, and characteristics. The category of *structure* includes such variables as size, density and migration. *Composition* includes the variables of age, sex, religion, ethnicity, and race. The category of *characteristics* includes the variables of income, education, occupation, housing, and marital status. Demographic studies usually are applied not only to current variables, but also to trends within each of the three major categories (e.g., growth or shrinkage; change in age/sex distributions; trends in income and occupation).

Many of the potential impacts of alternative water-related plans will be partially contingent on changes in the demographic characteristics of the population which arise as a result of the plan, i.e., indirect effects. For example, changes in the relative size of the population may call for alterations in the housing supply. Changes in the age distribution of a population may call for changes in the types of social services needed by that population: a relative increase in the size of the elderly population may require homemaker services and elderly nutrition programs, while a relative increase in the number of children and teenagers may lead to a need for child guidance counselors and day care centers. The overall composition of local population is very important. A high percentage of elderly to working age adults means a higher "dependency ratio" of the population—with more people requiring financial support and fewer people involved in producing income. An imbalance in male/female ratios, especially in the young adult age group, has important social consequences. Impacts of the plans which alter composition, therefore, should be carefully examined. These are just a few of the most typical examples of the secondary impacts which the implementation of a plan might have on the overall population of an area.

Primary impacts on the demographic characteristics and trends in an area might occur in a number of different plan-related circumstances. A plan which involves the construction of a new hydroelectric power plant, for example, might lead to a population increase through an increase in power supply for business and residential uses. If new businesses do, in fact, come into the area, they might bring with them more young couples of working age, with resulting changes in demand for housing, social services, recreational facilities, and so on.

Rating the impacts and social effects of alternative plans. In Table 1, Section II, Part A, a set of indicators is presented to suggest possible changes which might occur in the demographic profile of a community as a result of the implementation of a water resource plan. In relation to demographics, potential negative and beneficial effects of a water resource project would be of two general types: changes in the dependency ratio of the population (i.e., the ratio of those individuals who are able to earn a living wage to those who are dependent on wage earners) and changes in the "normal balance" of the population in relation to age/sex percentages. Negative effects in the former case occur when the number of elderly people and/or children becomes large enough to make their support difficult or infeasible by the number of young adults and middle-aged persons in their income-productive years. Negative effects in the latter case occur when an abnormally large proportion of a particular age/sex group is found in the community. Positive demographic effects would, of course, be the opposite of the negative ones described above. Thus, an NED plan could be considered to have potential positive effects if it created jobs within the community, encouraged younger people who would otherwise have left the area to stay, or encouraged those who had already left to come back. Under these circumstances, the following entries would be appropriate in Table 1 in the area of demographics.

Examples of NED Plan Effects

Items in Evaluation Categories	Measures of Impact	Effects ++,+,0,-,--
1. Changes in general demographic makeup of the population		
a. Size	Potential increase of approximately 150 individuals.	0
b. Migration trends	Reduction in the out-migration of men and women.	++
c. Age/sex distribution	Increased balance of men and women in the 20-34 age group.	++

Education

Scope of concern. Education may be defined as all those activities which transmit information, contribute to knowledge, or aid the learning of the people of a community. Taken as such, education obviously goes beyond the activities of the school system and other formal education; it is an ongoing dynamic force in the lives of all members of the community, regardless of their age. However, the consideration of the effect on education of various water-related plans will probably focus primarily on the operations of and conditions in the educational system(s) of the area under consideration. The term "school system" as it is used here can include not only public elementary and secondary schools, but also private and parochial schools, and, in some cases, institutes of higher education such as colleges, universities, and technical training institutes.

Water-related plans can have considerable impact on the educational system of the area in which they are implemented. For example, if the project involves the closing of an existing road or roads, school buses may need to be rerouted, thereby either increasing or shortening the travel time of students to and from school. Various aspects of the project may also become study material in the schools, for example, in biology or physics classes.

Less immediate and direct, but equally important, impacts can also occur as a result of the implementation of a water-related plan in the area. For example, if the plan is for a dam or reservoir which will take several years to build, it is likely that a considerable number of construction workers and other personnel will move into the area during the construction period, many of them bringing their families with them. This, in turn, will likely place an increased strain on the existing school system, but one which does not necessarily justify the hiring of new teachers or the building of new facilities, since the workers and their families may leave the area upon completion of the project. The resulting temporary strain can considerably reduce the quality of education in the system during the construction of the project. Conversely, if the plan will bring about a permanent increase in population in the area (for example, by creating new industrial or agricultural opportunities), the increased tax base resulting from the larger population may well permit the enlargement and improvement of existing school facilities and staff. A new influx of population into the area of the project may also involve the introduction of new cultures and folkways, which could also affect the types of educational opportunities offered and demanded. New populations can bring new values and educational aspirations. The new job picture can also be a factor. Thus, the new composition of student body may result in changes in curricula for college, trades, and commercial career courses. The long-term implications for negotiation and for career choice become critical here. The school system, therefore, has much at stake as a direct consequence of any plan which promises to change the nature of the population.

Rating the impacts and social effects of alternative plans. In Table 1, Section II, Part B, items are presented to indicate possible changes which might occur in the educational system of an area as a result of a given water-related plan. The planner might have determined, for example, that the construction of a multi-purpose reservoir under the NED plan will encourage considerable industrial development in what is currently a rural, agricultural community. There are indications that some 200 new industrial jobs will be created within the five years following construction of the plant. Some of these jobs will be filled by community residents, but others will have to be filled by people who will move into the area, many of whom will bring their families with them. Since this is primarily a farming community, the emphasis in the local school system—especially in the community's single high school—has been on a vocational, agriculturally-oriented curriculum, with a variety of courses in plant and animal husbandry and the like. Although such courses are likely to continue to be in demand, a new curriculum—one which places more emphasis on college preparation and/or different kinds of vocational education—will probably be required for the children of urbanites or suburbanites who move into the community. It is likely that the school system will not immediately be responsive to this demand, and this can be rated as a negative effect, at least in the short run. Under these circumstances, the following entries in Table 1 would be appropriate for the NED plan.

Examples of NED Plan Effects

Items in Evaluation Categories	Measures of Impact	Effects ++,+,0,-,--
20. Distribution of school curricula (academic vs. vocational)	No immediate change from current agricultural emphasis in the curriculum.	-
2. Type of enrollment in schools, by age, income, ethnicity, etc.	Influx of less agriculturally-oriented, more "urbanized" students.	0

Government Operations and Services

Scope of concern. The operations of and services provided by government to its citizens encompass a wide range of areas and may be said to affect almost every aspect of the lives of those citizens to some extent. In one way or another, government operations and services touch upon almost all the other sectors discussed in this document–education, health, environment, law and justice, etc. Moreover, several levels of government may be involved in the provision or regulation of services, including government at the federal, state, county, and local (city or town) levels. Special governing bodies such as school districts, water districts, port authorities, and the like may overlap or intercede between traditional government levels as well.

The number and level of governing bodies to be considered in an assessment of a water-related plan will, of course, depend upon the nature and size of the plan itself. For example, the construction of a levee on a small river may affect only the population of a single town located on that river and thus concern only its municipal government; on the other hand, the building of a large dam may have such far-reaching influence on economics, ecology, etc. (as in the case of Hoover Dam) that its construction and regulation becomes the concern of state or even national government. We will limit the discussion here, however, to examples of how a water-related plan may affect government operations and services at the local level. Effects, as in most cases, can be either positive or negative, direct or indirect. For example, in the case of a plan which requires construction on a certain amount of land located within a town, the people residing on that land will obviously have to move. If these people decide to leave the area rather than settling in another part of the town, a reduction in the tax base is likely to occur. Moreover, the departure of a large number of people is likely to have fairly significant effects on the economies of scale of operation of municipal services such as water, electricity, and sewage treatment. Conversely, if the new project increases employment opportunities and prosperity in the area, thus bringing an influx of new residents, both the tax base of the town and the economies of scale in government services may be increased. A growth in the population may bring about other changes affecting government operations and services as well. If the size of the community increases dramatically, services which were not formerly provided by the local government, such as garbage disposal and street paving, might be required. The necessity to provide such services would obviously place a strain on the government if it remained at its previous size and with its previous structure; therefore, parts or even the entire structure of local government might eventually be altered as an indirect impact of the water-related project. In an even more dramatic example, an influx of people into a previously sparsely settled area may in fact require the incorporation of a town in that area and the creation of a local government which did not exist before the implementation of the water-related plan. Of course, the impact of a water-related plan on the governmental sector of a community need not necessarily be as dramatic or pervasive as those described above. Only one feature of government services might be affected, as in the case of a plan which improves or stabilizes the municipal water supply, or one which reduces the need for flood control activities by local government.

It should be noted that the examples cited above can conceivably occur at a higher level than local government. County governments may also be affected by reductions or increases in the population, with similar direct and indirect consequences. As has been suggested, this depends on the size and nature of the project planned.

Rating the impacts and social effects of alternative plans. In Table 1, Section II, Part C, seventeen items are listed as indicators of possible changes which might take place in government operations and services as a result of a particular water-related plan. For example, the NED plan might call for the construction of a new dam, which will in turn require the flooding of five square miles. This area includes one-third of the incorporated community of Brownsville, a mixed commercial and residential area. Within the area are located fifty homes, as well as a small drygoods store and a motel-restaurant. Interviews have indicated that at least half of the families whose homes are in the flood pool area will probably move to the nearby city of Lyons, as will the drygoods store; the owner of the motel-restaurant plans to retire. Brownsville will therefore lose a considerable portion of its tax base, and economies of scale for government services will be reduced as well; it is probable that the Brownsville Town Council will either have to raise taxes to support its garbage collection and street-cleaning services, or discontinue these services altogether, while costs for police and sewage, among other things, will certainly be raised. Since the city of Lyons is a fairly large one, the effects on its economy of the influx of Brownsville people will probably be negligible. Under these circumstances, the following entries in Table 1 would be appropriate for the NED plan.

Examples of NED Plan Effects

Items in Evaluation Categories	Measures of Impact	Effects ++,+,0,-,--
13. Services provided by local government (sewage, garbage collection, police, fire protection, etc.) service priorities	Brownsville may discontinue garbage collection and street cleaning because of reduced tax base.	--
16. Efficiency and effectiveness of local governments, services provided by local governments	Cost of sewage and police protection will be raised due to reduced economies of scale.	--
4. Population of the area	Brownsville will lose approximately 25 out of 200 families.	-

Housing and Neighborhood

Scope of concern. The effect of a water-related plan upon the housing and neighborhood situation in a given area can be substantial and, if so, must be the subject of serious consideration in any analysis of this type. The effect can, of course, be of either a positive or negative nature, but the types of effects which most often come to mind in this context are more or less negative. The possible solution to housing problems, as well as the persons, agencies, or groups responsible for implementing these solutions, can also be highly varied.

The most obvious direct effect of a water-related plan would occur in a case where construction of a new facility—such as a sewage treatment plant or a hydroelectric plant—requires the displacement of some residents or a change in the quality of a neighborhood. If residents must be displaced, new homes must, of course, be found. Complications will frequently arise in regard to the fact that many residents will want to remain in the general area because of family or friendship ties, or because their present housing is close to their jobs or their children's schools. Such people will often find it difficult, if not impossible, to replace their previous housing at a reasonable cost, since the price of housing construction or even rental has risen drastically in recent years; thus people who built or bought their homes in the 1950s may be unable to find similar accommodations at current prices and may be forced to move to housing which is considerably inferior, at least in their opinion. In some areas which are already fairly well settled, it may not even be possible, regardless of cost, to find or construct alternative housing for displaced persons. Added to such considerations are the problems involved in building new housing quickly when there are insufficient numbers of craftsmen and residential construction workers in the area. To a lesser degree, displacement may also be a problem in the case of persons living in mobile homes when there is no land available on which to relocate their homes. The change in the character of a neighborhood which might occur when a large water-related facility is constructed nearby may also be considered a negative effect under some circumstances.

Less direct but equally serious problems may arise when a plan does not require the displacement of residents. One of these problems, for example, may relate to the influx of construction workers into the area for the period of construction. These people, as well as their families, will also need housing. In most cases, however, it would be economically infeasible to build adequate temporary housing for the workers; thus, if the housing in the area is already scarce, the situation is likely to be exacerbated, at least temporarily, by an influx of construction workers. Wherever these workers are housed, it is likely that they will have some effect, again only temporary perhaps, on the neighborhood(s) where they live. Construction workers are, in general, younger and more transient than people likely to be found living in established communities; their values and behavior may therefore also be different from neighborhood residents. As a result, they may possibly have a disruptive effect on the neighborhoods where they live during the period of construction

Similar but more long-term problems can also arise in the housing sector if the plan is expected to bring a wave of permanent settlers into the area. If there is not sufficient land or if the cost of housing construction is exceptionally high at the site, crowded conditions—or even a real crisis in housing—can occur. The first to suffer in such a situation would be the poor, who are often likely to be moved out of their housing to make way for new construction.

This is not to say, however, that the effect upon housing of an alternative plan must always be problematic or negative. If the plan provides increased or improved water supply to the area, it will, of course, be advantageous to residents and may even encourage the addition of new plumbing or sewage facilities in some neighborhoods. Moreover, if the plan brings increased economic prosperity to the area, the construction of new housing may, in fact, be made more attractive and economically feasible. An influx of construction workers may not be a serious problem if the construction period will be short and if these persons (and their families) can be housed in mobile homes for which adequate provisions exist.

Rating the impacts and social effects of alternative plans. In Table 1, Section II, Part D, a list of twenty-one indicators of changes which might potentially occur in the area of housing under a given water-related plan is provided. The EQ plan, for example, might involve the construction of a new sewer system. The plan would thus have numerous positive effects in an area which previously did not have a sewer system and was served only by outhouses and septic systems. One such effect would obviously be the increase of the percentage of housing units with all plumbing facilities in the area served by the system (the increase being equal to the number of homes which previously had only outhouses). In addition, a sewage system would be likely to increase the diversity of types of housing potentially available to the area. In many cases, it is impossible to build high-rise apartments or to construct low-cost housing developments in areas served only by septic systems, since septic systems usually require low-density (e.g., two-acre) zoning in order to accommodate leaching fields. If zoning were changed to accommodate new low-cost housing developments, it might be possible to clear run-down and dilapidated neighborhoods to make way for this new housing construction. These and related effects would make the following entries in Table 1 appropriate under the EQ plan.

Examples of EQ Plan Effects

Items in Evaluation Categories	Measures of Impact	Effects ++,+,0,–,––
17. Diversity of types of housing available (apartments, duplexes, one-family units, etc.)	Possible construction of two high-rise apartment buildings.	+
20. Acres of run-down or dilapidated neighborhoods	Ten acres will be cleared for a new housing development on one-acre lots.	++
21. Percent of housing units with all plumbing facilities	Twenty homes will be able to convert from outhouses to indoor bathroom facilities.	++

Law and Justice

Scope of concern. The various sectors of the law and justice evaluation category—the police, the courts, lawyers, and institutions of correction (jails, prisons, youth detention centers)—have the responsibility of preserving peace in the community and assuring that standard rules of conduct are preserved for the welfare of all citizens. In most cases, the effect of a water-related plan upon the law and justice sector, as well as the effect of the sector upon the plan, can be expected to be fairly indirect, although still important. An example of such indirect influence could be seen in a situation in which implementation of a proposed plan would bring an influx of new population into the area. In such a case, a strain could conceivably be placed on the law enforcement segment of the community; that is, a large number of new people from urban areas coming into a previously primarily rural district might in turn be expected to bring with them an increase in certain types of crime. Even if this were not the case, an important increase in population might at least be expected to increase the need for traffic regulation and similar services by police officers. Another example of such an indirect effect would be the case where the water-related plan brought increased employment opportunities to residents of a particular area; since it has been suggested that there is a connection between high unemployment and higher crime rates, such a plan might have the indirect benefit of reducing certain types of crime in an area. Periods of drought, which are obviously dangerous to if not destructive of crops, are times of considerable tension in agricultural communities in particular. A plan which helped to assure a more continual supply of water to an area might in turn lead to a decrease in tension among members of the agricultural community, thus once again reducing the incidence of water shortage-related crime.

The effect of a water-related plan on law and justice is more direct in situations which involve lawyers in water-related litigation of various sorts—between private parties and the government, between two sets of private parties or companies, etc. Such litigation may relate to old and new water rights, to reimbursements for land, housing, or moving expenses, or to other "inconvenience" actions. However, cases of this type, whether they last for a month or for three years, are by definition only temporary and cannot be viewed as having a long-range effect on the law and justice of the community.

Rating the impacts and social effects of alternative plans. In Table 1, Section II, Part E, a list of eighteen indicators of changes which might potentially occur in the law and justice system of an area as a result of the implementation of a water-related plan is provided. Many of these indicators will be difficult to quantify, since there is no concrete proof that a given demographic change will lead to a definite increase or decrease in civil and criminal code violations. However, certain correlations have been made between the incidence of poverty and crime. Therefore, if the implementation of a planned project inadvertently increases the number of families or individuals below poverty level, there might, in turn, be an increase in the incidence of certain types of crime. A plan which will significantly increase non-taxpaying population for the short term can result in rise in crime, with no rise in law enforcement capabilities. In rare cases, the income of a certain segment of the population could, in fact, be reduced by the implementation of a water-related plan. If, for example, the NED plan involved an irrigation project which would encourage capital-intensive farming, small farmers and workers on smaller, labor-intensive farms could lose their source of income; if these people did not leave the area, their income could be reduced to one which is below poverty level. It is possible, then, that criminal violations such as shoplifting and burglaries might rise in the area. This would, in turn, place a strain on the local criminal justice system, and if circumstances (lack of funds, regulations, etc.) mitigated against increasing the staff (police officers, public defenders, etc.) of that system, the negative effects could be fairly serious. Under these somewhat unusual circumstances, the following entries in Table 1 would be appropriate for the NED plan as shown on the following page.

Social Services

Scope of concern. Social services may be defined as all those services or activities which help the members of a community to live a more rewarding and enjoyable life through individual or

Examples of NED Plan Effects

Items in Evaluation Categories	Measures of Impact	Effects ++,+,0,-,--
7. Number of full-time equivalent judges, police officers, prosecutors, public defenders	No immediate changes in the size of the criminal justice staff due to lack of funds.	-
4. Percent of families below poverty level	Increase by 20% in the number of families below poverty level.	--
1. Civil and criminal code violations as a function of new population and economic characteristics	Increase by an unknown percent in the number of criminal code violations.	-

group development, or through the alleviation of personal or family problems. Such services may be provided by public agencies and supported by taxes, they may be provided free of charge by private groups such as social service organizations, churches or philanthropical societies, or they may be offered for a fee by private individuals or groups. They affect a large number of individuals in one way or another and cover a wide variety of areas, including day care, homes for the elderly, employment and vocational counseling, child guidance, marital counseling, and homemaker services for the house-bound, to name just a few. The capacity and diversity of social service agencies and groups differs widely from community to community. In populous urban areas they may include all of the types mentioned above and more, while in rural communities they may be limited to agricultural extension services and counseling by the local clergy.

The impact upon the social service sector of a community is likely to be quite considerable in the case of some water-related plans. This would be true, for example, in the case of a plan which involved the flooding of an area, which, in turn, would require some families to move. In such an instance, a wide variety of services might be needed. Vocational guidance and employment counseling might be needed by adults who are forced to leave their jobs; child guidance services might be required for children who suffer readjustment problems because of the move; home-finding services might be necessary for families having problems finding a new place of residence. Such relocations are likely to be especially hard on older people who have lived in the community for long periods of time; in some cases, these people might even have to be placed in elderly-care institutions. All of these problems are likely to place a strain on existing social service resources and might also call for resources which did not formerly exist in the community. An equal strain might be placed on existing services even if the plan did not require families to move. An increase in population, which might accompany new employment opportunities or new prosperity in the area, would also bring about the demand for more extensive, and perhaps more diverse, social services. This would be the case, for example, if a large influx of previously urban residents entered a rural area where social services were formerly of a fairly simple and limited nature. The increased tax base in the community would probably afford the creation of some services which had not previously existed; however, it might be necessary to introduce some agency such as the United Way or the Community Chest in order to provide additional support. In the long run, the demand for and resulting creation of more extensive or varied services is likely to be of benefit to the community.

Rating the impacts and social effects of alternative plans. In Table 1, Section II, Part F, a list of seventeen variables is presented as possible indicators of changes which might take place in the social services of an area in the event of the implementation of a water-related plan. The demand for various types of social services and the ability of a community to provide them may depend on a number of factors, including changes in the community's demographic and economic profiles. For example, if the NED plan leads to an increase in the community's tax base through the influx of new industry, new recreational facilities, or the like, the introduction of new social services, such as marriage counseling, a small homemaker program for the elderly, or a teen center, might become possible. The introduction of even one such service or an increase in the capacity of an already existing service would be of substantial benefit to the community. Under these circumstances, the following entries in Table 1 would be appropriate for the NED plan in relation to social services.

Examples of NED Plan Effects

Items in Evaluation Categories	Measures of Impact	Effects ++,+,0,-,--
8. Total expenditures on social services	Increase of $10,000 annual local expenditures on social services.	+
12. Types of social services provided by social service agencies	Introduction of a new community day-care center within the local Human Resources Center.	++
1. Number of persons receiving social services, by type of services received	Twenty-five children ages two months to five years served from 8:00 a.m. to 3:30 p.m.	++

Religion

Scope of concern. Of the sectors under consideration, religious life might at first glance seem to be one of those least applicable to the subject of water-related plans. However, the religious community in a given location may, in fact, have considerable influence on the activities and attitudes of residents of that location and so must be a topic of consideration in any planning effort. Moreover, changes in population composition can have major implications for churches in terms of their membership. Although less so than in former times, religious bodies still make considerable contributions to the educational, recreational and social—as well as the spiritual—lives of their members. Many churches regularly hold educational classes for the adults and the children in their congregations; many also sponsor various types of recreational clubs and activities, from bowling leagues to Boy Scout and Girl Scout troops. These enterprises, along with such traditional events as church suppers, ladies' auxiliaries, and men's clubs, form a central part of the lives of many people—especially those in rural areas—and can provide an important forum for the exchange of opinions and the formation of attitudes towards various subjects. Ministers, priests, and rabbis can also serve as poweful "opinion makers" or educational agents for members of their congregations. In addition to these important "socialization" functions, religious bodies may serve other important social support functions in the community. Churches may own valuable land or other holdings in the area; they may also run various health- and welfare-oriented services, including hospitals, guidance clinics, nursing homes, homes for orphans, and food distribution centers for the needy. Religious leaders, their congregations, and the activities in which these people engage must thus be a subject of concern for anyone planning a project which is expected to have an effect on the community.

Rating the impacts and social effects of alternative plans. In Table 1, Section II, Part G, a list of thirteen indicators of possible changes which might occur in the religious life of a community in the event of the implementation of a water-related plan is presented. Changes in this component of society might take place, for example, in the event of an NED plan—perhaps a reservoir or canal system—which would encourage the development of capital-intensive, as opposed to labor-intensive, farming. The growth of large, capital-intensive farms might mean the loss of jobs for many farm laborers. Such an event might force these laborers to leave the community in search of other jobs. If, as is true in some cases, the majority of farm laborers belonged to a particular ethnic group (e.g., Mexican-Americans), their departure might considerably reduce the membership in one or more local congregations. This, in turn, could eventually force the church to close its doors and/or relocate, if indeed the membership was sufficiently reduced. In such circumstances, the following entries would be appropriate for the NED plan in the area of religion as shown on the following page.

Examples of NED Plan Effects

Items in Evaluation Categories	Measures of Impact	Effects ++,+,0,-,--
5. Number of churches, synagogues, etc.	Local Catholic church may be forced to leave the community because of a decline in membership.	--
4. Change in ethnic composition of the population	Considerable reduction in the Mexican-American community, possibly by as much as 75%.	0
1. Size of church membership, by denomination	Size of local Catholic church membership reduced from 200 to approximately 80.	--

Culture

Scope of concern. Culture, as defined here, includes two major considerations: (1) the "culture" of the population, which includes its ethnic composition and associated folkways, as well as the values and unique institutions of the people; and (2) the "cultural" materials present in the area(s) under consideration for plan implementation, including archeological, historical and scientific sites and artifacts. It is usually highly desirable that these cultural aspects of an area not be disturbed or destroyed.

Water-related plans may affect the culture of an area in numerous ways. The culture of the population, for example, will definitely be touched in either of two cases: if new people come into the area as a result of increased opportunities for employment, or if some or all of the existing population is forced to vacate the area because of plan implementation. The places in which such effects will be most noticeable will, of course, be those communities or sites in which specific ethnic enclaves are located, such as Indian reservations or European-American communities. Such communities usually have highly distinctive behavior, inter-community relations, and even language characteristics which it may be desirable to preserve, both for the well-being of their members and because they are unique and therefore valuable. A large influx of non-ethnic people into the community may have a serious diluting effect on the area's culture, as these people bring with them new values, traditions, and ways of behaving. Likewise, if plan implementation forces people to move out of their former communities, the characteristics which made their home unique may be so dispersed as to become non-operational.

Cultural materials may also be affected in one way or another by water-related plans. The construction process, for example, may require the destruction of historical trails and archeological sites (burial mounds, campsites, etc.) or the removal of artifacts from their original surroundings. Less serious, but also worthy of consideration, would be a case in which the accessibility of an archeological, scientific, or historical site is reduced by the implementation of the plan.

Rating the impacts and social effects of alternative plans. In Table 1, Section II, Part H, a list of ten variables is presented to indicate possible cultural changes which might arise as the result of a planned water resource project. Large-scale changes in unique ethnic populations or in historical and archeological sites will probably be avoided whenever possible, although they may, in some rare cases, be necessitated by extenuating circumstances. For example, the building of a dam at a particular river site under an NED plan might require the flooding of an area in which a number of Indian burial sites are located. As an even more drastic example, the flood pool area might include a small settlement of American Indians. In such a case, the settlement would, of course, have to be relocated; if possible, the settlement would be moved as a whole. However, its members might choose instead to disperse themselves into different areas. This would eventually represent a threat to the traditional behavior, values, and folkways which formerly were preserved by the members of the settlement when they were living as a group. Under these circumstances, the following entries in Table 1 would be appropriate under the NED plan as shown on the following page.

Examples of NED Plan Effects

Items in Evaluation Categories	Measures of Impact	Effects ++,+,0,-,--
1. Ethnic composition of the population	Small settlement (50 members) of Indians would be relocated from the flood pool area; possible dispersion of the population to scattered areas.	--
3. Traditional behavior, values, folkways	Dispersion would result in a threat to the preservation of Indian culture as a result of assimilation in other areas.	--

Recreation

Scope of concern. Recreation and leisure represent an important part of the lives of people in a community. This is the time during which people can get away from the world of work, to replenish or "re-create" themselves, to improve their minds and bodies, to broaden their knowledge and skills, and, perhaps most important, to relax and enjoy themselves. Recreation facilities and the possible impact upon them by water-related plans will thus be of great concern to the residents of a community touched by the plan. The possible displacement or removal of an important recreation facility is likely to meet with considerable disapproval on the part of local citizens, while the introduction of a new water-related recreation area with attendant increases in tourism and influx of monies into the area may (or may not) be viewed positively. In most cases, the possible impacts on recreation of a water-related project will be felt most keenly in the outdoor recreation sector: a man-made lake might include, among its other uses, recreational facilities such as boating and swimming areas; or, conversely, damming up a segment of a river formerly used for white-water canoeing would change that recreational resource into one for boating, waterskiing, and so forth.

Rating the impacts and social effects of alternative plans. In Table 1, Section II, Part I, eighteen indicators of change are presented which might take place in the recreation facilities and uses of an area under a given water-related plan. In the vast majority of cases, recreation in the area will be improved by the implementation of water-related plans, although there may be some exceptions to this rule. For example, an NED plan might involve the construction of a dam on a river formerly used for white-water canoeing. The lake associated with the dam will be used for boating and swimming and is likely to attract a large number of tourists to the site from nearby metropolitan areas. However, the flood pool area for the reservoir will also cover one-third of the area of a site which was formerly popular for pheasant hunting. Under this rather complex situation, the following entries would be appropriate for Table 1.

Examples of NED Plan Effects

Items in Evaluation Categories	Measures of Impact	Effects ++,+,0,-,--
9. Area in miles of land used for outdoor recreation (hunting grounds, picinic areas, etc.)	Five square miles of land used for pheasant hunting will be in reservoir flood pool area.	-
10. Area in miles of water-related recreation areas	Twenty-mile strip of the Quinn River, formerly used for white-water canoeing, will no longer be available for this purpose.	--
	Fifty square miles of associated new lake area will be available for pleasure boating and swimming.	++
13. Types of recreation available in public facilities and water and land areas	Pheasant hunting and white-water canoeing eliminated in plan area; swimming and boating made available.	0

Informal Organizations and Groups

Scope of concern. Informal organizations and groups, as we refer to them in this context, include those groups which are organized around social, personal, or political interests, or which are a result of ethnic or organizational characteristics. They include, in other words, various collections of people at the community or neighborhood level, but are distinct from political, public agencies, and institutions of a more formal nature, such as government departments, social service and welfare agencies, and health institutions. Informal organizations and groups as we have defined them range from fraternal orders such as Rotary and Elks Clubs, to Boy and Girl Scout troops, to the League of Women Voters, to the Sierra Club.

Since such groups are quite important to the social viability of a community, it is of considerable importance that they be included in an assessment of the possible impacts of alternative water-related plans. The effects of such plans on informal groups may be highly varied according to the group in question, and alternative plans can have distinctly different impacts on the same group within a community. For example, the NED plan may serve to further the interest of a group such as the Junior Chamber of Commerce or the local farm cooperative, while being distinctly contrary to the position of the Sierra Club. Conversely, the EQ plan might have the opposite effect. In an indirect manner, any of the alternative plans might serve to strengthen the cohesiveness of these informal groups and to increase their activity level by serving as a rallying point for members of the group who see the plan as either beneficial or inimical to their interests. Water-related plans may even serve to stimulate the formation of various advocate groups, such as associations of landowners, hunting and fishing clubs, and consumer unions, when individuals with common interests see those interests as potentially threatened or furthered by various alternatives.

Rating the impacts and social effects of alternative plans. In Table 1, Section II, Part J, a list of nine indicators of changes which might occur within informal organizations and groups as a result of the implementation of a water-related plan is provided. For example, preliminary interviewing to determine community members' reactions to a particular water resource project may have indicated that numerous people will be opposed to certain aspects of the NED plan, which will require the clearing of five square miles of forest land. Opposition seems sufficiently strong that one or more advocate groups will be formed to fight the plan. At the same time, businessmen and the local Chamber of Commerce are strongly in favor of the plan, since it will provide a boost to the community's economy. In either case, public interest in the plan has clearly been aroused, and participation by both proponents and opponents in the planning process is likely to be increased. Under these circumstances, the following entries in Table 1 would be appropriate.

Examples of NED Plan Effects

Items in Evaluation Categories	Measures of Impact	Effects ++,+,0,-,--
3. Number and types of informal organizations and groups (ethnic, religious, service-oriented, environmentally oriented, etc.)	Probable formation of at least one environmental advocate group to oppose aspects of the NED plan.	0
9. Coordination and conflict among various informal organizations and groups	Increase in conflict between environmental groups and businessmen in the community.	-
2. Extent of public participation in the planning process as a result of membership in/activities of informal organizations and groups	Probable increase in the planning process by both proponents and opponents of the NED plan.	+

Community and Institutional Viability

Scope of concern. Various types of formal groups and institutions such as governmental bodies, social service agencies, and schools have been dealt with, to this point, in their own right. The purpose of the discussion here is to view the community and its institutions as a whole and to determine what overall impacts alternative water-related plans might have on this complex. The focus of institution-related concern is on the capacity of the community's institutions to meet demands for a range of services and on the inter-relationships between institutions. The focus of community-related concern is on how residents view their community as a whole, their pride in the community, their belief in its vitality, etc. Data collection on other sectors will allow the planner to obtain a good overview of the institutional complex in the community as regards its size, quality, and diversity. It will be necessary to determine also (if possible, through conversations with agency personnel) what types of inter-relationships are common to institutions in the community—whether they are informal, based on personal acquaintance or familiarity among agency employees, or whether they are more formalized, involving exchanges of information by means of printed forms. The former case will probably be more common in small communities which have a limited number of institutions than in larger communities or towns, where the diversity and number of institutions obviates the possibility of conducting on an informal, person-to-person basis.

Whatever the makeup of the institutional complex in the community, it is likely that alternative water-related plans will have some impact on it. If a plan is one which will require relocation of some residences or businesses, it is obvious that institutions will feel its effects; if they are located in the area specified for use in the plan, they will naturally have to relocate or discontinue services. If many of their clientele must relocate, the impact could be almost as serious, since it is the clients of the institutions—students in the schools, patients of hospitals or clinics—who constitute the institutions' reason for existence. Even if only some of the institutions or agencies in the community are severly affected in this manner, the loss of such groups can have negative effects on the institutional support structure, as would be the case if a counseling center to which schools referred their problem students were to close.

If, on the other hand, the plan will bring about a significant increase in population in the area, the institutional complex could also experience substantial impacts. A large increase in population usually implies an increased demand for both service capacity and diversity of services. Government structure, for example, may have to be changed to some degree to afford the provision of more municipal services; this might, in turn, affect private agencies which had previously provided such services at a fee. Other institutions or agencies might also be required to expand or diversify their services, and the whole structure and complex of institutions in the community might thus eventually be changed. In some cases, whole new institutions or service agencies may have to be introduced into the community, complicating the relationships among older agencies and between these older agencies and the new ones, and leading to overall strains in the institutional complex. Finally, when the institutional structure of a community becomes larger and more diversified than it had been previously, informal relationships among agencies and casual methods of exchanging information and clients are often no longer viable. Thus, an increase in population in the area may lead not only to changes in its individual institutions, but also to changes in the relationships between these institutions.

Apart from the potential impacts of the plan on institutional viability, consideration must also be given to its possible effects on the viability of the community itself. If relatively large numbers of people relocate out of the community or if there is an influx of new population, community cohesiveness could be affected. However, if the plan brings increased prosperity to the area, a sense of community vitality which previously did not exist could be instilled in the community's residents. New prosperity and the changes which it brings (new services, land improvement, etc.) could also contribute to residents' pride in their community.

Rating the impacts and social effects of alternative plans. In Table 1, Section II, Part K, a set of indicators is provided of possible changes which might occur in community and institutional viability in relation to a water resource plan. Changes in the institutional viability of a community might be brought about, for example, in the case of an NED plan whose implementation is expected to bring a new influx of people into the area. If the area is currently sparsely populated, it is likely that the number of formal institutions and their capacity for service are limited. Moreover, coordination among the institutions is probably fairly loose and informal. An increase in population will lead to demands for an increase in the number and diversity of services in most cases. If these demands cannot be quickly met—and it is unlikely that they can—the effects would clearly be negative, at least in the short run. Moreover, once new institutions are added to the community structure and the old ones are expanded, it is likely that some strain will be placed on the coordinative mechanisms in the community and that the old, informal ways of carrying on inter-institution business will become less viable. Under these circumstances, the following entries would be appropriate for Table 1 under the NED plan.

Examples of NED Plan Effects

Items in Evaluation Categories	Measures of Impact	Effects ++,+,0,-,--
1. Changes in individual institutions as they affect each other		
a. Size (number of staff, facilities, service capacity)	No immediate change in institutional size to meet demands of increased population; increase in institutional size may take several years.	--
g. New institutions created	Demands of new population will eventually lead to the creation of a new health care facility.	+
2. Changes in institutional interrelationships		
a. Coordination	Initial strain in coordinative mechanisms of local government; strain on informal relationships.	-

The Area, Socioeconomic Effects Component

In the following section, attention is given to seven evaluation categories which exist at a higher level of aggregation than either the individual/family or the community levels. Although several categories seem to contain aspects which may be applicable at the community, institutional level, the categories have been grouped under this particular component because their consideration may involve more than one community, or because they are important enough to pervade several aspects of community life at once; i.e., consideration of transportation, for example, cannot be limited to the community level alone, since transportation by definition frequently relates to exchanges among communities. Likewise, a discussion of the economic base of a community and the changes which might occur in the economic base as the result of a water resource plan's implementation, must give consideration to the more far-reaching effects which accompany changes in the economy, such as changes in housing and public and private sector services. The categories discussed here are thus of a fairly broad, comprehensive nature, although their focus will sometimes be within the community context. The seven evaluation categories which make up the Area, Socioeconomic Effects component of the Social Well-Being Account are as follows:

Employment and Real Income deals with the means by which people in the area earn their living and the amount of income which they receive.

Welfare and Financial Compensation deals with the quality and quantity of benefits (including money and services) provided to people who, for various reasons, are unable to support themselves.

Communications discusses various inter- and intra-community methods of communications, including personal and media methods, and considers how a water-related plan may affect communications and may be affected by them.

Transportation deals with public and private transportation, both within and between communities, as well as with the condition and location of roads and waterways used for various types of transport.

Economic Base deals with the overall economy of the area, including types of industry (and/or agriculture) which exist in the community, the changes which might occur in industry and agriculture as a result of a water-related project, and the extent to which these changes will have a social impact in the community.

Planning deals with the period during which alternative plans are formulated and analyzed, and the effects which the planning period might have on the community(ies) under consideration for plan implementation.

Construction concerns the potential short- and long-term effects of construction, ranging from temporary noise and other annoyances to long-range economic and social impacts.

The complete table listing the items for this component is presented on pp. 235-245 in Part 3.

Employment and Real Income

Scope of concern. In most cases, trends in employment and real income follow fairly closely along with those for the economic base of an area, for obvious reasons, and the data collected for the latter area can certainly be useful in the consideration of employment and income in the community. However, we have separated out employment and income from economic base to emphasize that the former focuses on the individual and family rather than on the industry and business of the community. Moreover, data collected for an assessment of the economic base sector are relevant only to those jobs for which wages or salaries are paid. Individuals and families in a community may receive some or all of their income from sources other than wages, such as self-employment, real estate, etc.

Except in those rare cases where a neighborhood is located inside the take line of a proposed reservoir and individuals and families must leave the area (and thus the place of self-employment), the impact of a water-related plan on the employment and income of individuals and families who receive money from self-employment is not likely to be as direct or immediate as in the case of wage or salary earners. However, the indirect, long-range impact may be equally great. For example, if a water-related project brings new population into the area, self-employed persons such as artists and craftsmen and small store owners might find their businesses and income growing. The increased tax base resulting from new population and industry coming into the area may reduce the cost of services such as utilities, thereby increasing the ability of self-employed persons to purchase other necessities and amenities. Conversely, the possible decrease in population and businesses which may result when large employers are forced to leave an area, and the concomitant reduction in tax base and services, is likely to create difficulties for the self-employed person or one receiving his or her income from sources other than wages. Data collection in the employment and income sector should also include some indication of the community resources (e.g., employment counselors, job placement services, vocational training centers) available to aid persons who lose their jobs due to implementation of a water-related plan.

Rating the impacts and social effects of alternative plans. In Table 1, Section III, Part A, twenty-four indicators are provided to suggest possible changes which might occur in the employment and real income of the people in a community as a result of a water resource plan. These changes might be quite substantial, as in the case of an NED plan which calls for the construction of a new hydroelectric power plant on a river running near a community. The availability of power will, in many cases, attract new industry or enable existing factories to expand. For example, the (imaginary) town of Anas currently has two major employers: a packing plant, which employs eighty-five people, and a small grain processing plant, which employs eighteen. Unemployment in the town has been at a high 12.5% since the local textile factory closed six months ago, leaving sixty-five men and women (mostly assembly line workers and knitting machine operators) out of work. Word of the possible construction of a new power plant has led the packing plant, which is actually a subsidiary of a large company in another part of the state, to consider expanding its operations, providing new employment for twenty people. Furthermore, there are indications that a company which makes hand calculators is thinking of moving to Anas; this would create approximately thirty new jobs, in addition to the ones which would be filled by employees of the company in its present location, who would move to Anas with the company. Obviously, this industrial expansion will have multiplier effects as well, with new secondary service facilities (restaurants, stores, etc.) springing up to serve the enlarged population. Under these circumstances, the following entries would be appropriate for Table 1.

Examples of NED Plan Effects

Items in Evaluation Categories	Measures of Impact	Effects ++,+,0,-,--
9. Total employers by employment size class (small: 1-19; medium: 20-99; large: 100 or more)	Potential increase by one medium size employer (Addeze Calculators); expansion from medium to large size by another (Newmark Packing Co.).	++
2. Number of persons unemployed as a percent of total labor force	Possible reduction from 12.5% to approximately 4.0% in the area.	++

Welfare and Financial Compensation

Scope of concern. Welfare is traditionally defined as the provision of income or services to individuals or families who would otherwise be unable to support themselves, for reasons of age, disability, lack of employment, etc. Under U.S. law, individuals and families are entitled to receive welfare benefits when their income fails to achieve a legally defined minimum level. Welfare so defined does not include Social Security, Workmen's Compensation, or unemployment benefits; these are considered to be forms of insurance, paid for by the individual and/or his employer at some time prior to the dispensation of benefits.

Welfare benefits may be provided by either public or private sources. Private welfare agencies and groups, including churches, the Salvation Army, the Red Cross, and local fraternal organizations such as the Rotary and Kiwanis Clubs, may dispense their benefits in the form of money, housing, food, or goods. In almost all cases, however, these private groups or agencies have limited resources and are therefore able to provide only minimum service to a relatively small number of people. The prime source of support for needy individuals and families is thus public, including agencies at the local, county, state, and national levels. Major welfare programs at the state and national levels include Supplemental Security Income (which subsumes the former categories of Old Age Assistance and Aid to the Blind and Disabled), Aid to Families with Dependent Children, Medicaid, General Relief, and the Food Stamps program. Many state, county, and local governmental units operate additional programs or provide supplemental funds to the needy.

Under a variety of circumstances, the effect of a water-related plan on the welfare and public assistance system of a community can be considerable in either the positive or negative sense. If implementation of the plan increases employment opportunities in the area, for example, there is a good chance that some persons previously collecting either welfare or unemployment benefits may be able to find jobs; this would obviously reduce the burden on local and state welfare agencies. On the other hand, if the plan requires relocation of a major source of employment, the strain on local, state, and county welfare agencies may be substantially increased, as individuals who were formerly employed lose their ability to support themselves and their families, at least temporarily.

More indirect effects can also be foreseen, as in the case of a plan which brings an influx of people into the area. In such a case, housing demand is likely to increase, and with it the cost of housing. Rents may thus be raised, forcing formerly self-supporting individuals or families onto the welfare rolls. Some families may be forced to leave their homes altogether, causing additional problems. In fact, a large increase in population is likely to raise prices in many other areas—food, clothing, etc.—producing similar difficulties for marginal income families or individuals. Those who will be hardest hit in such a situation include the aged, handicapped, or infirm who are living on fixed incomes provided by Social Security, Railroad Retirement, Workmen's Compensation, etc.

Rating the impacts and social effects of alternative plans. In Table 1, Section III, Part B, seventeen indicators are provided which suggest changes that might occur in the welfare and financial compensation sector of a community as a direct or indirect result of a water-related plan. As an example, an EQ plan might call for the construction of an irrigation system in an agricultural community which greatly increases the potential for local agricultural productivity. However, as larger, more mechanized agribusiness is attracted to the area by increased availability of water, smaller farmers may find that they can no longer compete. In many cases, these smaller farmers may be strongly attached to their own land and unwilling to leave the area, particularly if they are no longer young. In such a case, these people might be forced, however unwillingly, to apply for welfare payments. The increased clientele at the local or county welfare agency might also cause problems if this is a fairly small office with few caseworkers. Case overloads could considerably reduce the efficiency and effectiveness of welfare services. Under these circumstances, the following entries would be appropriate for the welfare and financial compensation section of Table 1.

Examples of NED Plan Effects

Items in Evaluation Categories	Measures of Impact	Effects ++,+,0,-,--
8. Staff size of welfare agencies	No immediate change in number of caseworkers serving at the county welfare office.	-
16. Efficiency and effectiveness of welfare agencies	Decrease in effectiveness of county welfare operations due to case overloads.	-
1. Number of persons receiving welfare payments as a percent of total population	Potential increase of approximately 3%.	-

Communications

Scope of concern. Communications may be broadly defined as the exchange of information, knowledge, and ideas. Two general types of communication exist: person-to-person communication, involving conversations, letters, small group bulletins, etc., and mass media forms of communication such as radio, television, newspapers, and books. Person-to-person communications may well have an impact on the formulation of a water-related plan if such exchanges involve extremely negative or positive attitudes toward it; i.e., word may pass from one person or small group to another within the community, eventually resulting in the formation of advocacy groups to support or contest one alternative plan or another. In small communities especially, discussion of the pros and cons of alternative plans may well dominate many conversations among residents for some time. Mass media communications may have a similar impact; for example, a positive or negative stand by the local newspaper or television station on the subject of the plan(s) might have an important influence on the citizenry of the area. The mass media might themselves be affected or influenced by one or more of the alternatives. For instance, if a plan is expected to bring an increase in population to a largely rural area, this increased population might in turn swell the circulation of the local newspaper or make it economically feasible to start a radio station or even a small television station.

Rating the impacts and social effects of alternative plans. In Table 1, Section III, Part C, a set of indicators is provided to suggest possible changes which might take place in the communication sector in relation to the implementation of a given water-related plan. Since the operations of the communications media in relation of size, political orientation, sophistication, etc. depend to a large extent on their audiences, a change in the population of an area (its size, ethnicity, educational level, political orientation, etc.) will be certain to influence the media to some extent. For example, an NED plan might call for the introduction of high voltage transmission lines into a community. The availability of additional power would make the area more attractive to industry as well as residents. If, in turn, a new industry were to locate in or near the community, the additional population which it would bring might eventually cause considerable alterations in the local media. The increase in size alone might lead to the creation of a local newspaper where none existed before, or to the expansion (in size, sophistication, etc.) of the existing local newspapers; i.e., an increase in circulation of the local newspaper might enable it to add more staff, such as an extra reporter, a political columnist, or the like. If the area is primarily a small, rural one, the influx of a more urbanized population might eventually influence the newspaper to take a different stance on community and political issues, although this would be difficult to predict in the short run. Under such circumstances, the following entries would be appropriate in Table 1.

Examples of NED Plan Effects

Items in Evaluation Categories	Measures of Impact	Effects ++,+,0,-,--
4. Circulation of newspapers per 100 residents (local and out-of-town)	Potential increase of approximately fifty subscribers to the local newspaper.	+
2. Total population	Potential increase of approximately 200 persons as a result of new industry in the area.	0

Transportation

Scope of concern. The transportation system within an area or community is vital to the community's existence for a variety of reasons. In most cases, roads and/or rails bring important goods and commodities into the area for the use of its residents. Roads are also important to people who work outside of the immediate area in which they live and who must commute to their place of work. The transportation system of an area may be limited to a number of small streets and roads, or it might include railways, water systems, airports, and major highways. Depending on the nature of the water-related plan under consideration, the effect of the plan on any or all of the transportation systems of an area—in both their commercial (freight and passenger) and private uses—may need to be investigated.

Water-related plans are likely to have considerable effects on the transportation systems of an area. A dam on a river in the area, for example, might displace or cut off important commercial river transportation activities, as well as private use activities such as recreational boating. On the other hand, such a dam, if built on another part of the river or in another area, might well augment such activities. Other types of plans might necessitate the washing out of local roads or might even cause the rerouting of a major highway in the area. Creation of navigable water channels can have important effects on cargo transportation. The creation of a major recreational facility might place a considerable strain on the existing road system of an area, if this facility will bring large numbers of tourists into the area from outside locales. Secondary effects might also occur which must be considered in an assessment of impact on the transportation system. For example, if the plan involves a major new irrigation project which will considerably increase the productivity of farms in the area, the roads and other systems needed to transport agricultural products outside of the area may need to be improved.

Rating the impacts and social effects of alternative plans. In Table 1, Section III, Part D, seventeen variables are presented which suggest changes that might take place in the transportation sector of a community in the event of the implementation of a water-related plan. For example, the EQ plan might call for the diversion of a river which formerly flooded a given stretch of land once every three or four years. The planned diversion route might in turn intersect for a certain distance—perhaps ten miles—with a paved road leading into and out of a community. Since the road itself would then have to be diverted from the river's path, the new segment of roadway built may represent a considerable improvement over the old one (wider, more even, etc.). This might, in turn, improve the ability of large commercial carriers to carry goods into and out of the community. Under these circumstances, the following entries would be appropriate for the transportation section of Table 1 as shown on the following page.

Examples of EQ Plan Effects

Items in Evaluation Categories	Measures of Impact	Effects ++,+,0,-,--
8. Total tons of commercial freight carried into, out of the area in a year period	Potential increase of approximately 25% in commercial tonnage.	++
16. Condition of streets, roads, and highways	Route 20 diverted for a ten-mile segment, widened and repaved.	+

Economic Base

Scope of concern. Economic base may be defined as an area's production and service institutions, the substance of the local economic condition. As such, it is both a key factor in the nature of a community and its quality of life, as well as in determining that quality; i.e., the economic base is a prime determinant of the size of a community's population, the type of people who make up that population, the tax base in the community, and thus the services and amenities available there. But perhaps most important, the economic base determines employment and amenities, as well as the necessities of life such as food and shelter. Much information concerning the economic base of the community will be available in the NED plan and account.

The effect of a water-related plan on the economic base of an area can be highly varied and of either a direct or indirect nature. The plan might itself involve a new industry or center of employment in the area, as would be the case with a desalinization facility or a power plant. Agricultural or industrial expansion can bring new population to the area and increase its tax base. Likewise, if the plan involves an increase in water pumping or electrical power production capacity, other new industry is likely to be attracted to the area. As new industry enters the area, it brings with it a new population of workers; both industry and population contribute to the tax base of the community and make possible an increase in community services provided by local government (street paving, garbage disposal, sewerage facilities, etc.). This increase in community services can, in turn, attract even more business and population to the area.

If the plan increases recreational opportunities in the area, new businesses such as sporting equipment retailers are likely to enter the scene, creating similar benefits for the local economic base. The same would be true for an agricultural community if the plan improves irrigation, livestock watering, or other agriculture activities; farm production can be increased, thereby bringing new prosperity to the area and making it more attractive to new business. Even the temporary presence of construction workers connected with the project may bring about increased services in the community which may remain after the workers have departed, making the area more attractive to businesses and population than formerly.

However, negative effects can also result from a water-related plan. Mining companies, for example, may be forced to move if the plan raises the local water table sufficiently to make those mines or wells unsafe, inoperative, or too costly to operate. If the community has a fairly strong, diversified economic base (i.e., a reasonable variety and number of businesses or industries), this may be only a minor problem, primarily affecting those residents who stand to lose the jobs they held with the relocating company. If, however, this occurs in a single-industry community or "company town," such as is often connected with the mining industry, the relocation of the company could seriously impair the community's economic base. As a less drastic example, the plan may require the closing of an area previously used for recreational activities such as boating or fishing. This could make the area less attractive to both residents and tourists, resulting in a long-range negative effect on the economic base of the area.

Rating the impacts and social effects of alternative plans. In Table 1, Section III, Part E, twenty indicators are provided to suggest possible changes which might take place in the economic base in the event of the implementation of a water-related plan. For example, after the introduction of new, high-voltage power lines into an area under the NED plan, new industry may well be attracted to the area by the increased availability of power. The presence of new industry will, in turn, proportionately expand the economic base of the community with a variety of potential results, from an increase in services available from the government sector (because of an expanded tax base) to more services available from the private sector (because of the demands of increased population). Thus, for example, the amount of retail trade carried on outside the plan area by residents of the area may be reduced, as more grocery stores, clothing stores, car dealers, and the like are attracted to the area by the increased population and prosperity. Under these circumstances, the following entries would be appropriate in Table 1.

Examples of NED Plan Effects

Items in Evaluation Categories	Measures of Impact	Effects ++,+,0,–,––
8. Number of establishments by SIC (Standard Industrial Code) category	Contract construction: increase of one establishment.	+
	Manufacturing: increase of three establishments.	+
	Retail trade: increase of establishments.	+
6. Percent of retail trade carried on outside the area by residents of the area (shopping for food, clothes, household goods and services, automobiles).	Potential reduction by 30% in amount of retail trade carried on outside the area.	++

Planning Effects

Scope of concern. The entire period of planning may last anywhere from a few years to a decade, from the time when alternatives are first formulated until the time when actual construction begins. First, the phase during which alternative plans are being considered itself requires a number of time-consuming activities, including data gathering and analysis which are necessary in order to produce the NED, EQ and alternative plans and finish the four accounts. Added to this will be the time required to finalize the technical specifications for the recommended water-related plan. Obviously, both of these phases involve complex tasks and cannot be expected to be completed in a matter of months. But what is likely to be occurring in the communities under consideration as possible sites for plan implementation during the data collection, analysis, and decision-making phases? Most probably this will be a period of disruption in the communities for a number of reasons. The primary cause of problems will be the uncertainty felt by both individuals and institutions as to the outcome of planning and decision-making processes. The uncertainty is likely to be especially great if one or more of the alternative plans involve a large area of land, or relocation of a neighborhood or community. In any event, it is likely to have substantial negative effects on the community. Not the least of these is the tension which will be experienced by residents who might be forced to move from the plan area because of land acquisition for a reservoir or construction; the period between the time the idea for the project is first introduced and the time when the final decision is made as to whether to implement a plan in the area is likely to be one of considerable strain for the people in the community.

Another negative effect of uncertainty can be expected in the economic sector. While businessmen are unsure as to whether they will be able to maintain their activities in the area, it is unlikely that they will make any attempts to substantially improve or expand their business; the same is true of farmers (especially owners of small farms) in relation to their land and crop production. Thus, a state of economic stasis can be expected to some degree in the areas under consideration for project construction; if one accepts the definition of economic stability as one in which the economy grows steadily to keep pace with increasing population or inflation, then this stasis has serious negative implications for the economy of the communities during the time of data collection, analysis, and decision-making. Obviously, the longer this period lasts, the more serious its negative effects will become.

Once an alternative plan has been selected, the uncertainty of the preceding period will end; however, the next phase of the project, technical planning, can also produce disruptive effects. People will know where and how the plan will be implemented, but even if implementation (i.e., construction) requires that they eventually move, this move will probably not have to take place for a number of years. Thus, continued economic stasis can be expected, as well as continued tension for residents of the community as they make decisions as to where and when to move. On the other hand, this period may prove valuable to the residents in allowing them time to make new plans and find new homes under a condition of certainty about the prospective move. Numerous people may even have to change their life plans completely. Late middle-aged and elderly people who hold jobs or who farm in the area are likely to opt for an earlier retirement than they had envisioned, under the conviction that when the move finally takes place, they will be too old to begin again. Farmers, in particular, will suffer the disruptive effects of a move. In most cases, farmers who have been working the same land for a number of years have learned to optimize, or nearly optimize, for the particular soil conditions, water retention, and runoff characteristics of their land. The process of learning these conditions for new land will be difficult at best, and will undoubtedly result in a temporary decrease in production efficiency.

Rating the impacts and social effects of alternative plans. In Table 1, Section III, Part F, a set of variables is presented to indicate changes which might occur in the community as a result of the planning for a water resource project. As has been mentioned above, many of these changes are likely to be negative primarily because of the uncertainty which exists during the planning period; negative results may increase over time, if the period of planning and uncertainty is extended. Thus, for example, people may hold their personal plans in abeyance for an uncomfortable and costly length of time, as they wait to see whether the NED plan (which calls for relocation of a certain segment of the community in connection with a proposed dam) is implemented, or whether the EQ plan (which places the reservoir further upstream) is chosen. On a broader community level, the effects may be similar, with the local government waiting to begin urban renewal activities until a plan is decided upon. Under these circumstances, the following entries would be appropriate for Table 1.

Examples of NED Plan Effects

Items in Evaluation Categories	Measures of Impact	Effects ++,+,0,-,--
1. Effects of planning activities for water resource project on the local population c. Personal plans	Residents in the NED plan flood pool area will wait to decide whether or not to move and will begin no new personal projects of major proportions; some degree of personal anxiety and stagnation will result.	--
2. Effects of planning activities for water resource project on local a. Community planning	Planned urban renewal activities will be held in abeyance until choice of plan is reached.	--

Construction

Scope of concern. Construction associated with plan implementation is likely to have considerable effects on the plan area; under different conditions and from different points of view, these effects can be either positive or negative, short- or long-term. One of the most obvious effects of construction will be physical disruption. Roads and railroads may be diverted; there will be increased dust and noise in the area. The physical attractiveness of the community may be either temporarily or permanently impaired. The influx of construction workers—and, in some cases, the workers' families—into the community during the period of construction can also have substantial effects in many sectors. These people will temporarily swell the population of the area, resulting in an increased demand for services of all kinds: schools may be strained by the addition of the workers' children to their classrooms, stores and businesses may be required to expand to meet the needs of new customers, the call for health and other social services may rise, and housing demand may increase. All of these factors may create a "boom town" atmosphere, either at the construction site or in neighboring communities. Although the additional money that arrives with the workers and the additional services that they require may benefit communities in the short term, the knowledge that the prosperity will be temporary may have significant social effects among permanent residents of the communities. Included among these effects may be fear of the future, resentment of the transient workers, and polarization of the communities into "permanent" and "transient" sections. Once the construction workers leave, there may be longer-range negative effects on the communities. The experience of boom towns in the past suggests that benefits are hard to hold onto, while damages remain. Most likely, the towns that expand rapidly during the construction phase will find that they have excess capacity in housing, schools, and commercial enterprises after construction ends. These unnecessary facilities will require expenditure of public or private monies, either to be maintained or to be removed. Use of mobile homes may alleviate housing problems, but may also result in increases in education, legal, and other services without contributing to the tax base.

Rating the impacts and social effects of alternative plans. In Table 1, Section III, Part G, a set of variables is presented to indicate possible changes which might occur in connection with the construction period for a water resource project. Once again, as has been mentioned above, most of these effects are likely to be negative; the main point of consideration will be the *relative* disruption to communities which is caused by the various alternative plans; i.e., if the NED plan calls for construction near one community which is fairly large and which can fairly easily absorb a temporary increase in population, while the EQ plan calls for construction near another community which is small and would feel a relatively greater disruptive effect, then from the viewpoint of construction, the former (NED) plan would be preferable. However, comparisons between plans are to be reserved for Table 2; therefore, the following entries, with explanatory discussion, would be appropriate for Table 1.

Examples of NED Plan Effects

Items in Evaluation Categories	Measures of Impact	Effects ++,+,0,-,--
1. Short-term effects a. Influx of workers	Influx of 50 construction workers into a community of approximately 3,000 will cause relatively minor temporary disruption.	-
b. Change in demand for public and private services associated with short-term influx of workers	Community service base adequate to accommodate 50 construction workers without significant changes.	0

The National, Emergency Preparedness Effects Component

In the first three components of the Social Well-Being Account, attention is focused on the potential changes which might occur in the evaluation categories of individual and community life as a result of the implementation of alternative water resource plans. Consideration of the evaluation categories of these three components is essentially limited to a given geographical locale that includes the area which will be directly affected by the implementation of a water resource plan and any communities and/or municipalities therein. However, another important consideration is the way in which the changes brought about by the plan would have selected national impacts. In many cases, these changes will, in fact, be limited to the geographical area covered by the plan; in others, however, changes could contribute to (or detract from) national viability, especially in the case of emergencies such as drought, floods, or attacks by hostile forces. For example, plans which will contribute to the stability of a water supply over a large area or which will enable the conservation of scarce fuels have important implications for national goals. The National, Emergency Preparedness component includes nine evaluation categories which must be considered in all applicable cases for alternative water resource plans; they are as follows:

Water Supplies deals with questions of the quantity, stability, distribution, etc., of water.

Food Production concerns provision of reserve food production potential, as well as questions of exportability of crops.

Power Supplies deals with questions concerning the quantity, stability, and responsiveness of available power.

Water Transportation discusses tonnage support capacity and network location characteristics, as well as the area covered by water transportation routes.

Scarce Fuels concerns the use of abundant fuels to conserve scarce ones and the use of alternative power supplies.

Population Dispersion relates to potential for settlement of areas in the event of a national emergency.

Industrial Dispersion is concerned with the potential for dispersion and relocation of industry in the event of a national emergency.

Military Preparedness relates primarily to the potential of a given area to house military bases and/or support military operations in a national emergency.

International Treaty Obligations deals with the questions of boundaries, use of common bodies of water, treaty obligations governing quantity and/or quality of water crossing international boundaries, etc., among neighboring nations.

In contrast to the earlier sections, examples of the various impacts and ratings of their beneficial and adverse social effects will be given in one complete set at the end of this section. The complete table listing the items for this component is presented on pp. 245-248 of Part 3.

Water Supplies

Scope of concern. In some cases, the alternative plans under consideration will have little relevance to national, emergency preparedness concerns in the area of water supplies. However, relatively large projects on water bodies which cover or connect a wide area (e.g., large lakes and rivers) will have potential impacts on water supplies outside the immediate project area. This would certainly be true of a dam or reservoir which stabilizes water supplies for a region of the country. Considerations of national impact would also apply in the case of a sewage treatment plant which improves the quality of water available from a lake or river supplying a large region. Plans involving desalinization plants, trans-mountain diversion systems, and large canals must also be analyzed from the standpoint of the impact they will have on water supplies as they affect national, emergency preparedness. All such projects have the potential of assuring a larger and more stable water supply to a large or important area of the country under emergency situations of various types.

Food Production

Scope of concern. Irrigation systems, reservoirs and similar projects have the potential of stabilizing or increasing water supplies in agricultural areas, with a concomitant stabilization or increase in crop production, whether it be crops for human, animal, or industrial (e.g., fiber) consumption. When reasonably large agricultural areas are to be affected, plans for these areas must therefore take into consideration the effects which increased crop production will have on national concerns. For example, increased crops can be exported to other areas of the country in the event of food shortages caused by droughts, floods, or other disasters. In assessing the possible impact of increased food and other crop production, several variables—including type and use of the crops, exportability, and various increases in quantity—should be taken into consideration.

Power Supplies

Scope of concern. Changes in capacity of hydroelectric dams and power production capability, transmission lines, and similar facilities which might be implemented through a water-related plan have the potential of assuring a larger and more stable power supply for a region in the event of a national emergency. In assessing the potential impact of plan alternatives in this area of concern, a number of variables must be taken into consideration; these include the relevant conditions, aggregate and peak demand in the region, and the kilowatt generation capacity of the planned facility, both for internal (to the immediate area) and external use. The possibilities for and means of transmission to outside areas must also be touched upon in an assessment of the potential impact of power supply facilities on national, emergency preparedness.

Water Transportation

Scope of concern. Alternative water-related plans can involve a variety of changes in the local and regional character of waterways used for transportation, including enlargement of riverbeds, diversion of rivers, and the construction of canals and connecting locks. In the majority of cases, such changes will, in turn, have the potential of considerably affecting the capacity of such waterways to support transportation in the event of national or regional emergencies. Enlarged capacity may be important or even vital in a number of circumstances, including national or regional strikes in other transportation sectors (e.g., railroad and truck shipping) or natural disasters which temporarily reduce or eliminate the transportation usages of other waterways. Among the considerations which must be assessed in relation to potential changes in capacity for water transportation of a given waterway are the changes which the plan is likely to effect in the areas of mileage and tonnage support capacity, and network location characteristics (i.e., how and where various waterways connect with one another).

Scarce Fuels

Scope of concern. Reduction in consumption of scarce fuels such as oil and natural gas (which is becoming increasingly important today) is likely to be vital in the event of a national or regional emergency which might reduce production capacity and availability of such fuels. Conservation of such scarce fuels is dependent on the creation and/or use of methods which either facilitates the consumption of more available fuels (e.g., coal) or increases the potential for employing other power sources such as hydroelectric or nuclear power. The extent to which a water-related plan involves a reduction in the consumption of scarce fuels is thus of considerable importance in the assessment of the impact of that plan from the standpoint of national, emergency preparedness. Among the aspects of alternative plans which must be studied in light of this goal are whether the plan involves the use (or facilitates the use) of abundant fuels, or whether it will lead to the effective utilization of alternative power sources.

Population Dispersion

Scope of concern. In certain rare emergency circumstances, it may become necessary to disperse the population of an area, or even an entire region, from their residences into other sections of the country. The possibility of dispersion of population to new, previously unsettled, or sparsely settled areas depends on the ability of those areas to support human life. This ability is, in turn, contingent to a great degree on the existence of an ample and reasonably stable water supply for human consumption, crop production, etc. The extent to which a water-related plan, such as a reservoir, dam, etc., will change the supply of water in an area and assure the viability of human settlement there is thus an important consideration for national, emergency preparedness. Among those variables which must be studied in an assessment of the potential impact of a water-related plan are the size of the potential water supply (e.g., how large a population it could possibly support), its quality (e.g., whether it can be used for crop production or drinking water), its accessibility, and its potential for distribution.

Industrial Dispersion

Scope of concern. As in the case of population dispersion, it may, on rare occasions, become necessary to disperse one or more industries of an area from their original location. The ability of an area to support new industry and the type and volume of industry which can be supported are important national emergency considerations. A plan involving a new hydroelectric plant, for example, would increase the ability of the area in which the plant is to be located to support industry; the existence of treatment plants capable of handling industrial wastes would also increase the viability of an area for industrial location. In assessing the potential feasibility of a plan in relation to industrial dispersion, a number of variables must be considered, including the change in volume of power it might effect, its possibilities for industrial waste treatment, the kinds of wastes which might be handled, and the volume of industry which might be supported and the availability of water for industrial cooling processes.

Military Preparedness

Scope of concern. In times of potential or actual attack on the country or a region of the country by hostile forces, it may become necessary to set up emergency military bases for defense purposes. The potential of an area for location of such bases depends on the availability of water for human consumption and possibly power supply, among other things. A plan which would increase the water supply in an area, or create a supply where none existed before, would naturally enhance that area's potential for the location of emergency military bases. Among the variables which must be studied in an assessment of the possible impact of a plan are the size of the water supply which would be available, its accessibility, and the quality of the water available.

International Treaty Obligations

Scope of concern. Any assessment of the potential impact of alternative plans in relation to international treaty obligations must, by definition, be treaty-specific. Treaties regarding water rights and water usage exist between the United States and Mexico and between the United States and Canada in relation to specific systems of water which extend across common borders. Naturally, the type of impact which a water-related plan might have on such treaty obligations depends wholly on the type of plan involved and on the nature of the treaty. The treaty involved must, of course, be studied thoroughly to determine what alternative plans are in compliance with all of its clauses. Consideration should also be given to other, non-legal effects which the plans might have in terms of international goodwill and relations.

Rating the impacts and social effects of alternative plans. In Table 1, Section IV, Parts A through I, a number of variables are presented in order to suggest potential impacts which might occur in relation to national, emergency preparedness in the event of implementation of a water-related plan. Such impacts might occur, for example, in the case of a large dam built in a sparsely settled area. Such a dam, with an associated hydroelectric plant, could have the potential to greatly improve various aspects of national, emergency preparedness. Such a dam would not only improve the stability of the water supply for an entire region, but would also make settlement of the immediate area more feasible, given the assurance of available water which previously did not exist. The associated hydroelectric plant would also insure a more stable power supply for the region, which would be needed in the event of a national emergency. In the long term, the increased availability of electric power would contribute to a change in fuel use patterns, thus preserving scarce fuels such as petroleum and natural gas. Under these circumstances, the following types of entries would be appropriate for various parts of Table 1, Section IV as shown on the following page.

The Aggregate Social Effects Component

The final component to be dealt with involves the aggregation of potential impacts of water resource projects as they re-

Examples of NED Plan Effects

Items in Evaluation Categories	Measures of Impact	Effects ++,+,0,–,––
A. Water Supplies 2. Changes in stability of the water supply	Water supply stabilized in a 500 square mile area previously subject to frequent droughts.	++
C. Power Supplies 1. Changes in the amount of power produced	Associated hydroelectric power plant will produce an estimated 500,000 kilowatts daily.	++
E. Scarce Fuels 2. Changes in use patterns of scarce vs. abundant fuels (e.g., coal)	Long-term reduction in petroleum and natural gas consumption in favor of hydroelectric power.	++
F. Population Dispersion 1. Changes in the amount of water available in sparsely settled areas	Large, stable water supply available in 500-square mile area with a current population of 1,000 persons.	++

late to social effects as a whole. While the previous components have focused on more practical concerns for the most part, it is also desirable to be able to consider the more general social implications of alternative water resource plans. The measures of impact will, in this case, be of an almost entirely qualitative nature, and the rating given to potential effects will be based, in large part, on observations made at the more practical level in the preceding four components. Three evaluation categories are of interest here:

Quality of Life deals with the physical and mental well-being of the individual and family and with their perceptions of the opportunities for further development of individual and family life in the future.

Relative Social Position concerns the extent to which the various social benefits and adverse effects of plan implementation would be equitably distributed among various individuals or groups in the community, and the capacity of individuals and groups to bear social costs.

Social Well-Being refers to the overall impacts on the character and capacities of the community and its institutions, both formal and informal.

The complete table listing the items for this component is presented on pp. 248-249 of Part 3.

Quality of Life

Scope of concern. In the most fundamental sense, quality of life refers to the nature of a person's inner state of mind, and to his or her interpersonal relations. This can be understood both from the individual perspective and in terms of the individual and his family and small group contexts. Three dimensions would seem to be important in assessing the impacts of proposed alternative plans on quality of life. First, the person's stage of life. Second, the overall economic security of his or her situation. Third, his or her geographic location in relation to the projects under consideration. In turn, the fundamental question is how, given the above considerations, the quality of life of individuals is affected in relation to the water development decision as opposed to quality of life in general.

Rating the impacts and social effects of alternative plans. In Table 1, Section VI, Part A, six indicators are presented to suggest the types of aggregate social impacts which might occur in the quality of life of individuals and families in an area in the event of the implementation of a given water-related plan. For example, the NED plan might call for bringing new high voltage lines into the area to improve its power supply. This, in turn, is expected to bring about increased economic development in the area due to the availability of power which will allow already existing industries to expand; one plant has already indicated that it plans to expand its operations by almost 50%, and another factory foresees at least a 30% expansion within the five years following the construction of the new lines. These two expansions will create approximately 150 new jobs, some of which will be filled by outsiders, but many of which can be filled by currently unemployed residents of the community.

New population coming into the area will create a demand for new and more diverse services in both the public and private sectors; hopefully, the expanded tax base will enable the local government to provide some new services, while increased demand will encourage the development of services in the private sector. Under these circumstances, the following entries would be appropriate in Table 1.

Examples of NED Plan Effects

Items in Evaluation Categories	Measures of Impact	Effects ++,+,0,-,--
1. Quality of self-development	Due to the increase in opportunities resulting from increased and more diverse services, many new paths for personal development will emerge.	++
6. Perceived equality of opportunity to benefit from changes in the community	Visibility of new opportunities and access to them should increase perceived equality of opportunity to benefit from community changes.	++

Relative Social Position

Scope of concern. Basically, considerations of relative social relationships are those involving questions of equity: Which of the alternative plans distributes benefits and costs most equitably across various actor groups and which, if any, of the alternatives distributes more benefits (or fewer costs) to one group at the expense of another? If, as is likely, some groups bear more costs than others, are these former groups the ones which are best able to bear higher costs, or are they already too heavily burdened?

Clearly, it is desirable that governmental actions, such as the implementation of water resource plans, be such that benefits and costs are equitably distributed across various layers of society. But if this is not possible, then the next desirable situation is one in which the greater costs are borne by those who are better able to bear them rather than by those who are less able to do so. (An example of a governmental action that is supposed to distribute its burdens in this fashion is the progressive income tax, even though in practice this does not always work out because of loopholes and special legislation.)

Rating the impacts and social effects of alternative plans. In Table 1, Section VI, Part B, a set of indicators is presented to suggest the types of aggregate effects which might occur in relation to the relative social position of groups within a community. For example, the NED plan might have the potential for considerably increasing the economic base of the area by attracting new industry or agribusiness. With increased prosperity, the majority of the community is likely to reap a number of benefits, such as increased services in the public and private sectors, etc. However, there will be groups in the community who do not benefit from the expanded economy and whose relative position will therefore suffer; i.e., as the economic base expands, prices may rise. Those who are participating in or benefiting from the expansion will have no problem paying the increased costs of services, while those who are unemployed and poverty-level individuals and families will find it more difficult to obtain the services which they need. As another example, the majority of new jobs which come into the area with new industry may not be open to people without the proper training and/or education. Thus, unemployed persons who do not have the proper training will not benefit from the improved economic situation and, in fact, will actually suffer because of rising costs. Under these circumstances, the following entries would be appropriate for Table 1, as shown on the following page.

Social Well-Being

Scope of concern. Social well-being is an important evaluative dimension in assessment of social impact. While *quality of life* is an expression of the degree to which individuals and families enjoy their lives in good health, in economic security, and in

Examples of NED Plan Effects

Items in Evaluation Categories	Measures of Impact	Effects ++,+,0,-,--
1. Equal opportunity to receive benefits from plan implementation and relationship to need	Certain groups, notably the poor, will not find various benefits equally available to them.	--
2. Equity of distribution of social and economic costs and relationship to ability to pay	Certain groups, particularly those with little education and/or training will absorb a disproportionately high cost and receive disproportionately low benefits.	--

general peace of mind about their present and future situation, *social well-being* is evaluative at a higher level of aggregation and is an expression of social values at the level of the community and its constitutent groups. Social well-being does *contribute* to quality of life, however. The following are some of the components of social well-being.

- The viability and stability of organizations and institutions such as schools, churches, clubs, colleges, and the like, especially as they contribute to the quality of life of individuals.
- The stability of the society in terms of the distribution of population and of employment opportunities.
- The stability of the economy.
- The security of the people as it is affected by government and social structure.
- The viability and stability of social service institutions which provide assistance to the needy or disadvantaged and to those requiring medical treatment.

Rating the impacts and social effects of alternative plans. In Table 1, Section VI, Part C, a set of four indicators is presented to suggest the types of aggregate impacts which might occur in the social well-being of an area as a result of the implementation of a water resource plan. For example, the NED plan might call for a new hydroelectric power plant to be built on a river running nearby a given community. The plan is expected to attract a good deal of industry to the area, but because of the supply characteristics of the locale, the new industry is likely to be of the same type as that already existing (i.e., more shoe manufacturers, as opposed to the diversification of industry to other manufacturing sectors.) Thus, although there will be new people coming into the area as a result of the availability of new jobs, the new population is likely to be of approximately the same composition (in relation to socioeconomic position, occupation, etc.) as that already existing in the community. The expanded economic base which will result from the new industry is expected to lead to an increase and diversification of services. Under these circumstances, the following entries would be appropriate for Table 1.

Examples of NED Plan Effects

Items in Evaluation Categories	Measures of Impact	Effects ++,+,0,–,––
1. General improvement in the quantity and quality of public and private services available to the public	Increase in service supply will keep pace with demand; there will be a greater diversification of services	+
4. Improvement in stability of values and norms in the community	The population will expand, but basic characteristics and composition will remain constant; the community should remain stable.	+

Summary of Rating the Social Effects of Alternative Plans

The above descriptions have covered each of the Social Well-Being Account components and their evaluation categories. Items in the account can be substituted, but as it now stands, it assures a comprehensive and thorough social assessment. The complete Table 1 is presented in Part 3. The planner is now in a position to complete Table 1 for each of the water development plans under consideration, as well as for a future in which no plan is to be implemented. Once this has been accomplished, the planner will be able to compare the beneficial and adverse social effects across the plans as described in Chapter 10.

10
Summary of Social Benefits and Adverse Effects Across Plans

In the preceding chapter, guidelines were presented for assessing the potential future impacts of each of the alternative water resource plans across the evaluation categories of the Social Well-Being components. These impacts were, in turn, rated for their likely social effects. Once this assessment has been completed and Table 1 has been filled out in full for each plan, the planner proceeds to the next step of the social assessment process, which involves comparing the beneficial and adverse social effects across all of the plans under consideration. The purpose of this activity is to compare the effects which have been attributed to various plans and assessed according to present-day needs. The comparison will be based on the subjective estimations of "very positive" to "very negative" effects which were entered in the third column of Table 1. These estimations should, in turn, be carefully reviewed for each component, in order to obtain a sense of the broader social implications of each plan when taken as a whole, and for the relative merits of the alternative plans when viewed in comparison to one another. In other words, the planner cannot simply aggregate plus and minus ratings for each component and expect to arrive at a final "decision" concerning the relative social costs and benefits of a plan, for the ratings are not, in fact, additive. For example, ratings for each of the evaluation categories of the Individual, Personal Effects Component might all be positive (+), while the Community, Institutional Effects Component might contain both positive and negative ratings. However, the implications of one or two very positive (++) ratings in the latter component may cause it to outweigh the former in the overview. Only by considering all positive and negative ratings can the necessary sense of the broad social implications of each plan be obtained; in turn, only a comparison of the positive and negative aspects of each plan as a whole can enable the planner to reach some final recommendations concerning the status of plans according to the Social Well-Being Account.

Table 2, which is presented in full on pp. 250-287 in Part 3, is intended to aid the comparison among plans by presenting a visual array of values/ratings across plans. The ratings in the columns with the main title "Beneficial & Adverse Effects of Plans" are drawn from the ratings of effects assigned to individual plans in column 3 of Table 1. It will be remembered that these ratings derive from a subjective comparison of the data in column 2 of Table 1 with what is known about present-day conditions in the community. Present conditions are, in turn, rated in column 2 of Table 2 on the basis of comparison with national and regional averages. Ratings for present conditions range from below average (BA) to average (A) to above average (AA). It is important to note that there will not always be ratings in this column, as the ratings are based on the description of present-day community life in Chapter 8, which does not require the degree of explication of Tables 1 and 2.

The ratings in Table 2 thus allow the planner not only to compare the plans with one another, but also to predict their potential overall effects in relation to present conditions. These overall effects essentially fall into four groups: (1) present-day conditions are below average, and these conditions will be exacerbated by a particular plan; (2) present-day conditions are average, and will remain unchanged in the event of plan implementation; (3) present-day conditions are below average or average, and will be improved by the plan in question; or (4) present-day conditions are above average and will be further improved by the plan.

Table 2. *A Summary Comparison of the Beneficial and Adverse Effects of the Alternative Plans for the Social Well-Being Account*

Items in Evaluation Categories	Present Conditions	Beneficial & Adverse Effects of Plans					
		No Plan	NED Plan	EQ Plan	ALT "X"	ALT "Y"	RECCO Plan

***Conditions (Above to below Average: AA,A,BA); Effects (Beneficial to Adverse: ++,+,0,-,--).**

In the following sections, discussion will focus on a description of cross-plan comparison across the five components of the Social Well-Being Account.

Comparing the Beneficial and Adverse Social Effects of the Alternative Plans, and their Relationship with Present-day Social Conditions

Data from both the social profile and narrative sections of Chapter 8 (rated from Above to Below Average) and from the social effects ratings of the various impacts presented in column 3 of Table 1 (rated from Very Positive to Very Negative) are utilized in this section. All of these ratings are now displayed side by side, under the five components:

- Individual, Personal Effects
- Community, Institutional Effects
- Area, Socioeconomic Effects
- National, Emergency Preparedness Effects
- Aggregate, Social Effects

Table 2 is first prepared by making these transfers; then the appropriate narrative is prepared to accompany the tables.

The narrative is divided into five sections, one for each of the SWB components. The attention here is on the comparative social merit of each of the plans, on balance, with respect to the five concerns of beneficial and adverse social effects on the individual, community, area, nation, and in the aggregate. The narrative must be prepared in order to (1) explain how the various entries in the tables were derived and (2) explain what implication the table entries have for the Feasibility Study, for whose sake the investigation of the Social Well-Being Account was undertaken. In the narrative, the planner explains why the effects found in certain evaluation categories of the components were considered important, but not others. Some explanation should also be given of why the future impacts were assessed as having an effect that warranted whatever rating was assigned (++,+,0,–,––). It is not enough, in other words, simply to say (or to indicate on the tables) that under individual, personal effects, health is the most significant area. The planner should indicate in the narrative what assumptions were made (usually based on present-day social characteristics), what secondary data were used, where these data were obtained, and what, if any, primary data were used, together with an estimate, if possible, of the reliability of the forecasts. These statements must be completed before consideration is given to trade-offs among effects, which are discussed in the section below.

Various Trade-Offs Among Effects

This section focuses on the potential trade-offs among effects, both within plans and across plans, for four sets of measures: (1) short-term vs. long-term effects; (2) direct vs. indirect effects; (3) geographical distribution; and (4) groups affected. (These trade-offs have been described in detail on pp. 60-64.)

Different plans can have substantially different potentials for both direct and indirect effects. For example, both the NED and the EQ plans might involve construction of a multi-purpose reservoir on a river, although the EQ plan, for various reasons, calls for the reservoir to be located at a site near a small community, while the NED plan calls for construction of the reservoir in an almost wholly unpopulated area. In terms of the direct effects of construction-related disruption and associated indirect effects, the NED plan would be given a more positive rating. Thus, the SWB Task Group should evaluate the plans according to their direct and indirect beneficial and adverse social effects.

Different plans may also vary considerably in relation to the short- and long-term effects they will have. For example, the NED plan might call for the construction of a dam and hydroelectric power plant within ten miles of a given community. The short-term effects associated with this plan would relate to disruption during construction (e.g., blockage of roads going into the community, and air pollution). The long-term effects of the NED plan would be a potential increase in industrial activity due to increased availability of power and associated expansion of the community's population and economic base. The EQ plan, on the other hand, might call for the construction of a dam without a hydroelectric power plant (but with potential recreational uses) some sixty miles up-river from the NED site, in an area where there is only very sparse population. The short-term social effects of the EQ plan would be minimal, since no roads would have to be blocked, air pollution would not spread to the community, etc. On the other hand, the long-term effects in terms of improving the community's economic base or expanding its population would also be minimal, since industrial workers are not likely to settle in the community, although long-term effects might also include increased recreational activity in the area. Such short- and long-term effects should be carefully described and compared for each plan, and the results should be included in the final analysis.

Two types of geographic trade-offs can be present. First, there can be trade-offs within the planning area; i.e., some communities will benefit while others suffer. Second, there can be trade-offs between the plan area and the "outside world"; i.e., with benefits and costs distributed unequally between the two. Some plans might result in significant positive effects for one area and negative or no effects in another, while others might have the opposite, or at least different, effects. For example, the location of a secondary sewage treatment plant on the river bordering Community X, according to the EQ plan, might have significant beneficial effects for that community; in that locale, hotels and other commercial establishments could switch from leaching fields to a sewer system and thereby would be able to expand their facilities. On the other hand, the sewage from the plant would flow downstream to a recreational fishing area thirty miles away and force the closing of that area for fishing. An alternative plan, however, might call for the construction of a tertiary treatment plant which would cost both the federal and local government more money, but which would leave the downstream fishing area unpolluted. As another example, the NED plan might call for a large irrigation system to be built in an agricultural area, which is expected to have the long-term effects of encouraging more capital-intensive farming and possibly having adverse effects on less efficient farmers in the area. Thus, this plan would have both negative and positive long-term effects for the immediate area. However, the increased productivity of farms in the area due to irrigation would imply increased benefits for the whole region in terms of an expanded crop production for exportation. In this case, then, the local benefits and adverse effects would have to be weighed carefully against the benefits for the region as a whole and compared to the similar beneficial and adverse effects of the EQ plan, which calls for a smaller irrigation system which would help small farmers but which would probably be insufficient to encourage a great deal of large-scale, capital-intensive agricultural activity. The SWB Task Group should specify the trade-offs which exist comparatively among the plans of this variable.

Yet another dimension to be considered in the cross-plan assessment relates to the *trade-offs among groups* and how they will be affected by the various plans. Different special groups may be uniquely affected in a negative way by the implementation of one plan, while the general population will benefit. The implementation of another plan may have negative effects for one group, positive for another, and not affect the general population at all. For example, an NED plan might call for the construction of a multipurpose reservoir which would have associated recreational uses, thus benefiting a large majority of the local population as well as that in nearby communities. However, the flood pool area of the reservoir would touch a small section of low-income houses and force the residents of this section to move, causing them considerable hardship. The EQ plan, on the other hand, might call for no reservoir to be built. The residents of the low-income housing would not be affected in this case, but the absence of the reservoir would not yield the positive effects in terms of recreation for the general population of the community in question. Once again, the effects of different plans on all special groups within the community are to be considered, and particularly those plans which might have negative implications for groups which are already carrying a considerable social burden, such as the poor and the elderly.

The intensity and direction (i.e., positive or negative) of these different types of effects may vary widely within and among plans, and the trade-offs among them must therefore be given serious consideration. Although most of the effects will be closely associated with one or more of the components and will be included within the component ratings in many cases, the trade-offs should also be considered separately. For example, the extent of disruption caused by construction associated with plan implementation will make up part of the rating for the Area, Socioeconomic Effects component. However, this particular measure should also be considered separately as a potential direct effect of plan implementation. As has been mentioned, the sets of trade-offs delineated here may apply both within and/or across plans; both must be taken into consideration.

A Summary Comparison of the Plans

In the final step of the cross-plan analysis, all of the various plans under consideration, including the alternative of no plan implementation, should be viewed together according to the ratings which have been made in former analysis phases. Table 3 has been designed to facilitate this process. As will be seen, the first column of this table is divided into two parts; the first part lists the five components of the Social Well-Being Account, and the second part lists the four categories of trade-offs discussed in the section above. Two types of ratings are called for. Ratings for each plan according to the various components of the Social Well-Being Account should be made according to the system used throughout the analysis: from ++ for very positive ratings, to + for positive, 0 for neutral, - for negative, and -- for very negative effects. As has been noted before, these ratings will be drawn from the individual evaluation category ratings described in Chapter 9. The final rating given to each plan for each component will not represent an aggregation of the evaluation category ratings, but rather an estimate of the overall intensity and direction of the effects, the "social meaning" or "social implications" of each plan in the evaluation categories. This rating can be facilitated by observing the correspondence between where the beneficial and adverse effects fall and the present-day relative social conditions (i.e., above average, average, below average). As an example, the NED plan might have received:

- A ++ rating in the Life, Protection and Safety category, due to its potential for reducing the destruction of life and property through flood control;
- A 0 rating in the Health category, because it has no foreseeable effects in this area;
- A + rating in the Family and Individual category, because of its potential for creating new recreational facilities which would lead to personal satisfaction and family enjoyment;
- A - rating in the Attitudes, Values, and Beliefs category, because it is predicted to have some negative effects on people's attitudes toward the federal government;
- A -- rating in the Environmental Contributions category, due to the fact that it would destroy a scenic river reach previously valued highly by many residents of the area.

The planner would review all of these ratings in the evaluation categories for the Individual, Personal Effects component to get a feeling for what the overall implications were; having weighed all factors, including present-day needs, it might be decided to assign a + rating to the component, due to the fact

Table 3. *Summary of Effects Across Plans*

		No Plan	NED Plan	EQ Plan	Alt "X"	Alt "Y"	RECCO
Components of the Social Well-Being Account[a]	I. Individual, Personal Effects II. Community, Institutional Effects III. Area, Socio-Economic Effects IV. National, Emergency Preparedness Effects V. Aggregate Social Effects						
Trade-offs[b]	Direct vs. Indirect Effects						
	Short-Term vs. Long-Term Effects						
	Geographic Distribution						
	Special Groups Affected						

[a]Rate: ++ (very positive); + (positive); o (neutral); - (negative); -- (very negative).

[b]Brief verbal descriptions (e.g., direct positive effects on recreation vs. indirect negative effects on employment).

that the potential benefit in terms of lives and property saved from destruction over a wide area overrides the negative effects assigned to the other categories of that component.

Ratings for the various plans according to the four categories of trade-offs should be entered in a narrative shorthand; i.e., for an NED plan which calls for the creation of a multi-purpose reservoir which would include recreational facilities but which would also necessitate the relocation of a local industry from the flood pool area, the entry in the "Direct vs. Indirect Effects" row might read "direct positive effects for recreation; indirect negative effects for employment and economic base."

The Appendix to the Social Well-Being Account

The Social Well-Being Account should have an appendix containing the relevant support materials that were gathered during the social assessment and the construction of the Social Well-Being Account. These materials might include a listing of the secondary data sources used, a listing of the interviews conducted (such as the kind of person interviewed, age, sex, socio-economic status, and by education), any other survey data collected by the Social Well-Being Task Group, any charts, maps, tables, etc. In general, the appendix should contain all the back-up materials on which the assessment (and consequently the Social Well-Being Account) was based.

11

The Recommendation of a Plan with Optimal Balance of Beneficial and Adverse Effects

The Social Well-Being Task Group (SWBTG) is now in a position to make a recommendation to the rest of the planning team among the various plans *insofar as social well-being factors are concerned.*

With the help of Table 2, the group can see which plan affects a given evaluation category positively or negatively. The recommended plan will be that plan which has the most positive effects together with the least negative effects, provided that all of the evaluation categories are of equal importance. Since, however, it is likely that some categories will be considered more important than others, they may have to be weighted (either in a formal or informal procedure) in order to arrive at a recommendation. The SWBTG may feel, for example, that real income effects should be weighted more heavily than effects on national, emergency preparedness, and so would give less weight to a plan that, however useful from a national, emergency preparedness point of view, might lead to only slight increases in real income for the population of the plan area. However, this kind of reasoning must be made explicit; it cannot be taken for granted that real income effects should always be more heavily weighted than others; such an assumption, for example, would probably downgrade all EQ plans.

In making the recommendation, the condition of No Plan is one of the alternatives that must be considered. It should be apparent from the effects displayed in Table 2 that the decision not to implement a plan cannot be assumed to mean that no impacts will occur. Indeed, a No Plan decision can have far-reaching effects, of either a positive or negative nature. For example, in an area which has been subject to serious droughts during the past decade, the decision not to build a reservoir to ameliorate this situation can have serious long-range negative effects on the demographics of the area, as people in the farming community decide to move on to places which have a more constant water supply. This, in turn, would have similar negative effects on the economics of the community and on various other social sectors as well. On the other hand, the decision not to build a dam which would have required the flooding of a particular river reach can have substantial positive effects on a population which uses that particular river reach for recreational purposes; people who were planning to leave the area because of the planned project are likely to maintain their residences there, and this would have concomitant benefits for the economy and other sectors of the community.

The effects of a No Plan decision may also be more subtle than those described above. For example, if people in the area had been counting on a planned project to boost the economy in some way (for example, by providing more electric power to attract new industry, or new irrigation lands), an attitude of pessimism about future growth could develop in the face of a decision not to implement the plan. Conversely, the decision not to implement a plan which would have destroyed a natural resource (e.g., a harbor or scenic riverfront) valued by the community may have quite positive effects on the attitudes of the population toward their community.

Particularly helpful in making a recommendation will be considerations of the effects in the aggregate; i.e., the effects which have been aggregated under the headings of Quality of Life,

Relative Social Position, and Social Well-Being. By considering these aggregate effects, the Social Well-Being Task Group will be able to ascertain which plan (including No Plan) has the most beneficial (and least adverse) effects on individuals and on communities, and most importantly, which plan distributes its effects most equitably; i.e., without unjust shifts in the relative social position of persons which occur because one group of persons reaps more benefits than another group, because one group suffers fewer of the costs than another group, or, in the worst case, because one group reaps most of the benefits while another group suffers most of the costs.

Since the Social Well-Being Task Group is concerned with beneficial and adverse social effects, its recommendations will be based on the distribution of those alone; i.e., on how the Task Group assesses the completed Social Well-Being Account. While the SWBTG's recommendation is only concerned with the Social Well-Being Account, its social assessment will be considered along with the other three accounts in reaching a decision about which plan to recommend to decision-makers for implementation.

Part 3
Tables to be Used in Preparing the Social Well-Being Account

Table 1. *Beneficial and Adverse Effects on Social Well-Being Under the Plan for* ___________

Items in Evaluation Categories	Measures of Impact	Effects ++,+,0,–,––
I. INDIVIDUAL, PERSONAL EFFECTS		
A. LIFE, PROTECTION, AND SAFETY		
Change in State Variables		
1. Number of persons served by each agency, by services received		
2. Property loss due to water-related natural disasters		
3. Life loss due to water-related natural disasters		
Change in Relevant Condition Variables		
4. Climatic trends over next decade (based on past trends)		
Change in System Variables (Quantity & Structure)		
5. Number and type of agencies which deal with natural disasters (e.g., Civil Defense, flood control agencies)		
6. Staff size and budget of agencies which deal with natural disasters		
7. Location of agencies which deal with natural disasters (distance from population centers of communities under consideration for plan implementation)		
(Function & Purpose)		
8. Governmental level at which agencies dealing with natural disasters are located (e.g., local, county, state)		
9. Staff types of agencies dealing with natural disasters (i.e., professional or volunteer)		
10. Services provided by agencies which deal with natural disasters (e.g., financial, medical)		

Table 1. *Beneficial and Adverse Effects on Social Well-Being Under the Plan for* ___________

Items in Evaluation Categories	Measures of Impact	Effects ++,+,0,-,--
A. LIFE, PROTECTION, AND SAFETY (cont'd.)		
11. Coordination or conflict among agencies dealing with natural disasters		
(Quality & Character)		
12. Accessibility of agencies which deal with natural disasters		
13. Efficiency and effectiveness of agencies which deal with natural disasters		
Change in Other Variables (Specify)		
B. HEALTH		
Change in State Variables		
1. Morbidity levels, by type of disease		
2. Mortality levels, by type of mortality (type of disease, accident, natural causes, etc.)		
Change in Relevant Condition Variables		
3. Distribution of pollution levels in terms of noxious stimuli (air, noise, water, land)		
4. Number of disease-carrying organisms		
5. Provision of various sanitation services (sewage, garbage disposal, etc.)		
Change in System Variables (Quantity & Structure)		
6. Number of out-patient care facilities		
7. Number of in-patient beds per 1,000 population		

Table 1. *Beneficial and Adverse Effects on Social Well-Being Under the Plan for* ____________

Items in Evaluation Categories	Measures of Impact	Effects ++,+,0,-,--
B. HEALTH (cont'd.)		
8. Number of health care personnel in area		
9. Budgets of in-patient, out-patient care facilities		
10. Location of health care facilities		
(Function & Purpose)		
11. Organization and administration of local or county health department		
12. Types of staff in local health care facilities (ratio of doctors to nurses to aides; ratio of GPs to specialists); staff type of health care personnel overall in area		
13. Services provided by health care facilities (e.g., special services such as radiation therapy); activities of health agencies		
14. Diversity of types of health care facilities		
15. Coordination and conflict among health service providers		
16. Cost of health care services		
17. Physical distribution of types of health care services (private physicians, hospitals, etc.)		
18. Equality of opportunity to receive health care		
19. Efficiency and effectiveness of health care facilities and agencies (e.g., time required to receive treatment, amount of preventive care provided)		
20. Satisfaction with health care services among residents		

Table 1. *Beneficial and Adverse Effects on Social Well-Being Under the Plan for* ___________

Items in Evaluation Categories	Measures of Impact	Effects ++,+,0,-,--
B. HEALTH (cont'd.)		
Change in Other Variables (Specify)		
C. FAMILY AND INDIVIDUAL		
Change in State Variables		
1. Number of families in the area		
2. Number of single persons in the area		
3. Family composition (percent husband-wife, female-headed)		
Change in Relevant Condition Variables		
4. Number of families below poverty level		
5. Number of persons unemployed as a percent of total labor force		
6. Number of annual cases in juvenile courts, family courts		
7. Number of divorces as a percent of total marriages		
Change in System Variables (Quantity & Structure)		
8. Number of family-related service agencies in the area		
9. Staff size of family-related service agencies		
10. Number of family and personal counselors in the area (not in agencies)		
11. Location of family-related service agencies (distance from population centers)		

Table 1. *Beneficial and Adverse Effects on Social Well-Being Under the Plan for* ____________

Items in Evaluation Categories	Measures of Impact	Effects ++,+,0,-,--
C. FAMILY AND INDIVIDUAL (cont'd.)		
(Function & Purpose)		
12. Types of family and individual counselors in the area, both private and in agencies (e.g., ministers vs. psychologists vs. social workers vs. psychiatrists)		
13. Services provided by family-related agencies		
14. Coordination and conflict among family and individual services in the area		
(Quality & Character)		
15. Accessibility of family and individual services		
16. Equality of opportunity to obtain family and individual services		
17. Number of persons served annually by individual and family services		
18. Satisfaction with family and individual services among residents		
Change in Other Variables (Specify)		
D. ATTITUDES, BELIEFS AND VALUES		
1. Resident expectations of what will be the impacts of this plan, and their attitudes about the effects:		
a. Local environment		
b. Local economy		
c. Local community		
d. Population characteristics and composition		

Table 1. *Beneficial and Adverse Effects on Social Well-Being Under the Plan for* ___________

Items in Evaluation Categories	Measures of Impact	Effects ++,+,0,-,--
D. ATTITUDES, BELIEFS AND VALUES (cont'd.)		
e. Local participation in decision-making		
f. Local values, customs, and folkways		
g. Local opportunity to benefit from plan implementation		
h. Local absorption of adverse effects of the plan		
2. Resident perceptions of government agencies implementing this plan, and their reactions toward the agencies if the plan is implemented		
a. Federal agencies		
b. State agencies		
c. Local agencies		
3. Other attitudes (specify)		
E. ENVIRONMENTAL CONSIDERATIONS		
1. Changes in the environment as they affect residents' mental and physical well-being:		
a. Aesthetic (visual) quality		
b. Pollution levels (odor, land, water, etc.)		
c. Accessibility to scenic or recreational sites		
d. Land and water use patterns		
2. Changes in personal concern with environmental protection:		
a. Number, existence of groups involved in environmental issues		
b. Activities of groups involved in environmental issues		

Table 1. *Beneficial and Adverse Effects on Social Well-Being Under the Plan for* ___________

Items in Evaluation Categories	Measures of Impact	Effects ++,+,0,-,--
E. ENVIRONMENTAL CONSIDERATIONS (cont'd.)		
c. Coordination among groups involved in environmental issues		
d. Conflict among environmental groups, between groups and other institutions (local, state, national)		
3. Other changes (specify)		
II. COMMUNITY, INSTITUTIONAL EFFECTS		
A. DEMOGRAPHICS		
1. Changes in general demographic makeup of the population		
a. Size		
b. Density		
c. Migration trends		
d. Age/sex distribution		
e. Marital status		
f. Ethnic groups		
2. Secondary effects related to changes in general demographic makeup of the populations (if not discussed under another category)		
3. Other changes (specify)		
B. EDUCATION		
Change in State Variables		
1. Size of enrollment in schools		

Table 1. *Beneficial and Adverse Effects on Social Well-Being Under the Plan for* ___________

Items in Evaluation Categories	Measures of Impact	Effects ++,+,0,-,--
B. EDUCATION (cont'd.)		
2. Type of enrollment in schools, by age, income, ethnic group, etc.		
3. Level of education of general population		
4. School dropout rates		
Change in Relevant Condition Variables		
5. Birth rates in area		
6. Percent of population of school age		
7. Number of persons 25 and over with four years of high school or more		
Change in System Variables (Quantity & Structure)		
8. Enrollment capacity of schools, by type (elementary, middle, secondary, vocational)		
9. Enrollment capacity of institutions of higher education, by type (post-high school vocational, community college, university)		
10. Number of full-time equivalent teachers in public schools and institutions of higher education		
11. Budget of local Department of Education		
12. Number of instruction rooms in schools		
13. Geographic area of school districts		
14. Location of institutions of higher education		
(Function & Purpose)		
15. Organization and administration of local Department of Education		
16. Ratio of teachers to aides/para-professionals to teachers in public schools		

Table 1. *Beneficial and Adverse Effects on Social Well-Being Under the Plan for* ___________

Items in Evaluation Categories	Measures of Impact	Effects ++,+,0,-,--
B. EDUCATION (cont'd.)		
17. Non-academic services offered by schools (counseling, health, etc.)		
18. Diversity of courses offered in local schools, institutions of higher education		
19. Coordination and conflict among local schools, institutions of higher education		
(Quality & Character)		
20. Distribution of school curricula (academic vs. vocational)		
21. Equality of opportunity for education		
22. Achievement levels of students		
23. Satisfaction with schools among residents		
Change in Other Variables (Specify)		
C. GOVERNMENT OPERATIONS AND SERVICES		
Change in State Variables		
1. Citizen participation in local government (e.g., number and membership of citizen groups in the area whose purpose is assuring good government)		
2. Number of formal municipal government meetings during the last year, percent open to the public		
3. Voting trends (percent voting, party voted for)		
Change in Relevant Condition Variables		
4. Population of area		

Table 1. *Beneficial and Adverse Effects on Social Well-Being Under the Plan for* ___________

Items in Evaluation Categories	Measures of Impact	Effects ++,+,0,-,--
G. GOVERNMENT OPERATIONS AND SERVICES (cont'd.)		
Change in System Variables (Quantity & Structure)		
5. Number of incorporated municipalities, unincorporated communities, with population of each		
6. Number of persons employed by municipal governments		
7. Budgets of local governments		
8. Location of local governments		
9. Amount of revenue coming from local sources (property and sales taxes, sale of property, fines, assessments, fees and licenses, etc.)		
10. Value and purpose of state and federal aid to municipalities during the past year		
(Function & Purpose)		
11. Organization and administration of local governments (e.g., mayor, city council)		
12. Staff types in local government		
13. Services provided by local government (sewage, garbage collection, police & fire protection, etc.), service priorities		
14. Inter- and intra-governmental coordination and conflict		
(Quality & Character)		
15. Accessibility of local governments (location; meetings open to public)		
16. Efficiency and effectiveness of local governments, services provided by local governments		
17. Satisfaction with local government		
Change in Other Variables (Specify)		

Table 1. *Beneficial and Adverse Effects on Social Well-Being Under the Plan for* ____________

Items in Evaluation Categories	Measures of Impact	Effects ++,+,0,-,--
D. HOUSING AND NEIGHBORHOOD		
Change in State Variables		
1. Percent of persons living in substandard housing		
2. Percent of persons living in overcrowded housing		
3. Percent of owner-occupied dwellings		
Change in Relevant Condition Variables		
4. Percent of persons working outside county of residence		
5. Population growth rates		
6. Average income for families and individuals		
Change in System Variables (Quantity & Structure)		
7. Number of dwelling units occupied year round		
8. Number of vacant and seasonal dwelling units		
9. Number of occupied units, by persons per room (1.00 or less, 1.01-1.50, 1.51 or more)		
10. Cost of housing (median value, median monthly contract rent, construction costs)		
11. Location of residential areas		
12. Location of mobile home parks in the area, capacity		
13. Number of new housing starts during the last year		
14. Existence of large areas of land in areas suitable for residential construction		

Table 1. *Beneficial and Adverse Effects on Social Well-Being Under the Plan for* ___________

Items in Evaluation Categories	Measures of Impact	Effects ++,+,0,-,--
D. HOUSING AND NEIGHBORHOOD (cont'd.)		
15. Number of residential construction firms in the area		
(Function & Purpose)		
16. Activities of local housing-related agencies (Department of Housing, Department of Redevelopment, etc.)		
17. Diversity of types of housing available (apartments, duplexes, one-family units, etc.)		
18. Coordination and conflict among local housing-related agencies		
(Quality & Character)		
19. Equality of opportunity for housing		
20. Acres of run-down or dilapidated neighborhoods		
21. Percent of housing units with all plumbing facilities		
Change in Other Variables (Specify)		
E. LAW AND JUSTICE		
Change in State Variables		
1. Civil and criminal code violations as a function of new population and economic characteristics		
2. Civil and criminal code violations as a function of water availability		
3. Type and amount of water-related litigation		

Table 1. *Beneficial and Adverse Effects on Social Well-Being Under the Plan for* ___________

Items in Evaluation Categories	Measures of Impact	Effects ++,+,0,–,––
E. LAW AND JUSTICE (cont'd.)		
Change in Relevant Condition Variables		
4. Percent of families below poverty level		
5. Number of persons unemployed as a percent of total labor force		
Change in System Variables (Quantity & Structure)		
6. Number of courts, police departments, other criminal justice functions		
7. Number of full-time equivalent judges, police officers, prosecutors, public defenders		
8. Inmate capacity of local, county jails		
9. Budget of local criminal justice system		
10. Location of criminal justice functions (courts, police stations, jails, etc.)		
(Function & Purpose)		
11. Jurisdiction, administration of local criminal justice functions		
12. Services provided by local criminal justice system		
13. Coordination and conflict in criminal justice system		
(Quality & Character)		
14. Accessibility of courts, police services, etc.		
15. Opportunity to receive equal treatment under the law		
16. Number of arrests as a percent of reported crimes		

Table 1. *Beneficial and Adverse Effects on Social Well-Being Under the Plan for* ___________

Items in Evaluation Categories	Measures of Impact	Effects ++,+,0,-,--
E. LAW AND JUSTICE (cont'd.)		
17. Number of cases tried as a percent of arrests		
18. Satisfaction with the criminal justice system among residents		
Change in Other Variables (Specify)		
F. SOCIAL SERVICES		
Change in State Variables		
1. Number of persons receiving social services, by type of service received		
Change in Relevant Condition Variables		
2. Number of families below poverty level		
3. Number of families receiving welfare payments, social security, etc.		
4. Number of persons over 65 years of age as a percent of total population		
5. Number of persons unemployed as a percent of total labor force		
Change in System Variables (Quantity & Structure)		
6. Number of social service agencies (public and private)		
7. Service capacity, staff size of social service agencies		
8. Total expenditures on social services		
9. Location of social service agencies		

Table 1. *Beneficial and Adverse Effects on Social Well-Being Under the Plan for ___________*

Items in Evaluation Categories	Measures of Impact	Effects ++,+,0,-,--
F. SOCIAL SERVICES (cont'd.)		
(Function & Purpose)		
10. Organization and administration of social service agencies		
11. Types of staff employed by local social service agencies (professional counselors, volunteers, clergymen, etc.)		
12. Types of social services provided by social service agencies		
13. Coordination and conflict among social service agencies (public vs. public, public vs. private)		
(Quality & Character)		
14. Accessibility of social service agencies (location, provision of outreach services, etc.)		
15. Equality of opportunity to receive social services (by age, ethnic group, etc.)		
16. Efficiency and effectiveness of social service agencies		
17. Satisfaction among residents with social service agencies		
Change in Other Variables (Specify)		
G. RELIGION		
Change in State Variables		
1. Size of church membership, by denomination		
2. Size of parochial school enrollment		
3. Attendance rates at local churches as a percentage of membership		

Table 1. *Beneficial and Adverse Effects on Social Well-Being Under the Plan for* ____________

Items in Evaluation Categories	Measures of Impact	Effects ++,+,0,–,––
G. RELIGION (cont'd.)		
Change in Relevant Condition Variables		
4. Change in ethnic composition of the population		
Change in System Variables (Quantity & Structure)		
5. Number of churches, synagogues, etc.		
6. Number of clergymen per 1,000 population		
7. Budget of local congregations		
8. Location of churches		
9. Property owned by churches (location, size, value, current use)		
(Function & Purpose)		
10. Non-religious public services provided by churches (e.g., parochial schools, counseling services, relief services)		
11. Types of churches, by denomination		
(Quality & Character)		
12. Opportunity to attend services of one's choice		
13. Stands taken by churches in regard to community affairs, results		
Change in Other Variables (Specify)		
H. CULTURE		
Change in State Variables		
1. Ethnic composition of the population		
2. Languages spoken in the area		

Table 1. *Beneficial and Adverse Effects on Social Well-Being Under the Plan for* ____________

Items in Evaluation Categories	Measures of Impact	Effects ++,+,0,-,--
H. CULTURE (cont'd.)		
3. Traditional behavior, values, folkways		
Change in Relevant Condition Variables		
4. Condition of roads going to and from archeological, historical and scientific sites and artifact locations		
Change in System Variables		
5. Number and type of archeological sites (burial mounds, campsites, etc.) in the area		
6. Number and type of historical sites (trails, monuments, etc.) in the area		
7. Number and type of scientific sites in the area		
8. Number and type of preserved artifacts or artifact locations in area		
9. Location of archeological, historical, and scientific sites and artifacts in the area		
10. Accessibility to archeological, historical, and scientific sites and artifacts in the area		
Change in Other Variables (Specify)		
I. RECREATION		
Change in State Variables		
1. Annual use of (attendance at) public recreation facilities		

Table 1. *Beneficial and Adverse Effects on Social Well-Being Under the Plan for* ___________

Items in Evaluation Categories	Measures of Impact	Effects ++,+,0,–,––
I. RECREATION (cont'd.)		
Change in Relevant Condition Variables		
2. Types/condition of roads to and from recreation facilities		
3. Number and types of secondary service facilities in recreation areas (e.g., gas stations, retail stores, restaurants)		
4. Distance to major recreation areas outside the planning area; types of recreation available within a 50-mile radius of planning area		
Change in System Variables (Quantity & Structure)		
5. Number of public facilities used for outdoor recreation (including school facilities), such as golf courses, stadia, etc.		
6. Number of water-related recreation areas (reservoirs, rivers, lakes, etc.)		
7. Staff of local recreation agencies and of public recreation facilities		
8. Budget of local recreation agencies		
9. Area in miles of land used for outdoor recreation (hunting grounds, picnic areas, etc.)		
10. Area in miles of water-related recreation areas		
11. Location of recreation areas within the area		
(Function & Purpose)		
12. Activities and responsibilities of local recreation agencies		
13. Types of recreation available in public facilities and water and land areas		

Table 1. *Beneficial and Adverse Effects on Social Well-Being Under the Plan for* ___________

Items in Evaluation Categories	Measures of Impact	Effects ++,+,0,-,--
I. RECREATION (cont'd.)		
14. Coordination and conflict in public sector recreation		
(Quantity & Structure)		
15. Accessibility of recreation areas (distance from population centers)		
16. Cost of recreation, by type		
17. Equality of opportunity to use public recreation facilities		
18. Satisfaction among residents with recreation areas, facilities		
Change in Other Variables (Specify)		
J. INFORMAL ORGANIZATIONS AND GROUPS		
Change in State Variables		
1. Size, composition of membership in various informal organizations and groups		
2. Extent of public participation in the planning process as a result of membership in/activities of informal organizations and groups		
Change in System Variables		
3. Number and types of informal organizations and groups (ethnic, religious, service-oriented, environmentally-oriented, etc.)		
4. Organization and administration of informal organizations and groups		
5. Types of activities engaged in by informal organizations and groups		
6. Stands taken on community issues, including on plan(s) by informal organizations and groups		

Table 1. *Beneficial and Adverse Effects on Social Well-Being Under the Plan for* ____________

Items in Evaluation Categories	Measures of Impact	Effects ++,+,0,-,--
J. INFORMAL ORGANIZATIONS AND GROUPS (cont'd.)		
7. Power position in the community of different informal organizations and groups		
8. Cohesion, solidarity within informal organizations and groups		
9. Coordination and conflict among various informal organizations and groups		
Change in Other Variables (Specify)		
K. COMMUNITY AND INSTITUTIONAL VIABILITY		
1. Changes in individual institutions as they affect each other		
a. Size (number of staff, facilities, service capacity)		
b. Type		
c. Location		
d. Organization and administration		
e. Services provided		
f. Accessibility		
g. New institutions created		
2. Changes in institutional inter-relationships		
a. Coordination		
b. Conflict		
c. "Balance of power"		
3. Changes in community viability		
a. Residents' image of their community		
b. Outside image of the community		

Table 1. *Beneficial and Adverse Effects on Social Well-Being Under the Plan for ____________*

Items in Evaluation Categories	Measures of Impact	Effects ++,+,0,-,--
K. COMMUNITY AND INSTITUTIONAL VIABILITY (cont'd.)		
c. Community solidarity		
4. Other changes (specify)		
III. AREA, SOCIOECONOMIC EFFECTS		
A. EMPLOYMENT AND REAL INCOME		
Change in State Variables		
1. Percent of workers by type		
2. Number of persons unemployed as a percent of total labor force		
3. Percent of persons unemployed by occupational category		
4. Percent of families and unrelated individuals by income level		
5. Mean income by class of worker or recipient		
6. Estimated percent of non-residents in area labor force		
7. Percent of persons below poverty level		
Changes in Relevant Condition Variables		
8. Number of business establishments opened, closed during a year period		

Table 1. *Beneficial and Adverse Effects on Social Well-Being Under the Plan for ___________*

Items in Evaluation Categories	Measures of Impact	Effects ++,+,0,–,––
A. EMPLOYMENT AND REAL INCOME (cont'd.)		
Change in System Variables (Quantity & Structure)		
9. Total employers by employment size class (small: 1-19; medium: 20-99; large: 100 or more)		
10. Number of job placement agencies, vocational education schools (school-related, post-high school)		
11. Staff size of job placement agencies and vocational education schools (including job placement officers & employment counselors)		
12. Total employed persons 16 years of age and over		
13. Total amount spent for job placement activities, vocational education		
14. Location of job placement agencies, vocational education schools		
(Function & Purpose)		
15. Percent of employed population by occupational category		
16. Types of job training and vocational education offered		
17. Activities of local office of U.S. Employment Service		
18. Coordination and conflict among employers; among vocational schools; among placement agencies		
19. Accessibility of vocational education schools (distance from population center; cost to attend)		

Table 1. *Beneficial and Adverse Effects on Social Well-Being Under the Plan for* ___________

Items in Evaluation Categories	Measures of Impact	Effects ++,+,0,-,--
A. EMPLOYMENT AND REAL INCOME (cont'd.)		
20. Accessibility of job placement agencies (distance from population center)		
21. Opportunity for equal employment		
22. Efficiency and effectiveness of vocational education schools (e.g., number of persons trained)		
23. Efficiency and effectiveness of job placement agencies (e.g., number of persons placed)		
24. Satisfaction among residents with employment, income		
Change in Other Variables (Specify)		
B. WELFARE AND FINANCIAL COMPENSATION		
Change in State Variables		
1. Number of persons receiving welfare services as a percent of total population		
2. Percent of persons receiving different types of welfare services		
3. Number of persons receiving financial compensation as percent of total population		
4. Percent of persons receiving different types of financial compensation		
Change in Relevant Condition Variables		
5. Number of persons below poverty level		
6. Number of persons unemployed as percent of total labor force		

Table 1. *Beneficial and Adverse Effects on Social Well-Being Under the Plan for* ___________

Items in Evaluation Categories	Measures of Impact	Effects ++,+,0,−,−−
B. WELFARE AND FINANCIAL COMPENSATION (cont'd.)		
Change in System Variables *(Quantity & Structure)*		
7. Number of public and private welfare agencies		
8. Staff size of welfare agencies		
9. Public welfare expenditures		
10. Location of public and private welfare agencies		
(Function & Purpose)		
11. Types of staff employed by public, private welfare agencies (professionals vs. volunteers)		
12. Services provided by public, private welfare agencies		
13. Coordination and conflict among welfare agencies (public vs. public, public vs. private)		
(Quality & Character)		
14. Accessibility of welfare agencies		
15. Distribution of welfare benefits (by income level, ethnic groups, age, etc.)		
16. Efficiency and effectiveness of welfare agencies		
17. Satisfaction with welfare system among residents		
Change in Other Variables (Specify)		
C. COMMUNICATIONS		
Change in State Variables		
1. Communications pathways		

Table 1. *Beneficial and Adverse Effects on Social Well-Being Under the Plan for* ____________

Items in Evaluation Categories	Measures of Impact	Effects ++,+,0,-,--
C. COMMUNICATIONS (cont'd.)		
Change in Relevant Condition Variables		
2. Total population		
Change in System Variables *(Quantity & Structure)*		
3. Number of households with at least one television set, radio, telephone		
4. Circulation of newspapers (local and out-of-town) per 100 residents		
5. Equipment of news, communications media		
6. Budget of news, communications media		
7. Location of radio and television broadcasting stations in the area; location of local newspaper publisher(s)		
(Function & Purpose)		
8. Number of local television, radio and newspaper reporters		
9. Number of television, radio stations (AM/FM) received in the area at 6 pm		
10. Number of minutes per week of radio and television reporting time devoted to local news		
11. Coordination, conflict among local communications media (e.g., stands taken by different radio or television station, newspapers)		
(Quality & Character)		
12. Effectiveness of local news, communications media in the area in regard to local issues		
13. Satisfaction among residents with local news, communications media		
Change in Other Variables (Specify)		

Table 1. *Beneficial and Adverse Effects on Social Well-Being Under the Plan for* ___________

Items in Evaluation Categories	Measures of Impact	Effects ++,+,0,-,--
D. TRANSPORTATION		
Change in State Variables		
1. Number of licensed drivers in the area		
2. Transportation use patterns		
Change in Relevant Condition Variables		
3. Percent of workers by place of work (inside, outside county of residence)		
Change in System Variables (Quantity & Structure)		
4. Size of water transportation facilities in the planning area, by type		
5. Number of major highways into, out of the area		
6. Total street miles in the area		
7. Number of cars registered in the area		
8. Total tons of commercial freight carried into, out of the area in a year period		
9. Total passengers coming into the area by means of public transportation		
10. Number of miles from population center of the area to major facilities (train station, retail center, schools, etc.)		
(Function & Purpose)		
11. Types of public transportation available in the area		
12. Coordination and conflict among public transportation operations		

Table 1. *Beneficial and Adverse Effects on Social Well-Being Under the Plan for ____________*

Items in Evaluation Categories	Measures of Impact	Effects ++,+,0,-,--
D. TRANSPORTATION (cont'd.)		
(Quality & Character)		
13. Accessibility of different forms of public transportation (distance to stations from center of population, costs of transportation)		
14. Equality of opportunity to use public, private transportation		
15. Efficiency and effectiveness of various forms of public transportation		
16. Condition of streets, roads, and highways		
17. Satisfaction among residents with public transportation		
Change in Other Variables (Specify)		
E. ECONOMIC BASE		
Change in State Variables		
1. Percent of persons employed by Standard Industrial Code (SIC) category		
2. Percent of persons employed in agriculture		
3. Tax dollars allocated to human services		
4. Number of persons unemployed as a percent of total labor force		
Change in Relevant Condition Variables		
5. Number of persons at work by place of residence		

Table 1. *Beneficial and Adverse Effects on Social Well-Being Under the Plan for* ___________

Items in Evaluation Categories	Measures of Impact	Effects ++,+,0,–,––
E. ECONOMIC BASE (cont'd.)		
6. Percent of retail trade carried on outside the area by residents of the area (shopping for food, clothes, household goods and services, automobiles)		
7. Percentage of owner-occupied dwelling units		
Change in System Variables (Quantity & Structure)		
8. Number of establishments by SIC category		
9. Number of farms in the area		
10. Number of government units in the area		
11. Size of establishments (small, medium and large)		
12. Percent of land used for grazing and farming		
13. Total taxable payroll by SIC category		
14. Total value of farm products (all crops, livestock and livestock products, dairy and dairy products, poultry and poultry products)		
15. Estimated full value of property		
16. Value of new capital investments in the area during past year		
17. Location of establishments by SIC category		
(Function & Purpose)		
18. Coordination and conflict among establishments, between industry and agriculture		

Table 1. *Beneficial and Adverse Effects on Social Well-Being Under the Plan for* ____________

Items in Evaluation Categories	Measures of Impact	Effects ++,+,0,–,––
E. ECONOMIC BASE (cont'd.)		
(Quality and Character)		
19. Accessibility (distance from population center to places of employment)		
20. Satisfaction with economic base		
Change in Other Variables (Specify)		
F. PLANNING		
1. Effects of planning activities for water resource project on the local population:		
a. Employment		
b. Land (e.g., farm) and home improvement		
c. Personal plans		
d. Other (specify)		
2. Effects of planning activities for water resource project on local government		
a. Community planning		
b. Equipment and facilities maintenance		
c. Intercommunity cooperation and conflict		
d. Other (specify)		
3. Effects of planning activities for water resource project on local economy		
a. Attraction for new industry		

Table 1. *Beneficial and Adverse Effects on Social Well-Being Under the Plan for* ____________

Items in Evaluation Categories	Measures of Impact	Effects ++,+,0,–,––
F. PLANNING (cont'd.)		
b. Attraction for investment in agriculture		
c. Attraction for new capital investments		
d. Other (specify)		
4. Effects of planning activities for water resource project on external investors		
a. Bond issues		
b. Quality of bond ratings		
c. Other (specify)		
5. Other effects of planning activities for water resource project (specify)		
G. CONSTRUCTION		
1. Short-term effects		
a. Influx of workers		
b. Change in demand for public and private services associated with short-term influx of workers		
c. Requirements for transient housing		
d. Physical disruption (noise, dust, road blockage or diversion, etc.)		
e. Other short-term effects (specify)		
2. Long-term effects		
a. Population change		

Table 1. *Beneficial and Adverse Effects on Social Well-Being Under the Plan for __________*

Items in Evaluation Categories	Measures of Impact	Effects ++,+,0,-,--
G. CONSTRUCTION (cont'd.)		
b. Changes in public and private services available		
c. Housing patterns		
d. Physical effects		
e. Other long-term effects (specify)		
IV. NATIONAL, EMERGENCY PREPAREDNESS EFFECTS		
A. WATER SUPPLIES		
1. Changes in amount of water available		
2. Changes in stability of the water supply		
3. Changes in quality of water available		
4. Other changes (specify)		
B. FOOD PRODUCTION		
1. Changes in potential for reserve food production		
2. Changes in types of crops produced (for human vs. animal vs. industrial consumption)		
3. Other changes (specify)		

Table 1. *Beneficial and Adverse Effects on Social Well-Being Under the Plan for ____________*

Items in Evaluation Categories	Measures of Impact	Effects ++,+,0,–,––
C. POWER SUPPLIES		
1. Changes in the amount of power produced		
2. Changes in the stability of the power supply		
3. Changes in transmission potential for power supplies		
4. Changes in response time for emergency power		
5. Other changes (specify)		
D. WATER TRANSPORTATION		
1. Changes in the number of miles of useable water transportation system		
2. Changes in tonnage support capacity of water transportation system		
3. Changes in network location characteristics of water transportation system		
4. Other changes (specify)		
E. SCARCE FUELS		
1. Changes in the amount of scarce fuels (oil and natural gas) consumed for various purposes		
2. Changes in use patterns of scarce vs. abundant fuels (e.g., coal)		
3. Changes in use of alternative power sources (e.g., solar, hydroelectric)		
4. Other changes (specify)		

Table 1. *Beneficial and Adverse Effects on Social Well-Being Under the Plan for* ____________

Items in Evaluation Categories	Measures of Impact	Effects ++,+,0,–,––
F. POPULATION DISPERSION		
1. Changes in the amount of water available in sparsely settled areas		
2. Changes in the quality of water available, and concomitant potential for human consumption and other uses		
3. Changes in water transportation routes for population dispersion		
4. Other changes (specify)		
G. INDUSTRIAL DISPERSION		
1. Changes in the amount of water available in previously nonindustrialized areas		
2. Changes in the quality of water available and concomitant potential for industrial uses		
3. Changes in water transportation routes for industrial dispersion		
4. Other changes (specify)		
H. MILITARY PREPAREDNESS		
1. Changes in the amount of water available		
2. Changes in the quality of water available and concomitant potential for human consumption and other uses		
3. Other changes (specify)		

Table 1. *Beneficial and Adverse Effects on Social Well-Being Under the Plan for* ____________

Items in Evaluation Categories	Measures of Impact	Effects ++,+,0,-,--
I. INTERNATIONAL TREATY OBLIGATIONS		
1. Changes in the water use patterns for bodies of water regulated by international treaties		
2. Changes in the inherent nature of bodies of water regulated by international treaties (e.g., riverbed diversion)		
3. Other changes (specify)		
V. AGGREGATE SOCIAL EFFECTS		
A. CHANGES IN QUALITY OF LIFE		
1. Quality of self-development		
2. Quality of family and interpersonal relations		
3. General health, peace of mind, motivation		
4. Standard of living (income, housing, recreation)		
5. Satisfaction with local culture and community		
6. Perceived equality of opportunity to benefit from changes in the community		
7. Other (specify)		

Table 1. *Beneficial and Adverse Effects on Social Well-Being Under the Plan for* ___________

Items in Evaluation Categories	Measures of Impact	Effects ++,+,0,-,--
B. CHANGES IN RELATIVE SOCIAL POSITION		
1. Equal opportunity to receive benefits from plan implementation and relationship to need		
2. Equity of distribution of social and economic costs and relationship to ability to pay		
3. Other (specify)		
C. CHANGES IN SOCIAL WELL-BEING		
1. General improvement in the quantity and quality of public and private services available to the public		
2. General improvement in the ability of community institutions to cooperate with one another		
3. Economic stability of the area		
4. Improved personal income levels		
5. Enhanced security of life through reduction in water-related risks		
6. Improved population distribution in terms of male/female balance among age groups, dependency ratios, etc.		
7. Improvement in stability of values and norms in the community		
8. Other (specify)		

Table 2. *A Summary Comparison of the Beneficial and Adverse Effects of the Alternative Plans for the Social Well-Being Account*

Items in Evaluation Categories	Present Conditions	Beneficial & Adverse Effects of Plans					
		No Plan	NED Plan	EQ Plan	ALT "X"	ALT "Y"	RECCO Plan
I. INDIVIDUAL, PERSONAL EFFECTS							
A. LIFE, PROTECTION AND SAFETY							
Change in State Variables							
1. Number of persons served by each agency, by services received							
2. Property loss due to water-related natural disasters							
3. Life loss due to water-related natural disasters							
Change in Relevant Condition Variables							
4. Climatic trends over next decade (based upon present trends)							
Change in System Variables (Quantity & Structure)							
5. Number and type of agencies which deal with natural disasters (e.g., Civil Defense, flood control agencies)							
6. Staff size and budget of agencies which deal with natural disasters							
7. Location of agencies which deal with natural disasters (distance from population centers of communities under consideration for plan implementation)							
(Function & Purpose)							
8. Governmental level at which agencies dealing with natural disasters are located (e.g., local, county, state)							

•Conditions (Above to below Average: AA,A,BA); Effects (Beneficial to Adverse: ++,+,0,-,--).

Table 2. *A Summary Comparison of the Beneficial and Adverse Effects of the Alternative Plans for the Social Well-Being Account*

Items in Evaluation Categories	Present Conditions	Beneficial & Adverse Effects of Plans					
		No Plan	NED Plan	EQ Plan	ALT "X"	ALT "Y"	RECCO Plan
A. LIFE, PROTECTION AND SAFETY (cont'd.)							
9. Staff types of agencies dealing with natural disasters (i.e., professional or volunteer)							
10. Services provided by agencies which deal with natural disasters (e.g., financial, medical)							
11. Coordination or conflict among agencies dealing with natural disasters							
(Quality & Character)							
12. Accessibility of agencies which deal with natural disasters							
13. Efficiency and effectiveness of agencies which deal with natural disasters							
Change in Other Variables (Specify)							
B. HEALTH							
Change in State Variables							
1. Morbidity levels, by type of disease							
2. Mortality levels, by type of mortality (type of disease, accident, natural causes, etc.)							
Change in Relevant Condition Variables							
3. Distribution of pollution levels in terms of noxious stimuli (air, noise, water, land)							
4. Number of disease-carrying organisms							

*Conditions (Above to below Average: AA,A,BA); Effects (Beneficial to Adverse: ++,+,0,–,– –).

Table 2. *A Summary Comparison of the Beneficial and Adverse Effects of the Alternative Plans for the Social Well-Being Account*

Items in Evaluation Categories	Present Conditions	Beneficial & Adverse Effects of Plans					
		No Plan	NED Plan	EQ Plan	ALT "X"	ALT "Y"	RECCO Plan
B. HEALTH (cont'd.)							
5. Provision of various sanitation services (sewage, garbage disposal, etc.)							
Change in System Variables (Quantity & Structure)							
6. Number of out-patient care facilities							
7. Number of in-patient beds per 1,000 population							
8. Number of health care personnel in area							
9. Budgets of in-patient, out-patient care facilities							
10. Location of health care facilities							
(Function & Purpose)							
11. Organization and administration of local or county health department							
12. Types of staff in local health care facilities (ratio of doctors to nurses to aides, ratio of GPs to specialists); staff type of health care personnel overall in area							
13. Services provided by health care facilities (e.g., special services such as radiation therapy); activities of health agencies							
14. Diversity of types of health care facilities							
15. Coordination and conflict among health service providers							
16. Cost of health care services							

*Conditions (Above to below Average: AA,A,BA); Effects (Beneficial to Adverse: ++,+,0,-,--).

Table 2. *A Summary Comparison of the Beneficial and Adverse Effects of the Alternative Plans for the Social Well-Being Account*

Items in Evaluation Categories	Present Conditions	Beneficial & Adverse Effects of Plans					
		No Plan	NED Plan	EQ Plan	ALT "X"	ALT "Y"	RECCO Plan
B. HEALTH (cont'd.)							
17. Physical distribution of types of health care services (private physicians, hospitals, etc.)							
18. Equality of opportunity to receive health care							
19. Efficiency and effectiveness of health care facilities and agencies (e.g., time required to receive treatment, amount of preventive care provided)							
20. Satisfaction with health care services among residents							
Change in Other Variables (Specify)							
C. FAMILY AND INDIVIDUAL							
Change in State Variables							
1. Number of families in the area							
2. Number of single persons in the area							
3. Family composition (percent husband-wife, female-headed)							
Change in Relevant Condition Variables							
4. Number of families below poverty level							
5. Number of persons unemployed as a percent of total labor force							
6. Number of annual cases in juvenile courts, family courts							

*Conditions (Above to below Average: AA,A,BA); Effects (Beneficial to Adverse: ++,+,0,-,--).

Table 2. *A Summary Comparison of the Beneficial and Adverse Effects of the Alternative Plans for the Social Well-Being Account*

Items in Evaluation Categories	Present Conditions	Beneficial & Adverse Effects of Plans					
		No Plan	NED Plan	EQ Plan	ALT "X"	ALT "Y"	RECCO Plan
C. FAMILY AND INDIVIDUAL (cont'd.)							
7. Number of divorces as a percent of total marriages							
Change in System Variables (Quantity & Structure)							
8. Number of family-related service agencies in the area							
9. Staff size of family-related service agencies							
10. Number of family and personal counselors in the area (not in agencies)							
11. Location of family-related service agencies (distance from population centers)							
(Function & Purpose)							
12. Types of family and individual counselors in the area, both private and in agencies (e.g., ministers vs. psychologists vs. social workers vs. psychiatrists)							
13. Services provided by family-related agencies							
14. Coordination and conflict among family and individual services in the area							
(Quality & Character)							
15. Accessibility of family and individual services							
16. Equality of opportunity to obtain family and individual services							

*Conditions (Above to below Average: AA,A,BA); Effects (Beneficial to Adverse: ++,+,0,-,--).

Table 2. *A Summary Comparison of the Beneficial and Adverse Effects of the Alternative Plans for the Social Well-Being Account*

Items in Evaluation Categories	Present Conditions	Beneficial & Adverse Effects of Plans					
		No Plan	NED Plan	EQ Plan	ALT "X"	ALT "Y"	RECCO Plan
C. FAMILY AND INDIVIDUAL (cont'd.)							
17. Number of persons served annually by individual and family services							
18. Satisfaction with family and individual services among residents							
Change in Other Variables (Specify)							
D. ATTITUDES, BELIEFS AND VALUES							
1. Resident expectations of what will be the impacts of this plan, and their attitudes about the effects:							
a. Local environment							
b. Local economy							
c. Local community							
d. Population characteristics and composition							
e. Local participation in decision-making							
f. Local values, customs, and folkways							
g. Local opportunity to benefit from plan implementation							
h. Local absorption of adverse effects of the plan							

*Conditions (Above to below Average: AA,A,BA); Effects (Beneficial to Adverse: ++,+,0,–,––).

Table 2. *A Summary Comparison of the Beneficial and Adverse Effects of the Alternative Plans for the Social Well-Being Account*

Items in Evaluation Categories	Present Conditions	Beneficial & Adverse Effects of Plans					
		No Plan	NED Plan	EQ Plan	ALT "X"	ALT "Y"	RECCO Plan
D. ATTITUDES, BELIEFS AND VALUES (cont'd.)							
2. Residents' perceptions of government agencies implementing this plan, and their reactions toward the agencies if the plan is implemented							
a. Federal agencies							
b. State agencies							
c. Local agencies							
3. Other attitudes (specify)							
E. ENVIRONMENTAL CONSIDERATIONS							
1. Changes in the environment as they affect residents' mental and physical well-being:							
a. Aesthetic (visual) quality							
b. Pollution levels (odor, land, water, etc.)							
c. Accessibility to scenic or recreational sites							
d. Land and water use patterns							
2. Changes in personal concern with environmental protection:							
a. Number, existence of groups involved in environmental issues							

*Conditions (Above to below Average: AA,A,BA); Effects (Beneficial to Adverse: ++,+,0,-,--).

Table 2. *A Summary Comparison of the Beneficial and Adverse Effects of the Alternative Plans for the Social Well-Being Account*

Items in Evaluation Categories	Present Conditions	Beneficial & Adverse Effects of Plans					
		No Plan	NED Plan	EQ Plan	ALT "X"	ALT "Y"	RECCO Plan
E. ENVIRONMENTAL CONSIDERATIONS (cont'd.)							
b. Activities of groups involved in environmental issues							
c. Coordination among groups involved in environmental issues							
d. Conflict among environmental groups, between groups and other institutions (local, state, national)							
3. Other changes (specify)							
II. COMMUNITY, INSTITUTIONAL EFFECTS							
A. DEMOGRAPHICS							
1. Changes in general demographic makeup of the population							
a. Size							
b. Density							
c. Migration trends							
d. Age/sex distribution							
e. Marital status							
f. Ethnic groups							
2. Secondary effects related to changes in general demographic makeup of the populations (if not discussed under another category)							

*Conditions (Above to below Average: AA,A,BA); Effects (Beneficial to Adverse: ++,+,0,–,––).

Table 2. *A Summary Comparison of the Beneficial and Adverse Effects of the Alternative Plans for the Social Well-Being Account*

Items in Evaluation Categories	Present Conditions	Beneficial & Adverse Effects of Plans					
		No Plan	NED Plan	EQ Plan	ALT "X"	ALT "Y"	RECCO Plan
A. DEMOGRAPHICS (cont'd.)							
3. Other changes (specify)							
B. EDUCATION							
Change in State Variables							
1. Size of enrollment in schools							
2. Type of enrollment in schools, by age, income, ethnic group, etc.							
3. Level of education of general population							
4. School dropout rates							
Change in Relevant Condition Variables							
5. Birth rates in area							
6. Percent of population of school age							
7. Number of persons 25 and over with four years of high school or more							
Change in System Variables (Quantity & Structure)							
8. Enrollment capacity of schools, by type (elementary, middle, secondary, vocational)							
9. Enrollment capacity of institutions of higher education, by type (post-high school vocational, community college, university)							
10. Number of full-time equivalent teachers in public schools and institutions of higher education							
11. Budget of local Department of Education							

•Conditions (Above to below Average: AA,A,BA); Effects (Beneficial to Adverse: ++,+,0,-,--).

Table 2. *A Summary Comparison of the Beneficial and Adverse Effects of the Alternative Plans for the Social Well-Being Account*

Items in Evaluation Categories	Present Conditions	Beneficial & Adverse Effects of Plans					
		No Plan	NED Plan	EQ Plan	ALT "X"	ALT "Y"	RECCO Plan
B. EDUCATION (cont'd.)							
12. Number of instruction rooms in schools							
13. Geographic area of school districts							
14. Location of institutions of higher education							
(Function & Purpose)							
15. Organization and administration of local Department of Education							
16. Ratio of teachers to aides/ paraprofessionals to teachers in public schools							
17. Non-academic services offered by schools (counseling, health, etc.)							
18. Diversity of courses offered in local schools, institutions of higher education							
19. Coordination and conflict among local schools, institutions of higher education							
(Quality & Character)							
20. Distribution of school curricula (academic vs. vocational)							
21. Equality of opportunity for education							
22. Achievement levels of students							
23. Satisfaction with schools among residents							
Change in Other Variables (Specify)							

*Conditions (Above to below Average: AA,A,BA); Effects (Beneficial to Adverse: ++,+,0,-,--).

Table 2. *A Summary Comparison of the Beneficial and Adverse Effects of the Alternative Plans for the Social Well-Being Account*

Items in Evaluation Categories	Present Conditions	Beneficial & Adverse Effects of Plans					
		No Plan	NED Plan	EQ Plan	ALT "X"	ALT "Y"	RECCO Plan
C. GOVERNMENT OPERATIONS AND SERVICES							
Change in State Variables							
1. Citizen participation in local government (e.g., number and membership of citizen groups in the area whose purpose is assuring good government)							
2. Number of formal municipal government meetings during the last year, percent open to public							
3. Voting trends (percent voting, party voted for)							
Change in Relevant Condition Variables							
4. Population of area							
Change in System Variables (Quantity & Structure)							
5. Number of incorporated municipalities, unincorporated communities, with population of each							
6. Number of persons employed by municipal governments							
7. Budgets of local governments							
8. Location of local governments							
9. Amount of revenue coming from local sources (property and sales taxes, sale of property, fines, assessments, fees and licenses, etc.)							
10. Value and purpose of state and federal aid to municipalities during the past year							

*Conditions (Above to below Average: AA,A,BA); Effects (Beneficial to Adverse: ++,+,0,-,--).

Table 2. *A Summary Comparison of the Beneficial and Adverse Effects of the Alternative Plans for the Social Well-Being Account*

Items in Evaluation Categories	Present Conditions	Beneficial & Adverse Effects of Plans					
		No Plan	NED Plan	EQ Plan	ALT "X"	ALT "Y"	RECCO Plan
C. GOVERNMENT OPERATIONS AND SERVICES (cont'd.)							
(Function & Purpose)							
11. Organization and administration of local governments (e.g., mayor, city council)							
12. Staff types in local government							
13. Services provided by local government (sewage, garbage collection, police & fire protection, etc.), service priorities							
14. Inter- and intra-governmental coordination and conflict							
(Quality & Character)							
15. Accessibility of local governments (location; meetings open to public)							
16. Efficiency and effectiveness of local governments, services provided by local governments							
17. Satisfaction with local government							
Change in Other Variables (Specify)							
D. HOUSING AND NEIGHBORHOOD							
Change in State Variables							
1. Percent of persons living in substandard housing							
2. Percent of persons living in overcrowded housing							
3. Percent of owner-occupied dwellings							

*Conditions (Above to below Average: AA,A,BA); Effects (Beneficial to Adverse: ++,+,0,–,– –).

Table 2. *A Summary Comparison of the Beneficial and Adverse Effects of the Alternative Plans for the Social Well-Being Account*

Items in Evaluation Categories	Present Conditions	Beneficial & Adverse Effects of Plans					
		No Plan	NED Plan	EQ Plan	ALT "X"	ALT "Y"	RECCO Plan
D. HOUSING AND NEIGHBORHOOD (cont'd.)							
Change in Relevant Condition Variables							
4. Percent of persons working outside county of residence							
5. Population growth rates							
6. Average income for families and individuals							
Change in System Variables (Quantity & Structure)							
7. Number of dwelling units occupied year round							
8. Number of vacant and seasonal dwelling units							
9. Number of occupied units, by persons per room (1.00 or less, 1.01-1.50, 1.51 or more)							
10. Cost of housing (median value, median monthly contract rent, construction costs)							
11. Location of residential areas							
12. Location of mobile home parks in the area, capacity							
13. Number of new housing starts during the last year							
14. Existence of large areas of land in areas suitable for residential construction							
15. Number of residential construction firms in the area							
(Function & Purpose)							
16. Activities of local housing-related agencies (Department of Housing, Department of Redevelopment, etc.)							

*Conditions (Above to below Average: AA,A,BA); Effects (Beneficial to Adverse: ++,+,0,-,--).

Table 2. *A Summary Comparison of the Beneficial and Adverse Effects of the Alternative Plans for the Social Well-Being Account*

Items in Evaluation Categories	Present Conditions	Beneficial & Adverse Effects of Plans					
		No Plan	NED Plan	EQ Plan	ALT "X"	ALT "Y"	RECCO Plan
D. HOUSING AND NEIGHBORHOOD (cont'd.)							
17. Diversity of types of housing available (apartments, duplexes, one-family units, etc.)							
18. Coordination and conflict among local housing-related agencies							
(Quality & Character)							
19. Equality of opportunity for housing							
20. Acres of run-down or dilapidated neighborhoods							
21. Percent of housing units with all plumbing facilities							
Change in Other Variables (Specify)							
E. LAW AND JUSTICE							
Change in State Variables							
1. Civil and criminal code violations as a function of new population and economic characteristics							
2. Civil and criminal code violations as a function of water availability							
3. Type and amount of water-related litigation							
Change in Relevant Condition Variables							
4. Percent of families below poverty level							
5. Number of persons unemployed as a percent of total labor force							

*Conditions (Above to below Average: AA,A,BA); Effects (Beneficial to Adverse: ++,+,0,-,--).

Table 2. *A Summary Comparison of the Beneficial and Adverse Effects of the Alternative Plans for the Social Well-Being Account*

Items in Evaluation Categories	Present Conditions	Beneficial & Adverse Effects of Plans					
		No Plan	NED Plan	EQ Plan	ALT "X"	ALT "Y"	RECCO Plan
E. LAW AND JUSTICE (cont'd.)							
Change in System Variables (Quantity & Structure)							
6. Number of courts, police departments, other criminal justice functions							
7. Number of full-time equivalent judges, police officers, prosecutors, public defenders							
8. Inmate capacity of local, county jails							
9. Budget of local criminal justice system							
10. Location of criminal justice functions (courts, police stations, jails, etc.)							
(Function & Purpose)							
11. Jurisdiction, administration of local criminal justice functions							
12. Services provided by local criminal justice system							
13. Coordination and conflict in criminal justice system							
(Quality & Character)							
14. Accessibility of courts, police services, etc.							
15. Opportunity to receive equal treatment under the law							
16. Number of arrests as a percent of reported crimes							
17. Number of cases tried as a percent of arrests							
18. Satisfaction with the criminal justice system among residents							

*Conditions (Above to below Average: AA,A,BA); Effects (Beneficial to Adverse: ++,+,0,-,--).

Table 2. *A Summary Comparison of the Beneficial and Adverse Effects of the Alternative Plans for the Social Well-Being Account*

Items in Evaluation Categories	Present Conditions	Beneficial & Adverse Effects of Plans					
		No Plan	NED Plan	EQ Plan	ALT "X"	ALT "Y"	RECCO Plan
E. LAW AND JUSTICE (cont'd.)							
Change in Other Variables (Specify)							
F. SOCIAL SERVICES							
Change in State Variables							
1. Number of persons receiving social services, by type of service received							
Change in Relevant Condition Variables							
2. Number of families below poverty level							
3. Number of families receiving welfare payments, social security, etc.							
4. Number of persons over 65 years of age as a percent of total population							
5. Number of persons unemployed as a percent of total labor force							
Change in System Variables (Quantity & Structure)							
6. Number of social service agencies (public and private)							
7. Service capacity, staff size of social service agencies							
8. Total expenditures on social services							
9. Location of social service agencies							
(Function & Purpose)							
10. Organization and administration of social service agencies							

*Conditions (Above to below Average: AA,A,BA); Effects (Beneficial to Adverse: ++,+,0,-,--).

Table 2. *A Summary Comparison of the Beneficial and Adverse Effects of the Alternative Plans for the Social Well-Being Account*

Items in Evaluation Categories	Present Conditions	Beneficial & Adverse Effects of Plans					
		No Plan	NED Plan	EQ Plan	ALT "X"	ALT "Y"	RECCO Plan
F. SOCIAL SERVICES (cont'd.)							
11. Types of staff employed by local social service agencies (professional counselors, volunteers, clergymen, etc.)							
12. Types of social services provided by social service agencies							
13. Coordination and conflict among social service agencies (public vs. public, public vs. private)							
(Quality & Character)							
14. Accessibility of social service agencies (location, provision of outreach services, etc.)							
15. Equality of opportunity to receive social services (by age, ethnic groups, etc.)							
16. Efficiency and effectiveness of social service agencies							
17. Satisfaction among residents with social service agencies							
Change in Other Variables (Specify)							
G. RELIGION							
Change in State Variables							
1. Size of church membership, by denomination							
2. Size of parochial school enrollment							
3. Attendance rates at local churches as a percentage of membership							

*Conditions (Above to below Average: AA,A,BA); Effects (Beneficial to Adverse: ++,+,0,-,--).

Table 2. *A Summary Comparison of the Beneficial and Adverse Effects of the Alternative Plans for the Social Well-Being Account*

Items in Evaluation Categories	Present Conditions	Beneficial & Adverse Effects of Plans					
		No Plan	NED Plan	EQ Plan	ALT "X"	ALT "Y"	RECCO Plan
G. RELIGION (cont'd.)							
Change in Relevant Condition Variables							
4. Change in ethnic composition of the population							
Change in System Variables (Quantity & Structure)							
5. Number of churches, synagogues, etc.							
6. Number of clergymen per 1,000 population							
7. Budget of local congregations							
8. Location of churches							
9. Property owned by churches (location, size, value, current use)							
(Function & Purpose)							
10. Non-religious public services provided by churches (e.g., parochial schools, counseling services, relief services)							
11. Types of churches, by denomination							
(Quality & Character)							
12. Opportunity to attend services of one's choice							
13. Stands taken by churches in regard to community affairs, results							
Change in Other Variables (Specify)							

*Conditions (Above to below Average: AA,A,BA); Effects (Beneficial to Adverse: ++,+,0,–,––).

Table 2. *A Summary Comparison of the Beneficial and Adverse Effects of the Alternative Plans for the Social Well-Being Account*

Items in Evaluation Categories	Present Conditions	Beneficial & Adverse Effects of Plans					
		No Plan	NED Plan	EQ Plan	ALT "X"	ALT "Y"	RECCO Plan
H. CULTURE							
Change in State Variables							
1. Ethnic composition of the population							
2. Languages spoken in the area							
3. Traditional behavior, values, folkways							
Change in Relevant Condition Variables							
4. Condition of roads going to and from archeological, historical and scientific sites and artifact locations							
Change in System Variables							
5. Number and type of archeological sites (burial mounds, campsites, etc.) in the area							
6. Number and type of historical sites (trails, monuments, etc.) in the area							
7. Number and type of scientific sites in the area							
8. Number and type of preserved artifacts or artifact locations in the area							
9. Location of archeological, historical, and scientific sites and artifacts in the area							
10. Accessibility to archeological, historical, and scientific sites and artifacts in the area							
Change in Other Variables (Specify)							

•Conditions (Above to below Average: AA,A,BA); Effects (Beneficial to Adverse: ++,+,0,-,--).

Table 2. *A Summary Comparison of the Beneficial and Adverse Effects of the Alternative Plans for the Social Well-Being Account*

Items in Evaluation Categories	Present Conditions	Beneficial & Adverse Effects of Plans					
		No Plan	NED Plan	EQ Plan	ALT "X"	ALT "Y"	RECCO Plan
I. RECREATION							
Change in State Variables							
1. Annual use of (attendance at) public recreation facilities							
Change in Relevant Condition Variables							
2. Types/condition of roads to and from recreation facilities							
3. Number and types of secondary service facilities in recreation areas (e.g., gas stations, retail stores, restaurants)							
4. Distance to major recreation areas outside the planning area; types of recreation available within a 50-mile radius of planning area							
Change in System Variables (Quantity & Structure)							
5. Number of public facilities used for outdoor recreation (including school facilities), such as golf courses, stadia, etc.							
6. Number of water-related recreation areas (reservoirs, rivers, lakes, etc.)							
7. Staff of local recreation agencies and of public recreation facilities							
8. Budget of local recreation agencies							
9. Area in miles of land used for outdoor recreation (hunting grounds, picnic areas, etc.)							
10. Area in miles of water-related recreation areas							
11. Location of recreation areas within the area							

*Conditions (Above to below Average: AA,A,BA); Effects (Beneficial to Adverse: ++,+,0,-,--).

Table 2. *A Summary Comparison of the Beneficial and Adverse Effects of the Alternative Plans for the Social Well-Being Account*

Items in Evaluation Categories	Present Conditions	Beneficial & Adverse Effects of Plans					
		No Plan	NED Plan	EQ Plan	ALT "X"	ALT "Y"	RECCO Plan
I. RECREATION (cont'd.)							
(Function & Purpose)							
12. Activities and responsibilities of local recreation agencies							
13. Types of recreation available in public facilities and water and land areas							
14. Coordination and conflict in public sector recreation							
(Quantity & Structure)							
15. Accessibility of recreation areas (distance from population centers)							
16. Cost of recreation, by type							
17. Equality of opportunity to use public recreation facilities							
18. Satisfaction among residents with recreation areas, facilities							
Change in Other Variables (Specify)							
J. INFORMAL ORGANIZATIONS AND GROUPS							
Change in State Variables							
1. Size, composition of membership in various informal organizations and groups							
2. Extent of public participation in the planning process as a result of membership in/activities of informal organizations and groups							

*Conditions (Above to below Average: AA,A,BA); Effects (Beneficial to Adverse: ++,+,0,-,--).

Table 2. *A Summary Comparison of the Beneficial and Adverse Effects of the Alternative Plans for the Social Well-Being Account*

Items in Evaluation Categories	Present Conditions	Beneficial & Adverse Effects of Plans					
		No Plan	NED Plan	EQ Plan	ALT "X"	ALT "Y"	RECCO Plan
J. INFORMAL ORGANIZATIONS AND GROUPS (cont'd.)							
Change in System Variables							
3. Number and types of informal organizations and groups (ethnic, religious, service-oriented, environmentally-oriented, etc.)							
4. Organization and administration of informal organizations and groups							
5. Types of activities engaged in by informal organizations and groups							
6. Stands taken on community issues, including on plan(s) by informal organizations and groups							
7. Power position in the community of different informal organizations and groups							
8. Cohesion, solidarity within informal organizations and groups							
9. Coordination and conflict among various informal organizations and groups							
Change in Other Variables (Specify)							

*Conditions (Above to below Average: AA,A,BA); Effects (Beneficial to Adverse: ++,+,0,–,– –).

Table 2. *A Summary Comparison of the Beneficial and Adverse Effects of the Alternative Plans for the Social Well-Being Account*

Items in Evaluation Categories	Present Conditions	Beneficial & Adverse Effects of Plans					
		No Plan	NED Plan	EQ Plan	ALT "X"	ALT "Y"	RECCO Plan
K. COMMUNITY & INSTITUTIONAL VIABILITY							
1. Changes in individual institutions as they affect each other							
a. Size (number of staff, facilities, service capacity)							
b. Type							
c. Location							
d. Organization and administration							
e. Services provided							
f. Accessibility							
g. New institutions created							
2. Changes in institutional interrelationships							
a. Coordination							
b. Conflict							
c. "Balance of power"							
3. Changes in community viability							
a. Residents' image of their community							
b. Outside image of the community							
c. Community solidarity							
4. Other changes (specify)							

*Conditions (Above to below Average: AA,A,BA); Effects (Beneficial to Adverse: ++,+,0,-,--).

Table 2. *A Summary Comparison of the Beneficial and Adverse Effects of the Alternative Plans for the Social Well-Being Account*

Items in Evaluation Categories	Present Conditions	Beneficial & Adverse Effects of Plans					
		No Plan	NED Plan	EQ Plan	ALT "X"	ALT "Y"	RECCO Plan
III. AREA, SOCIOECONOMIC EFFECTS							
A. EMPLOYMENT AND REAL INCOME							
Change in State Variables							
1. Percent of workers by type							
2. Number of persons unemployed as a percent of total labor force							
3. Percent of persons unemployed by occupational category							
4. Percent of families and unrelated individuals by income level							
5. Mean income by class of worker or recipient							
6. Estimated percent of non-residents in area labor force							
7. Percent of persons below poverty level							
Changes in Relevant Condition Variables							
8. Number of business establishments opened, closed during a year period							
Change in System Variables (Quantity & Structure)							
9. Total employers by employment size class (small: 1-19; medium: 20-99; large: 100 or more)							
10. Number of job placement agencies, vocational education schools (school-related, post-high school)							
11. Staff size of job placement agencies and vocational education schools (including job placement officers & employment counselors)							

*Conditions (Above to below Average: AA,A,BA); Effects (Beneficial to Adverse: ++,+,0,-,--).

Table 2. *A Summary Comparison of the Beneficial and Adverse Effects of the Alternative Plans for the Social Well-Being Account*

Items in Evaluation Categories	Present Conditions	Beneficial & Adverse Effects of Plans					
		No Plan	NED Plan	EQ Plan	ALT "X"	ALT "Y"	RECCO Plan
A. EMPLOYMENT AND REAL INCOME (cont'd.)							
12. Total employed persons 16 years of age and over							
13. Total amount spent for job placement activities, vocational education							
14. Location of job placement agencies, vocational education schools							
(Function & Purpose)							
15. Percent of employed population by occupational category							
16. Types of job training and vocational education offered							
17. Activities of local office of U.S. Employment Service							
18. Coordination and conflict among employers; among vocational schools; among placement agencies							
19. Accessibility of vocational education schools (distance from population center; cost to attend)							
20. Accessibility of job placement agencies (distance from population center)							
21. Opportunity for equal employment							
22. Efficiency and effectiveness of vocational education schools (e.g., number of persons trained)							
23. Efficiency and effectiveness of job placement agencies (e.g., number of persons placed)							
24. Satisfaction among residents with employment, income							
Change in Other Variables (Specify)							

*Conditions (Above to below Average: AA,A,BA); Effects (Beneficial to Adverse: ++,+,0,-,--).

Table 2. *A Summary Comparison of the Beneficial and Adverse Effects of the Alternative Plans for the Social Well-Being Account*

Items in Evaluation Categories	Present Conditions	Beneficial & Adverse Effects of Plans					
		No Plan	NED Plan	EQ Plan	ALT "X"	ALT "Y"	RECCO Plan
B. WELFARE & FINANCIAL COMPENSATION							
Change in State Variables							
1. Number of persons receiving welfare services as a percent of total population							
2. Percent of persons receiving different types of welfare services							
3. Number of persons receiving financial compensation as percent of total population							
4. Percent of persons receiving different types of financial compensation							
Change in Relevant Condition Variables							
5. Number of persons below poverty level							
6. Number of persons unemployed as percent of total labor force							
Change in System Variables (Quantity & Structure)							
7. Number of public and private welfare agencies							
8. Staff size of welfare agencies							
9. Public welfare expenditures							
10. Location of public and private welfare agencies							
(Function & Purpose)							
11. Types of staff employed by public, private welfare agencies (professionals vs. volunteers)							
12. Services provided by public, private welfare agencies							

*Conditions (Above to below Average: AA,A,BA); Effects (Beneficial to Adverse: ++,+,0,-,--).

Table 2. *A Summary Comparison of the Beneficial and Adverse Effects of the Alternative Plans for the Social Well-Being Account*

Items in Evaluation Categories	Present Conditions	Beneficial & Adverse Effects of Plans					
		No Plan	NED Plan	EQ Plan	ALT "X"	ALT "Y"	RECCO Plan
B. WELFARE & FINANCIAL COMPENSATION (cont'd.)							
13. Coordination and conflict among welfare agencies (public vs. public, public vs. private)							
(Quality & Character)							
14. Accessibility of welfare agencies							
15. Distribution of welfare benefits (by income level, ethnic groups, age, etc.)							
16. Efficiency and effectiveness of welfare agencies							
17. Satisfaction with welfare system among residents							
Change in Other Variables (Specify)							
C. COMMUNICATIONS							
Change in State Variables							
1. Communications pathways							
Change in Relevant Condition Variables							
2. Total population							
Change in System Variables (Quantity & Structure)							
3. Number of households with at least one television set, radio, telephone							
4. Circulation of newspapers (local and out-of-town) per 100 residents							
5. Equipment of news, communications media							
6. Budget of news, communications media							

*Conditions (Above to below Average: AA,A,BA); Effects (Beneficial to Adverse: ++,+,0,-,--).

Table 2. *A Summary Comparison of the Beneficial and Adverse Effects of the Alternative Plans for the Social Well-Being Account*

Items in Evaluation Categories	Present Conditions	Beneficial & Adverse Effects of Plans					
		*No Plan	NED Plan	EQ Plan	ALT "X"	ALT "Y"	RECCO Plan
C. COMMUNICATIONS (cont'd.)							
7. Location of radio and television broadcasting stations in the area; location of local newspaper publisher(s)							
(Function & Purpose)							
8. Number of local television, radio and newspaper reporters							
9. Number of television, radio stations (AM/FM) received in the area at 6 pm							
10. Number of minutes per week of radio and television reporting time devoted to local news							
11. Coordination, conflict among local communications media (e.g., stands taken by different radio or television stations, newspapers)							
Quality & Character)							
12. Effectiveness of local news, communications media in the area in regard to local issues							
13. Satisfaction among residents with local news, communications media							
Change in Other Variables (Specify)							
D. TRANSPORTATION							
Change in State Variables							
1. Number of licensed drivers in the area							
2. Transportation use patterns							

*Conditions (Above to below Average: AA,A,BA); Effects (Beneficial to Adverse: ++,+,0,-,--).

Table 2. *A Summary Comparison of the Beneficial and Adverse Effects of the Alternative Plans for the Social Well-Being Account*

Items in Evaluation Categories	Present Conditions	Beneficial & Adverse Effects of Plans					
		No Plan	NED Plan	EQ Plan	ALT "X"	ALT "Y"	RECCO Plan
D. TRANSPORTATION (cont'd)							
Change in Relevant Condition Variables							
3. Percent of workers by place of work (inside, outside county of residence)							
Change in System Variables (Quantity & Structure)							
4. Size of water transportation facilities in the planning area, by type							
5. Number of major highways into, out of the area							
6. Total street miles in the area							
7. Number of cars registered in the area							
8. Total tons of commercial freight carried into, out of the area in a year period							
9. Total passengers coming into the area by means of public transportation							
10. Number of miles from population center of the area to major facilities (train station, retail center, schools, etc.)							
(Function & Purpose)							
11. Types of public transportation available in the area							
12. Coordination and conflict among public transportation operations							

*Conditions (Above to below Average: AA,A,BA); Effects (Beneficial to Adverse: ++,+,0,-,--).

Table 2. *A Summary Comparison of the Beneficial and Adverse Effects of the Alternative Plans for the Social Well-Being Account*

Items in Evaluation Categories	Present Conditions	Beneficial & Adverse Effects of Plans					
		No Plan	NED Plan	EQ Plan	ALT "X"	ALT "Y"	RECCO Plan
D. TRANSPORTATION (cont'd.)							
(Quality & Character)							
13. Accessibility of different forms of public transportation (distance to stations from center of population, costs of transportaion)							
14. Equality of opportunity to use public, private transportation							
15. Efficiency and effectiveness of various forms of public transportation							
16. Condition of streets, roads, and highways							
17. Satisfaction among residents with public transportation							
Change in Other Variables (Specify)							
E. ECONOMIC BASE							
Change in State Variables							
1. Percent of persons employed by Standard Industrial Code (SIC) category							
2. Percent of persons employed in agriculture							
3. Tax dollars allocated to human services							
4. Number of persons unemployed as a percent of total labor force							
Change in Relevant Condition Variables							
5. Number of persons at work by place of residence							

*Conditions (Above to below Average: AA,A,BA); Effects (Beneficial to Adverse: ++,+,0,-,--).

Table 2. *A Summary Comparison of the Beneficial and Adverse Effects of the Alternative Plans for the Social Well-Being Account*

Items in Evaluation Categories	Present Conditions	Beneficial & Adverse Effects of Plans					
		No Plan	NED Plan	EQ Plan	ALT "X"	ALT "Y"	RECCO Plan
E. ECONOMIC BASE (cont'd.)							
6. Percent of retail trade carried on outside the area by residents of the area (shopping for food, clothes, household goods and services, automobiles)							
7. Percentage of owner-occupied dwelling units							
Change in System Variables (Quantity & Structure)							
8. Number of establishments by SIC category							
9. Number of farms in the area							
10. Number of government units in the area							
11. Size of establishments (small, medium and large)							
12. Percent of land used for grazing and farming							
13. Total taxable payroll by SIC category							
14. Total value of farm products (all crops, livestock and livestock products, dairy and dairy products, poultry and poultry products)							
15. Estimated full value of property							
16. Value of new capital investments in the area during the past year							
17. Location of establishments by SIC category							
(Function & Purpose)							
18. Coordination and conflict among establishments, between industry and agriculture							

*Conditions (Above to below Average: AA,A,BA); Effects (Beneficial to Adverse: ++,+,0,-,--).

Table 2. *A Summary Comparison of the Beneficial and Adverse Effects of the Alternative Plans for the Social Well-Being Account*

Items in Evaluation Categories	Present Conditions	Beneficial & Adverse Effects of Plans					
		No Plan	NED Plan	EQ Plan	ALT "X"	ALT "Y"	RECCO Plan
E. ECONOMIC BASE (cont'd.)							
(Quality & Character)							
19. Accessibility (distance from population center to places of employment)							
20. Satisfaction with economic base							
Change in Other Variables (Specify)							
F. PLANNING							
1. Effects of planning activities for water resource project on the local population:							
a. Employment							
b. Land (e.g., farm) and home improvement							
c. Personal plans							
d. Other (specify)							
2. Effects of planning activities for water resource project on local government							
a. Community planning							
b. Equipment and facilities maintenance							
c. Intercommunity cooperation and conflict							
d. Other (specify)							
3. Effects of planning activities for water resource project on local economy							
a. Attraction for new industry							

*Conditions (Above to below Average: AA,A,BA); Effects (Beneficial to Adverse: ++,+,0,–,– –).

Table 2. *A Summary Comparison of the Beneficial and Adverse Effects of the Alternative Plans for the Social Well-Being Account*

Items in Evaluation Categories	Present Conditions	Beneficial & Adverse Effects of Plans					
		No Plan	NED Plan	EQ Plan	ALT "X"	ALT "Y"	RECCO Plan
F. PLANNING (cont'd.)							
b. Attraction for investment in agriculture							
c. Attraction for new capital investments							
d. Other (specify)							
4. Effects of planning activities for water resource project on external investors							
a. Bond issues							
b. Quality of bond ratings							
c. Other (specify)							
5. Other effects of planning activities for water resource project (specify)							
G. CONSTRUCTION							
1. Short-term effects							
a. Influx of workers							
b. Change in demand for public and private services associated with short-term influx of workers							
c. Requirements for transient housing							
d. Physical disruption (noise, dust, road blockage or diversion, etc.)							
e. Other short-term effects (specify)							

*Conditions (Above to below Average: AA,A,BA); Effects (Beneficial to Adverse: ++,+,0,-,--).

Table 2. *A Summary Comparison of the Beneficial and Adverse Effects of the Alternative Plans for the Social Well-Being Account*

Items in Evaluation Categories	Present Conditions	Beneficial & Adverse Effects of Plans					
		No Plan	NED Plan	EQ Plan	ALT "X"	ALT "Y"	RECCO Plan
G. CONSTRUCTION (cont'd.)							
2. Long-term effects							
a. Population change							
b. Changes in public and private services available							
c. Housing patterns							
d. Physical effects							
e. Other long-term effects (specify)							
IV. NATIONAL, EMERGENCY PREPAREDNESS EFFECTS							
A. WATER SUPPLIES							
1. Changes in amount of water available							
2. Changes in stability of the water supply							
3. Changes in quality of water available							
4. Other changes (specify)							
B. FOOD PRODUCTION							
1. Changes in potential for reserve food production							
2. Changes in types of crops produced (for human vs. animal vs. industrial consumption)							
3. Other changes (specify)							

*Conditions (Above to below Average: AA,A,BA); Effects (Beneficial to Adverse: ++,+,0,–,––).

Table 2. *A Summary Comparison of the Beneficial and Adverse Effects of the Alternative Plans for the Social Well-Being Account*

Items in Evaluation Categories	Present Conditions	Beneficial & Adverse Effects of Plans					
		No Plan	NED Plan	EQ Plan	ALT "X"	ALT "Y"	RECCO Plan
C. POWER SUPPLIES							
1. Changes in the amount of power produced							
2. Changes in the stability of the power supply							
3. Changes in transmission potential for power supplies							
4. Changes in response time for emergency power							
5. Other changes (specify)							
D. WATER TRANSPORTATION							
1. Changes in the number of miles of useable water transportation system							
2. Changes in tonnage support capacity of water transportation system							
3. Changes in network location characteristics of water transportation system							
4. Other changes (specify)							
E. SCARCE FUELS							
1. Changes in the amount of scarce fuels (oil and natural gas) consumed for various purposes							
2. Changes in use patterns of scarce vs. abundant fuels (e.g., coal)							
3. Changes in use of alternative power sources (e.g., solar, hydroelectric)							

*Conditions (Above to below Average: AA,A,BA); Effects (Beneficial to Adverse: ++,+,0,–,– –).

Table 2. *A Summary Comparison of the Beneficial and Adverse Effects of the Alternative Plans for the Social Well-Being Account*

Items in Evaluation Categories	Present Conditions	Beneficial & Adverse Effects of Plans					
		No Plan	NED Plan	EQ Plan	ALT "X"	ALT "Y"	RECCO Plan
E. SCARCE FUELS (cont'd.)							
4. Other changes (specify)							
F. POPULATION DISPERSION							
1. Changes in the amount of water available in sparsely settled areas							
2. Changes in the quality of water available, and concomitant potential for human consumption and other uses							
3. Changes in water transportation routes for population dispersion							
4. Other changes (specify)							
G. INDUSTRIAL DISPERSION							
1. Changes in the amount of water available in previously nonindustrialized areas							
2. Changes in the quality of water available and concomitant potential for industrial uses							
3. Changes in water transportation routes for industrial dispersion							
4. Other changes (specify)							
H. MILITARY PREPAREDNESS							
1. Changes in the amount of water available							
2. Changes in the quality of water available and concomitant potential for human consumption and other uses							

*Conditions (Above to below Average: AA,A,BA); Effects (Beneficial to Adverse: ++,+,0,–,––).

Table 2. *A Summary Comparison of the Beneficial and Adverse Effects of the Alternative Plans for the Social Well-Being Account*

Items in Evaluation Categories	Present Conditions	Beneficial & Adverse Effects of Plans					
		No Plan	NED Plan	EQ Plan	ALT "X"	ALT "Y"	RECCO Plan
H. MILITARY PREPAREDNESS (cont'd.)							
3. Other changes (specify)							
I. INTERNATIONAL TREATY OBLIGATIONS							
1. Changes in the water use patterns for bodies of water regulated by international treaties							
2. Changes in the inherent nature of bodies of water regulated by international treaties (e.g., riverbed diversion)							
3. Other changes (specify)							
V. AGGREGATE SOCIAL EFFECTS							
A. CHANGES IN QUALITY OF LIFE							
1. Quality of self-development							
2. Quality of family and interpersonal relations							
3. General health, peace of mind, motivation							
4. Standard of living (income, housing, recreation)							
5. Satisfaction with local culture and community							
6. Perceived equality of opportunity to benefit from changes in the community							
7. Other (specify)							

*Conditions (Above to below Average: AA,A,BA); Effects (Beneficial to Adverse: ++,+,0,-,--).

Table 2. *A Summary Comparison of the Beneficial and Adverse Effects of the Alternative Plans for the Social Well-Being Account*

Items in Evaluation Categories	Present Conditions	Beneficial & Adverse Effects of Plans					
		No Plan	NED Plan	EQ Plan	ALT "X"	ALT "Y"	RECCO Plan
B. CHANGES IN RELATIVE SOCIAL POSITION							
1. Equal opportunity to receive benefits from plan implementation and relationship to need							
2. Equity of distribution of social and economic costs and relationship to ability to pay							
3. Other (specify)							
C. CHANGES IN SOCIAL WELL-BEING							
1. General improvement in the quantity and quality of public and private services available to the public							
2. General improvement in the ability of community institutions to cooperate with one another							
3. Economic stability of the area							
4. Improved personal income levels							
5. Enhanced security of life through reduction in water-related risks							
6. Improved population distribution in terms of male/female balance among age groups, dependency ratios, etc.							
7. Improvement in stability of values and norms in the community							
8. Others(specify)							

*Conditions (Above to below Average: AA,A,BA); Effects (Beneficial to Adverse: ++,+,0,-,--).

Table 3. *Summary of Effects Across Plans*

		No Plan	NED Plan	EQ Plan	Alt "X"	Alt "Y"	RECCO
Components of the Social Well-Being Account[a]	I. Individual, Personal Effects II. Community, Institutional Effects III. Area, Socio-Economic Effects IV. National, Emergency Preparedness Effects V. Aggregate Social Effects						
Trade-offs[b]	Direct vs. Indirect Effects						
	Short-Term vs. Long-Term Effects						
	Geographic Distribution						
	Special Groups Affected						

[a]Rate: ++ (very positive); + (positive); o (neutral); - (negative); -- (very negative).

[b]Brief verbal descriptions (e.g., direct positive effects on recreation vs. indirect negative effects on employment).

References

Barbour, E. "Multiobjective Water Resource Planning." Paper presented at the Second World Congress on Water Resources, International Water Resources Association, New Delhi, India, December 17, 1975.

Borts, G. H. "The Equalization of Returns and Regional Economic Growth." *American Economic Review* 50, June 1960.

Box, G. P., and Jenkins, G. M. *Time Series Analysis: Forecasting and Control.* San Francisco: Holden-Day, 1970.

Burdge, R. J. *A Summary of Sociological Studies of Water Resources Dealing with Social Goals and the "Quality of Life."* Lexington: University of Kentucky, 1973.

Fitzsimmons, S. J. and Salama, O. *Man and Water: A Social Report.* Washington, D.C.: U.S. Bureau of Reclamation, 1973.

Haggett, P. *Locational Analysis in Human Geography.* New York: St. Martin's Press, 1966.

Helmer, O. *Social Technology.* New York: Basic Books, 1966.

Maslow, A. *Motivation and Personality.* New York: Harper & Row, 1954.

Merton, R. K. *Social Theory and Social Structure.* Glencoe, Ill.: The Free Press, 1957.

Miller, D. C. *Handbook of Research Design and Social Measurement.* New York: David McKay, 1970.

Morgan, B. W. *An Introduction to Bayesian Statistical Decision Processes.* Englewood Cliffs, N.J.: Prentice-Hall, 1968.

Rosenberg, M. *The Logic of Survey Analysis.* New York: Basic Books, 1968.

U.S. Department of the Interior, Bureau of Reclamation. *Guidelines for Implementing Principles and Standards for Multi-Objective Planning of Water Resources.* Washington, D.C.: U.S. Bureau of Reclamation, December 1972.

U.S. Water Resources Council. "Principles and Standards for Planning Water and Land Resources." Special Task Force Report. Washington, D.C.: U.S. Water Resources Council, 1970.

1972 OBERS Projections. Washington, D.C.: U.S. Government Printing Office, 1972.

Proposed Principles and Standards for Planning Water and Related Land Resources. In the *Federal Register.* Washington, D.C.: U.S. Government Printing Office, 1973.

For Product Safety Concerns and Information please contact our EU representative GPSR@taylorandfrancis.com Taylor & Francis Verlag GmbH, Kaufingerstraße 24, 80331 München, Germany

Batch number: 10726322

Printed by Printforce, the Netherlands